STRAIGHT UP

Danny Dyer was born in 1977 in Canning Town, East London, and is a well-known film and television actor. A life-long player and fan of football, he is an ardent supporter of West Ham United FC. He currently lives with his partner and two young daughters in Essex.

DANNY
DYER
STRAIGHT
UP

arrow books

Published by Arrow Books 2011

2 4 6 8 10 9 7 5 3 1

First published in Great Britain in 2010 by
Century
Random House, 20 Vauxhall Bridge Road,
London SW1V 2SA

www.randomhouse.co.uk

Addresses for companies within The Random House Group Limited can be found at:
www.randomhouse.co.uk/offices.htm

The Random House Group Limited Reg. No. 954009

A CIP catalogue record for this book
is available from the British Library

ISBN 9780099552987

The Random House Group Limited supports The Forest Stewardship Council® (FSC®),
the leading international forest certification organisation. All our titles that are printed on
Greenpeace approved FSC® certified paper carry the FSC® logo. Our paper procurement
policy can be found at www.randomhouse.co.uk/environment

MIX
Paper from
responsible sources
FSC® C016897

Typeset in Adobe Garamond by Palimpsest Book Production Limited,
Falkirk, Stirlingshire
Printed and bound in Great Britain by
CPI Bookmarque, Croydon CR0 4TD

This book is dedicated to the three most beautiful girls in the world – Joanne, Dani and Sunnie. Thanks for putting up with me.

1

CHAMPAGNE SUPERNOVA

One of the most miserable times of my life was in the summer of 2000. I was just twenty-three years old and I'd moved into Noel Gallagher's old gaff – Supernova Heights – with a girl-friend who was worth millions and who was killing me with her non-stop party lifestyle.

She'd bought the place and had it redecorated in an amazing style – a floor-to-ceiling fish tank separated two rooms, an incredible kitchen stocked with all the beer you could drink, and a chill-out area in the basement with a massive TV and fuck-off sound system.

In the evenings I'd jump into her brand-new Range Rover and drive to a play I was in at the National Theatre – the top playhouse in the country. It was a role other actors would have cut their bollocks off to get and I'd been put into it at the personal insistence of the bloke who wrote it – Harold Pinter, the greatest playwright of the age. I was getting rave reviews for my performance and pats on the back from everyone who came to see it.

When the play was over, I'd sink a drink in the bar with the theatregoers and then do one out of there. They're not my sort of people, to be honest, nothing wrong with them but I just haven't got anything to talk to them about.

And why would I want to wait around? Back at Supernova Heights there would be a party going on – twenty or thirty people. I'm not going to go into exactly what went on there – lots of very, very famous people – but it was like the last days of Rome with added Charlie.

I'd get a hooter full of class As, a skin full of beer, talk bollocks all night and then take a couple of sleeping pills and crash out in bed at about ten in the morning. Then I'd wake up in the afternoon in time for the evening performance and start the whole thing again.

So why was I miserable? Because I didn't want to be there. I've always taken drugs and I probably always will, but there's a difference between having the odd crafty bump up the snout as a reward for a job well done and letting it rule your life. I wasn't respecting that difference and I hadn't been for the month before when I was in Ibiza shooting a film called *Is Harry On The Boat?*

At that stage of my life Ibiza was the wrong place for a geezer like me. I went fucking mad with drugs and drink and all-night partying, fucked up my relationship with the producers of the film and fucked up my body. If you look at the film now I seem quite fresh-faced but I was so run down I got an ulcer on my eye. The hospital had never seen anything like it. The director of the film had to shoot me from one side to stop it showing on-screen. It makes me heave nowadays to think how I was treating myself and, worse, how I was disrespecting the people who were paying my wages.

But none of that would really have mattered – or it would have been fixable – if I hadn't fucked up my relationship with

Joanne, my childhood sweetheart who I'd been with since I was fourteen, the only girl I'd ever loved and the mother of my daughter. In Ibiza I betrayed her with the rich bird – I won't say her name out of respect to Joanne – and Joanne found out through the papers. She went out one morning, bought the *Sun* and saw pictures of me with this girl splashed all over it.

I phoned her up and she gave me a straight red. Joanne's an aggressive little fucker, five foot tall and a right trap on her, a very strong woman. She told me I wasn't seeing my three-year-old again, my beautiful Dani, changed her phone number and cut me out of her life. It shattered me, knocked my feet out from under me. My own dad had left when I was nine years old and I vowed I'd never make my kid grow up in a single parent family. Now I had.

I had nowhere to go but Supernova Heights. I was home-less. Now I know going to Noel's old pad accompanied by a bird with a blank chequebook beats stopping at the fucking Salvation Army so I don't expect much sympathy. But I'd lost contact with everything – with Joanne and Dani, with the mates I grew up with, and even with my love of acting.

That, if anything, should have told me to turn it in. Acting is my passion; it's what I live for. I'm fascinated by it, how the great performers do what they do, how I can improve my performances, where to stand, how to move, everything. It gives me a bigger buzz than any drug I've ever taken. But in that summer of 2000, for the first time in my life it had become hard work. For me it had always come so easy. I used to wonder how other people found it difficult. But now I wasn't enjoying it at all. I was turning up, saying my lines and fucking off back home to get on with the party.

I was doing OK, no one noticed and the reviews were brilliant but I was cheating myself, the other actors and the audience. I could have done ten times better. Acting's about bouncing off other people, reading the other actors and the mood of the crowd. I was just reciting the lines I'd learned. It ain't the same.

I was desperate to see my little Dani again. I'd drive down to Custom House in the East End to stand outside our old maisonette when I knew Joanne would be bringing Dani back from her mum's. Joanne'd just blank me completely and usher Dani inside. The worst thing about it was that I didn't have a leg to stand on. It was all my own fault, completely. What's Joanne going to do? Let me walk all over her? I couldn't blame her in any way for elbowing me.

I'd stand there on the pavement with an empty feeling, looking around at those streets where I grew up. This was where I'd had such a laugh with my mates, where my mum and my nan still lived, where I'd lived until the spectacular OG in Ibiza. I felt like a shadow in my own life.

I was losing who I was in the company I was keeping and in the drugs I was doing. I missed Joanne and I missed little Dani, really, really badly. For a lot of lads from my background their ambition would have been to get out of the flats and into the rock star's mansion. I didn't realise it at the time – I was so fucked up with drugs that I didn't realise anything much – but mine was to get out of the mansion and back to the flats.

2

I FEEL LOVE

I was born on 24 July 1977 in Custom House in London's East End, near to the old docks on the Thames. Donna Summer's 'I Feel Love' was number one that day and it doesn't make a bad theme tune for my youth. The area I grew up in would be described by some as rough and ready and by others as a shithole. It was a tough neighbourhood, the most deprived in London, but that made no difference to me because I did feel love all around me.

I had my mum, my cockney nan, who we called Nanny Mother, my cockney granddad Jack and, out in Essex my dad's parents, the lovely Nanny Joyce and Granddad John.

I don't include my dad in this for two reasons. The first is that he's an old-fashioned dad and doesn't show his emotions very much, unless it comes to complaining about stuff – his job, the state of the country, anything. If Donna Summer did a song inspired by him it would be called 'I feel the country's going to the dogs and them cunts in the government are to blame'. Probably wouldn't have been as popular, though you never know.

The second reason is because he fucked off when I was nine so he wasn't around that much. I never felt as close to him as I did my mum. He wasn't a shit dad, far from it, but like a lot of blokes of his generation, he wasn't very good at expressing himself when it came to the more tender feelings. He never changed a nappy, never got involved with that side of it at all. I love him and I know he loves me but it's sad to say that the only time I really felt that from him was when he was drunk. You read a lot about how some kids suffer at the hands of big drinkers but it was never like that with Dad. He got a lot nicer when he was pissed which, luckily, was most nights. However, it wasn't all positive when he drank. Most people assume that my name is Daniel. It isn't. It's, in fact, Danial. My dad was so pissed when he filled out the birth certificate that he spelled the name wrong. That's why I changed my name to Danny smartish when I hit secondary school. Danial's a bit too near to Danielle.

Me and my dad do have a heart to heart about this sometimes – when we're both drunk. It's a strange feeling. When he has a few beers his face changes. There's a gentleness about him. When he's sober he's bitter, moaning about everything. And being the old-school fucking dad that he is, he don't show affection. It's not the done thing.

I used to feel safe when he'd hold my hand, though he'd hold it quite loosely. I got to an age, though, when he wouldn't do that no more.

Then there's the kissing thing. My mum would always kiss and cuddle us kids and my dad would too but there came a moment when he said, 'All right, boy, we shake hands now.' It hurt a little bit. You don't question it because you think it's normal. I remember once we were waiting to cross the road and he wouldn't hold my hand. He said, 'Go on, boy, go!'

and I went to go and there were cars coming and he grabbed my arm and pulled me back, laughing.

That laddy banter sort of set me up for the rest of my life, which is what it's about coming from East London. Men, we banter, we take the piss out of each other, we don't show emotion, we don't give too much away, otherwise it's a weakness and people jump all over you. I understand that. So it was nice for me to go home to a loving, caring affectionate mum where I could just lie there in her arms watching telly. I needed that in my life.

Although we didn't have a pot to piss in for most of my childhood – especially after my dad left – that never mattered. I had a great upbringing in many ways.

Weekends were best. On Saturday we'd all cram into Nanny Mother's little maisonette – twenty-five or thirty of us, all my aunts, uncles, all the kids.

Saturday's still my favourite day even now. I love getting up in the morning, fucking about, going over the betting shop and then down the drinker. I like an old-school boozer, few and far between nowadays. Old bit of carpet, little telly in the corner, same barmaid you get on well with, not that packed. I love the smell of the stale beer, the noise of people playing pool, the old boy sitting in the corner with his racing paper.

When I was a kid, of course, I didn't get to experience that. I stayed at my nan's and fucked about. The women would cook the dinner while the men went down the pub round the corner, The Angel, to have a booze. Then when the pub shut the men would come back and we'd all have a bit of dinner, watching the racing on the telly where the blokes would shout and scream for the horses they'd bet on. Then it was final score where we'd see how West Ham had got on.

Sometimes my dad would take me to the football. I remember my first game – West Ham against Coventry and we lost 1–0. David Speedie scored, I think. It was an over-whelming experience, the size of the crowd, the noise of it all. Everything about the football seemed big and I loved it – the cockiness and confidence of the men going in, the feeling that you were part of something really special. I know I'm a West Ham fan so I would say this but I think there's something unique about Upton Park – it's the people, the real East Enders, tough, colourful, hard and beautiful. You see some of them going in and everything about them says 'don't fuck with me', the way they munch their pies, the rolling way they walk, their beer-bloated faces, big bellies, big hearts, swearing up a storm. I fucking love them. They're people with a lust for life.

My dad was always a bit of a tight bastard and sent me in on my own through the Junior Hammers entrance – £2.50. Two pound fucking fifty! How much does it cost to take your kids today? Forty fucking quid. That's a disgrace. And back then the team was quality – McAvennie, Brooking, Devonshire, Alvin Martin, Billy Bonds. The opposition would fear the team as much as the fans. We finished fourth one season, that's my memory. In fact we finished fucking third. Third. It's like my brain can't actually believe that and has to move us down a position.

This was the days of the terraces and years before CCTV cut the amount of trouble down. I'd stand in the supposedly safe part of the ground looking out at the north and the south banks. That's when I first got a taste for what the ICF was all about – the Inter City Firm, West Ham's feared mob of dedicated hooligans. We were the club that started all that bollocks; we were the most game. My dad wasn't involved in all that, he was old school and just liked a piss up with his mates.

The south bank was where the ICF were. I'd watch as it would kick off between them and the rival fans. Sometimes some of the away supporters would infiltrate the West Ham terraces and then it would all come on top. I was fascinated by it as a young kid. I can remember the chants: 'You'll never make the station' and 'You're going home in a West Ham ambulance'. What I couldn't believe was that they'd start even if we were winning. I could see them wanting to get into the opposition fans if we were losing but that didn't make a difference to the ICF. Rain or shine, win or lose, they were going to have it.

I never felt tempted to join them, though. A lot of young kids would hang around them and try to prove themselves and become the next generation of hooligans. To be honest, I wanted to be a million miles away from that. I'm not a cunt and if someone has a go at me I'll be right back at 'em but I didn't have that bubbling aggression a lot of young blokes seemed to have. I was a happy-go-lucky kid.

Sometimes us kids would do the boot sales on a weekend with my dad. He'd buy us old *Beano* annuals. Well, sometimes. Most of the time he didn't buy us anything. There was a real old market in Brick Lane that would go through alleyways and through houses. I always remember the smell of it, leather, old things. This is why nowadays I love stuff like

Antiques Roadshow and *Time Team*. These are my guilty pleasures. I love anything to do with old stuff. My daughter Dani can't believe I watch them things but I don't give a fuck. I like 'em, I'll watch 'em.

On Sundays my dad would drop us at my Nanny Joyce's house in Hornchurch where I saw a glimpse of a different world. My Nanny Mother would eff and blind and loved the word 'cunt'. At my Nanny Joyce's house you couldn't say 'fart', you had to say 'blow off'. It was lovely there, though.

I can still remember the smell of the house, my nan's roll-ups mixed in with Shake 'n' Vac. Nanny Joyce's was immaculate. She used to roll all her cigarettes at one go and lay them out in a neat row, so precise. We had dinner round a table there and talked about stuff. Granddad was a security guard at Tate and Lyle's and I was impressed by his uniform. I used to kid the other lads that he was a policeman and say I'd get him to come and arrest them if they fucked around with me.

I have to say, nice as it was to all sit down for a proper meal, I don't believe all this bollocks about eating round a table bringing the family together. At home I never ate round a table in my life, and almost never with my mum and dad, and I'm as close to my family as anyone I know.

We did have a weird sort of little bond up over food, though. My dad used to get in from the pub, have his chops and then give me the bone to chew the last of the meat off, like a dog. That sounds awful but I loved it and it made me feel close to him.

So that's my early life, with my mum and dad and, eighteen months after I was born, my little brother Tony. I'm gonna come and say it from the off, I fucking hated him. Everything I was, Tony wasn't. I was a proper boy, into football, trying to be cool and in with all the hard kids. My brother was the complete opposite, very feminine, quite sensitive – a good talker and a good listener. We went to the Scott Wilkie school – a standard 1960s brick-and-metal-panels sort of place. In the school playground he'd go skipping with the girls and playing hopscotch. Skipping, in a fucking shithole primary school in the middle of East London! He didn't even gel down his hair and it all used to stick up in a big haystack. I'd call him Mullet and he'd call me Big Ears.

Why couldn't he just conform? But he wouldn't. He'd get battered and the next day, he'd be back at it, skipping away. I was trying to be cool and he'd make all that crash down round me earholes by doing something bollocky. He was always getting bullied, Tony, which meant I had to step in and defend him. I fucking resented that. Any chance I got I'd give him a slap or a dig. I beat him once with a wet flannel when he'd just got out of the bath. I didn't realise how much you can hurt someone with one of those. I gave him a couple of clumps with this flannel and it marked all his legs up so then I got a clump from Dad. I wasn't a violent kid but he just fucking irritated me.

My brother's always got on with women much better than he has with blokes, it's just the way he is. At home, after my sister Kayleigh arrived, he'd play with her dolls, combing their hair and stuff. My dad, who had left us by then, would come round to see us but end up going mad at him. He'd say 'He's queer that boy, fucking queer.' And then he'd start on at Tony:

'Look at you, fucking sitting there combing a dolly's hair. Give me that fucking doll, give it to me!' Tony would be defiant, Mum would say 'Leave him alone' and Dad would snap and try to grab the doll. Our old house was all corridors and Tony would run off with the doll in one hand and the brush in the other with my dad chasing him. Then he'd lock himself in the bog so Dad couldn't get at him, and sit combing its hair in there, just to wind him up. The irony is that, despite what my dad thought, Tony isn't gay at all – he's just had his first kid. He just liked playing with dolls and no one was going to tell him he couldn't.

I respect him now, really respect him. It takes some bollocks to be getting that sort of abuse at school and at home and just stick to your guns. I hated having to take him round with me, though. I'd sit him up the corner in the park while I played football and try to pretend he wasn't there.

He wasn't the only one tagging along with me, as it happens. My dog Sam would usually come with us too. He was a mongrel, bought for me when I was about five. He was a ginger dog with a big question mark in his fur. It curled all the way down his back and the dot was on his head.

This dog was my little mate. I never put him on a lead – he wouldn't have one. He'd come out with me and stay by my side when I was out and about. He was a very streetwise dog, like the Littlest Hobo. Sometimes in the morning I'd let him out and I'd see him around. I'd be out with my mates and he'd be out with his, he'd walk past me with half a burger hanging out his mouth. He was smart, very protective of me, but a real free spirit.

He would bark at everything, be lairy behind the back garden fence but when you came in he was dopey soft. I loved that dog and he loved me. Like I said, when you're a boy growing up in a man's world you sometimes need something to express your softer feelings to. I had my mum but I also had Sam. I felt I could tell him anything.

He used to live outside in the back garden. 'Garden' is probably not the right word. My mum and dad aren't exactly fans of Alan Titchmarsh, if you see what I mean. The back yard was always a shithole – holes everywhere that the dog had dug, a rotary clothes line leaning to one side and an old cupboard with one door off where the dog lived. My dad built a little shed out there once and started breeding zebra finches to sell. It was a little aviary. The birds got some disease, though, and I came in one morning to find all thirty of them dead at the bottom of it. He didn't bother after that.

Before he left us, my mum and dad used to argue – largely about him coming in pissed. There was never any domestic violence as such but, on the other hand, there wasn't one door in our house that hadn't got holes punched in it by my dad when he lost his temper.

Still, like I say, Dad wasn't a bad bloke, it's just that him and mum were so different. They met and had us when they were very young. They met one night in a pub called The Peacock. Mum's a 'peace to all nations' sort. She's left wing, believes in judging people on who they are, not the colour of their skin, and would give you the last coin out of her purse. My dad's the reverse of that, right wing and likes to hold on to his money.

An example of what my mum's like is that the other day this pregnant girl knocked on the door, said she wanted to use the toilet. She was obviously a crack addict. My mum let her in and, surprise surprise, she nicked all her jewellery. Mum felt sorry for her, though, wasn't angry at all. If she came back again she'd probably try to help her. My dad would have kicked her straight in the fucking head. To be fair, so would I. So why did they get together? Well, my dad is very funny and quite charming when he wants to be, and Mum fell for him.

I like to think I take the best from my mum and dad, kind and funny. That's what I was like as a kid – a bit scatty, a bit nutty, was always having a laugh.

I appreciate I may not have seemed so pleasant to some of the fellow residents of my estate as me and my mates were always up to some sort of mischief. There was fuck all to do when I was growing up, really fuck all. At all. I'm convinced that the reason areas like mine have such a high crime rate is because there's just nothing for the kids to do. They need some excitement. You have to keep your brain entertained. That's why you take drugs, that's why you fuck around. I don't understand the mentality of stabbing people for no reason but I totally understand the idea of breaking into cars, just generally trying to get some excitement into life. You've got nothing at home; you've got no discipline, no money, nothing other than the estate you live in. Therefore you go round robbing people – I'm not talking about mugging, I don't believe in that – or getting chases off people. It's quite a laugh to get a chase off the Old Bill.

Where I grew up is quite a depressing place to look at so

it's not like you could exactly lose yourself in the natural beauty. It's classic 1960s fuck-up architecture – a grey estate, rat runs and walkways, piss-soaked steps up to flats above, alleys with metal barriers to stop people dodging the Old Bill on motor-bikes, the whole thing clearly designed by some cunt who never had to live there. You've got one bit of scrubby park to play football in with a bunch of fucked swings and a cast of lunatics hanging about, the odd big square with a broken see-saw or a burned-out climbing frame. And that's it.

So what are you going to do for fun? Cause trouble, obviously. If you build a concrete jungle you can't be too surprised if you get a few monkeys swinging about in it. And me and my mates were them monkeys.

I don't mean we did anything particularly nasty, for the most part. To us it was just fucking about, but I can appreciate it seemed a bit more annoying if you were on the receiving end.

We'd play stupid things like Knock Down Ginger, mostly just winding people up. There were characters about the estate you could get a little chase off. There was one bloke called Elephant Man, so-called because he was an ugly fucker. He had two big dogs, an Alsatian and a Rottweiler. If you went outside his house and went 'Elephant Man!' he'd come out with the dogs.

If it weren't him it was another guy called Baldy, on account of his bald head, and he obviously didn't like it. If you threw a stone at his window and called him Baldy, that cunt would chase you all night. You'd run a few streets away and he would come out hunting. The cunt could pop up anywhere like Freddy fucking Krueger. He caught us one night and he had a spring cosh. He caught my mate round the legs. He hit my mate so hard the ball pinged off the end of the cosh. He made his fucking point and we never wound up Baldy again. It was always tempting, but no one ever had the bollocks to throw the stone because this geezer meant fucking business.

When people start going bald you don't mention it, it's an unspoken rule. So to have kids throwing stones at his windows, screaming 'Baldy', you can understand why he got so angry. I get a little bit of that myself nowadays because of who I am, kids ringing my bell and trying to get a chase. What goes around comes around.

As I grew older and started smoking weed, things did start turning a bit more serious. When we were eleven or twelve me and my mates – we called ourselves the Great Eight because there were eight of us – would start doing 'earners'. We'd say, 'Right, we're on the earn tonight.' This involved things like waiting for the Parcelforce van to pull up and the driver to go up to a front door. Then we'd nip in and nick what we could. Or we'd take the train out to Barking and wait outside a newsagent's until someone leaned their mountain bike up the window and then nick it.

You'd have to build yourself up. 'Right, I'm going to do this fucker, I'm going to get his mountain bike.' You never knew how long they'd be in the shop and your heart would be thumping. I never got a thrill from it, though. I got more of a buzz out of the fact that I'd be getting some puff later on. All we wanted was puff money, twenty Benson, and Rizlas.

As soon as the geezer was in the shop one of us would jump

on the bike and ride off. When it was my turn it got a bit hairy sometimes because I wasn't that big. I'd jump on the mountain bike and it would be too big for me, so I'd sort of wobble around on it and stay on as best I could. On a couple of occasions the bloke would come running out of the shop trying to catch me and I'd just have to wobble as quickly as I could, driving across traffic, through red lights – anything to get away. We never did get caught, though. We'd sell the bike for a fucking pittance to a bloke in Custom House and get a bit of money for weed.

I am ashamed of that now. It must be fucking horrible to come out and find the bike you've had for Christmas gone but I didn't think about it much then, though I'd have my little guilty moments. I don't really think crime was for me. Anything you do in life you need to get a buzz out of, and it just didn't happen for me when we were on the rob.

We were never into nothing serious. I think mugging people is disgusting. It makes you feel horrible if you're on the receiving end. Like when a mob of black kids mugged me for a computer game I'd bought in the shopping mall at Upton Park. I was a melt and I let them take the game off me. They could see I was a cunt. Bullies know who to bully, something I'd bear in mind later when meeting certain well-known actors who like to throw their weight about.

The other entertainment we had was videos. This was my first introduction to film. We didn't go to the pictures when I was a kid, we didn't have the money. But there were plenty of videos about. It was when that flood of American horror came into the country. We'd nick the video off my mum and dad's shelf and watch that. *Salem's Lot*, *Fright Night*, all that old slasher stuff.

I also saw *Scum* and *A Clockwork Orange* because I had a few pals a bit older who were naughty fuckers. *A Clockwork Orange* wasn't available in the UK at the time after someone set fire to a tramp after watching it, but my mate had managed to snag a pirated copy. I saw a snuff film round my mate's house when I was very young, about ten years old. I was fucking freaked out. I won't name the kid whose house it was, but it was his mum's snuff movie. A bit strange. She had a bit of porn too so she was clearly a dirty old bird.

The first scene has this kid bungee jumping off a block of flats but the rope he's using is too long. You watch him fall and splatter. That's the fucking opening scene. You can't believe what you're seeing. Then there's this montage of people being run over by motorbikes and shit. There was this other one with a magician who had to get out of this cage before this tray of spikes dropped on him – he didn't get out. You see the thing come down in his face. Another one was CCTV footage of a mental patient who's taken someone hostage. And he just cuts her throat.

I walked out of that house freaking the fuck out. I felt really vulnerable. As a kid you feel invincible. Suddenly, with watching something like that, you're alert to this sense of danger and feel incredibly guilty about watching it.

I couldn't tell my mum because I know she would have had a word with this other kid's mum about it. I took my brother round there to freak him out but he took it in his stride. He's so strong mentally, my brother. I thought he was going to sob his heart out, but he didn't. He just watched it, came home and went back to playing with the dolls.

Apart from videos it was TV. We watched all the usual stuff kids watched back in the eighties – *EastEnders*, *Grange Hill*. When I was really young my dad would let me sit up and watch *The Sweeney*, which I loved. My dad loved *Only Fools and Horses* and I can see why. He is a bit of a Del Boy. Take our house, a little box of a maisonette. In the living room he stuck wooden beams on the ceiling and hung fishing stuff off 'em – starfish, fishing rods, horseshoes, fish. It looked like the sort of thing Del Boy would have loved. My dad's also a big one for a bargain. He'd take us to all the boot sales and was always digging stuff out of skips.

My main mate when I was really young was a really sweet kid called John Guilder. I envied him, though, because he had proper holidays and his parents seemed quite well off. Our holidays were always the same – Canvey Island. I'd always think it would take hours to get there but, of course, it's only about forty-five minutes from where we live.

Dad would drop us at Canvey Island, fuck off for a week and leave us there. My nan had a caravan and my granddad and my aunt were all on the same site too, so it was a good little holiday.

Canvey Island had open space, grass, greenery, this mad smell in the air – the sea wall, the smell of the sea – seaweed, fish and chips and the freshness of it after East London. We'd walk from Thorney Bay caravan site to the sea wall and follow it round for twenty minutes and then you'd see the front – all the rides and the arcades. Just that smell of doughnuts and candyfloss would excite me. My mum would give me a couple of quid when it was 5p to have a go on an arcade game. Later on we'd meet up with the family and have a drink at the pub, The Monaco. It was great, going around on our own but knowing Mum was quite near.

One of the reasons I never complain about the fame side of my job is because I know what it can mean to people, especially kids, to see someone famous. The first time I saw someone famous was on holiday. I saw Zammo out of *Grange Hill*, Lee MacDonald, who was also in *EastEnders* later. It was by the arcades and it was a massive thing for me.

He looked so tall and big and smart and clean. I couldn't believe I'd seen him in the flesh. I ran to get my mum and grabbed her by the hand. She wasn't too interested, to be honest, but she came anyway. I took her back to the spot and he'd gone. I spent the afternoon searching the arcades but I never saw him again. It wasn't about me wanting to be an actor or wanting to be famous but I just remember this feeling it gave me.

It was excitement, like that Christmas type of feeling you have as a kid, and I just wanted to talk to him or touch him. I felt special just for being near him. It was my little moment. It was a weird tunnel vision – just me and Zammo.

The other person who would be at Canvey Island with us was my great friend, my uncle Gary, who was only three years older than me. He came along late – his brothers were twenty-five years older than him and they called him a power-cut baby. My nan was pregnant with him at the same time her own daughter Jackie was knocked up with her son Brian.

I thought Gary was the coolest thing. He was the one who gave me my hand-me-downs – he had Nike Air Max trainers and a yellow puffa jacket, a Chipie jacket – that was the stuff back then. He was a really good fighter as well. He was from Stratford. He went to a school called Lister school where there was a lot more black and Asian kids, and he hung around with this group of really tough black kids. He'd wear his jeans rolled up with his socks showing and people would always try to give it to him, but he'd tell them straight.

He's a hard fucker and once three kids tried it on with us on the crazy golf course at Canvey. I remember one kid saying to Gary, 'You think you're hard because you've got a golf club in your hand.' Gary said, 'Do you want it round your head then?' and that was it, I was off. I just ran for it while he stood there and had it with them. I must have only been about eight but I felt terrible for leaving him. He didn't have a go about me running away, though, which was nice of him.

So my entertainment when I was growing up was videos, TV and a week in Canvey Island. No wonder I ended up doing a bit of mischief. Unfortunately, one of the hazards of going around handing out shit is that you might encounter other people bent on the same idea. You might become their little bit of fun for the evening. That's exactly what happened to me with this bunch of gypsy kids.

For the most part I was OK with the hard kids in my area, of which there were a few, some from families of proper hard bastards. From a young age I knew the types that other adults feared. My dad used to drink in a pub called The Nottingham Arms on Prince Regent Lane that had been there since the

1700s. The pub got demolished not too long ago. It's where the dockers used to go because the Royal Victoria Docks are right next door. I'd be in the pub with my dad and this geezer called Jango would walk in, a boxer from years back – brick shithouse, big medicine ball head. He'd stride in and all the blokes, even my dad, would put their head down. Jango'd bowl in this pub and there'd be moments where he would turn on people and he'd slap 'em or smack 'em in the mouth or he'd just lose it and start throwing bottles into walls. It was almost accepted. There was a lot of characters like that. Sometimes it'd filter down to their kids and they'd be the kids you'd avoid.

I didn't get battered too much, not unless I went out of the area or some strangers came in. That was the problem when the gypsy kids got me – they were outsiders and I didn't know them.

The gypsies had plotted up next to a big building site near us. You knew they were something because a lot of the adults were wary of them. Remember, this ain't fucking Knightsbridge they've pulled up in. There are some right tasty fuckers about but even they were saying 'watch out for this mob'.

Me and my pals were swinging about on the building site after it had closed for the day, just for something to do. I went to go home but I got caught by some of these gypsy kids on the way. Five or six of them got hold of me and they tried to rob me but I had fuck all, just a pair of hand-me-down trainers three sizes too big for me. So they just thought they'd have a laugh with me and start bullying me. I remember feeling so skinny and vulnerable. They were taking turns holding my head down in this pile of building sand. I couldn't breathe and I was panicking. I felt I was fighting for my life so I wriggled free and punched one kid in the mouth. Then they were on me, kicking the shit out of me. Luckily, they took mercy on me in the end and let me go home.

I ran home sobbing my heart out, couldn't wait to see my mum. I was embarrassed to tell her, I don't know why because I knew that whatever I'd tell her she'd be sweet with, she always was. She held me and I just cried. I remember lying to my mates saying I put up a good fight but really, I was like a little girl.

Apart from that, and that time I got robbed by a bunch of black kids, I didn't get in too much bother. The hard kids liked me and would want to be around me. To be fair, it was probably helped by the fact I was quite naughty with the teachers. I never clicked with any of the subjects at school. I just couldn't get my head round 'em.

If, when I left primary school, you'd have asked my teachers what was going to become of me they'd have told you I'd make nothing of my life. I'd have agreed with 'em too. I couldn't see any future for myself other than doing what my dad did – going to work, hating it, coming home, getting pissed, going to sleep, repeat until retirement or death.

There was certainly no hope that I'd click with any of the subjects at senior school – the big Woodside Comprehensive. It all meant nothing to me, it was just a case of fucking around in lessons and being silly until I got kicked out at sixteen. maths, English, science, I just couldn't understand any of them. And then, on the first Tuesday afternoon at senior school, I walked into a class that was to change my life for ever. From the second I walked in I loved it like I loved nothing else, had a bigger thrill than any chase, any fight, any spliff could offer me. For the first time since I could remember, I had a reason to go to school – Miss Flynn's drama class.

3

QUICK CHANGE

I thought I was the first actor in our family. It turned out I was wrong – that was my dad. Up until age nine he was in our lives and after that he was out of them. I didn't really see all that much of him when he was at home. He was always at the pub, down the bookies, doing something else. Plenty of nights he didn't come home at all. I don't moan about this, it's just how blokes of his generation were. Or so we thought.

I can remember the very second he and my mum split up. It was a summer evening and we were all in the house, quite late I think because I was home and normally I'd be out and about for most of the night. She answered the phone, holding baby Kayleigh in her arms. I was at the other end of the corridor, fucking about, I can't remember what I was doing exactly.

Have you ever been in one of them situations where you just feel the air change, a chill come into the room? This was one of them. I stopped what I was doing and looked at my mum. I saw her on the phone, literally going white. And then she just said 'Oh no' and dropped to her knees, still holding my baby sister. That image sticks in my head, her there helpless, shaking and struck down, clinging on to the baby with the phone limp in her hand.

I still find it difficult to believe what had happened to this day. My dad had been working up west in Paddington at this woman's house – not a posh woman or anything, just a normal bird. Anyway, he'd ended up having an affair with her and had fathered not one but two kids with her. He had an entire separate family in Paddington. The mother of the kids knew about us but we didn't know about them. Obviously he'd been giving her some chat about how he intended to leave us eventually. In the end she'd got sick of waiting, called my mum and told her everything.

Mum wouldn't tell me what had happened, she didn't shout and scream, she didn't say anything at all. She didn't half give it him when he got in that night after work, though. Me and my brother lay in our bunk beds listening to them going for it. The next morning he wasn't there. When we asked where he was, she just said, 'Daddy's gone. He won't be coming back.'

When I did discover the truth, it suddenly made sense of a lot of his behaviour. Christmas morning he'd open our presents with us then drop us round Nanny Mother's. He'd fuck off, we presumed, up the pub. In fact, he'd been doing Christmas morning all over again with his other family. Then he'd come back later in the afternoon to us. Maybe that's where he was going when we were at Canvey. I don't know.

As much pain as it caused me as a child, the two kids he had have turned out to be beautiful human beings and I love them very much.

My brother Tony handled the whole thing really well, which irritated the fuck out of me. I needed someone to confide in, to cry to, but he wasn't bothered by it. Bottling it all up didn't do a lot for my behaviour. My mum took me to see a counsellor because I'd got so angry. She was the one there so she got the brunt of it. I'd tell her it was her fault – no way was it her fault – I'd tell her I'd rather be with Dad.

The counsellor did nothing for me. I had to draw stuff or play with shitty dolls that didn't even have any arms. He was this little Indian fella, he'd always be giving me stuff to colour in, all that. I think he was trying to see what my choice of colours said about my frame of mind. Well my choice of fucking colour was no colour at all. I just wouldn't cooperate. After about four sessions he told my mum he couldn't do anything for me and she took me out of there.

The area where I really got to use my experience was a few years down the line in drama class. From the second I walked in there I fell in love with it. It was all my dreams come true. I felt immediately at home, loved every second of being in the room.

The teacher was Miss Jane Flynn. I loved her. She was quite sexy in an old-school way – big bangers and voluptuous, quite posh for the school I went to. I used to love listening to her voice. Everything she said I totally agreed with and, unlike the other teachers, I wanted to do well for her.

I just found it so easy and natural. I would look around the room and think, 'Why do people struggle to do this?'

Why I love drama is that it's about expressing yourself, not using a pen, paper, calculators and dictionaries. It was about pulling things from within yourself, from your own experience, and being able to use them to become a different character than your own. I buzzed off that and I was always gutted when the lesson ended. To move on to maths was such a comedown.

You'd do little exercises – one of you would be the abused mum, the other the violent dad, some of the others the kids. Well I didn't have to do any research to act out how a man and a woman have a row.

I took to this class straight away. I'd never done any nativity plays at junior school, never done any acting before, so it was a revelation. And I knew I was good at it, much better than anyone else in the class.

It was like a drug to me. I couldn't get enough. I joined the after-school drama club at my school, which was a bit weird because it was full of the nerdy kids, not my normal crew at all. They were no good, though, and I couldn't wait until it was my turn when I could get up onstage and show what I could do.

Through Miss Flynn I found out about another after-school club at a nearby school, Star Lane. Now this is in Canning Town, across the A13, dodging the traffic. In interviews you'll always hear me say I'm from Canning Town but I'm not, I'm from Custom House. This is because people never understand what you're on about when you say you're from Custom House. They think you're talking about a house, a block of flats or something and they say, 'What was the area, though?' Eventually I got sick of it and just said I came from Canning Town.

Anyway, I was in enemy territory there and no fucking mistake. I was from Custom House, they were in Canning Town and the two are rivals. It's ridiculous but there it is.

My face was known over there too. I went to Woodside and

sometimes a group of us would get together and have a fight with Star Lane or Brampton or Eastleigh. Their boys would see it as a right gift if I got caught on their turf.

It was intimidating to go over there on my own at that age – about twelve, I think. Star Lane's a big old Victorian school, gothic, and I'd be going in with a mob of kids I'd never met before in my life.

Still, it was worth it. The love of drama made me take that risk of a beating and of ridicule. It was fantastic. We did a proper play about homelessness. I was a tramp. It was my first time onstage and my mum came to see me. I was so proud to show her something I was really good at, in a play with music and everything.

This is the thing, if you're a working-class kid who wants to get into acting, you haven't got Mummy and Daddy holding your hand, you just have to take any opportunity at all, anywhere, to get involved in it.

The teacher at Star Lane got talking to the teacher in Woodside. They both saw something in me and thought I was good enough to put me on to this other drama thing in Kentish Town called the Interchange Studios – it was set up for under-privileged kids, single parent families and all that who couldn't afford to go to drama school. It wasn't for the 'oh go and do it for Mummy' kid, it was for kids off the estate, like me.

Just to set the record straight, I always read in the press that I went to Sunday school. The kind of place where they teach you Bible stories and pray and sing songs. Of course I didn't go to fucking Sunday school. The class just happened to be on a Sunday.

I never had the money to get there so I'd jump the gates at Kentish Town tube station. If I got the overhead it would be easier because they didn't have barriers. But most of the time I'd go on the tube – twenty-odd stops – and I'd have to jump the barriers at the other end, which I had down to a fine art. I had a good technique of slipping in behind people. I'd never use old people because they took far too long to get through. I'd always look for someone who looked as though they were in a rush. I'd get so close without touching and I'd shuffle through behind them. I didn't care if I got caught on the way home. As long as I could get there and do my bit of acting I was happy.

The place in Kentish Town was all funky and punky and had graffiti all over the walls. You had to get a pass to be there, fill out a form, and I had this little pass clipped on to me. I felt so proud of that. This was another level up from drama club. I could pick between mime, dance, singing and audition technique.

I never wanted to do singing and dance and all that bollocks – that was never for me. I was into the drama side of it. So I went and did mime, which bored me eventually but I did learn a lot from it – how to express yourself using just your body.

I could never understand this shit that they get you to do at proper drama schools: 'be a piece of sizzling bacon' or 'be as light as a feather'. What the fuck is all that about? Where does that fit into the real world, and how does that help you act a kid who's just lost his mum, or a copper or a hard man – the kind of roles you'll be faced with as a working actor? I haven't got a fucking clue.

There I got closer to people who were actual actors, doing it in professional productions. There was a teacher at the Interchange who was on *Poirot* and I watched it, fascinated by it. It seemed so weird I could know someone who was on the telly. He was quite good as well.

They had a workshop at these studios where agents would come down to see the kids. That was always quite exciting, even though I only had half an idea of what an agent was.

The big thing for me, though, was just to be able to act. What I say to kids who want to be actors, who want to perform, who get a buzz out of it is this: it's not about money; it's not about being rich or famous. It's about having that desire to perform. You have something inside you that you can't explain and you need to channel that in whatever way you can. You should go to any little drama club, any fucking thing at all. Even if you haven't got any money, you find a way to get there. I'm not encouraging people to jump the barriers like I did but if you want it bad enough you will find a way.

That's why I think I got an agent pretty quickly – people could see I wasn't in it for money or fame or anything like that, they could see I just loved it, was good at it and wanted to absorb and learn more.

You always knew the agent would come down but you didn't know what they looked like or who they were. It'd be thirty kids, hanging around in little groups of six, all doing their thing, improvising scenarios. I'd sit there on the floor thinking, 'I can't wait to stand up and act.' I was never embarrassed or shy, I just wanted to show that there was something I was really good at. I think it was the second time the agents came down I got picked out by this woman called Charlotte Kelly. I didn't know it but, as she smiled at me and went to shake my hand, my life changed big style.

The days of being a no-hoper were over. I was going to see places and meet people that I had never dreamed of before. I was on my way to being the only thing that could make me happy – a professional actor. And the strange thing was I didn't have to wait. It was going to start the very next day.

4

PRIME SUSPECT

I'd never thought of acting as a career. To me it was always a hobby, something that kept me off the streets, something I was good at. I was good at football as well but I started smoking and taking drugs and all that, so football was never going to be the right discipline for me.

I even nearly gave up drama when I was about thirteen. My fucking school, shithole that it was, said I couldn't do both art and drama, I had to choose one. I was thinking of doing art because I loved drawing so much and I was thinking of that as a career. There seemed more chance of earning money out of art because there are so many things you can do with it.

Jane Flynn got wind that I was going to take art and she took me aside for a chat and said, 'Danny, seriously, you have to take drama as an option or you are really going to regret it.'

I put up a little bit of a fight but thought, 'Actually, fuck it, she's right.' So I elbowed the art. It's bollocks, why couldn't I do art and drama, two things I loved, instead of wasting my time – and annoying the teachers – in lessons I was no good at?

She didn't promise me a career out of it but she said she'd

never seen a pupil like me before, that I was a natural and that I'd give myself a better shot later on if I took it. I got a B in drama – my brother did most of the course work because I couldn't do it. I stood up and did the show no problem but a big part of it was writing it down and analysing my performance, which I was never any good at. I could never explain why I was playing a part the way I was, I'd just do it.

I was obviously excited when Charlotte pulled me aside, more for the fact that someone had recognised I was good than that I thought I was at the start of a career. Charlotte was a lovely little thing, short hair, kind face – she didn't seem like an agency type to me. I had no idea. I thought they all looked like movie stars themselves.

We were introduced and she said, 'I think you're incredibly talented and I'd like to represent you. This is quite a rare thing for me as an agent because I haven't got child actors on my books.'

I was confused by that. I thought, 'Books? what's she talking about?'

She said, 'Look, have you thought about this as a career?' I said I hadn't at all. She said she had a part for me to audition for tomorrow, how did I feel about going along? When she told me what it was I thought I was going to fall over. *Prime Suspect* with Helen Mirren: gorgeous Helen Mirren out of the brilliant *Long Good Friday*. It was one of my favourite films and I loved *Prime Suspect*. I'd seen the first two. I thought, 'I'm well up for it.'

I couldn't wait to get home and tell my mum. She was so

proud of me. This woman had given me her card and every-thing.

I rang her the next day. She was going to tell me where I had to go. My mum scraped up some money for a travel card. It was somewhere in Soho. I'd hardly ever been 'up London' as we called it.

I took the day off school and I went up on me jack. My mum was busy so she couldn't come. Also, and this has always been a very personal thing for me, it's something I've always done off my own back, I've never had a leg up. I don't think my mum would have helped by being there anyway. I turned up on my own – I had long greasy curtains by that stage because it was the time of acid house, the summer of love and all that bollocks. The travel card gave me a bit of confidence because I didn't have to jump the barriers for once.

There were a couple of other kids there with their mums. They had trousers on, a shirt, a tie. It didn't intimidate me; it spurred me on because I was the odd one out, the trampy kid in the corner. They'd clearly been to auditions many times and knew how it all went. You walk in, you get your lines and prepare. I could hear them all practising with their mums and I thought, 'You are shit.'

I wasn't scared at all going into that room. I had a little bit of nerves going on – you need a little bit of that – but I couldn't wait to get in and show off. I had no fear about it. I did feel a bit self-conscious sitting there a bit scummy, but I liked that; I like being the underdog. I had a pair of baggy jeans, a fucked up pair of Reebok Classics, nothing trendy.

The trendiest thing about me was my long hair but even then I couldn't be bothered to wash it.

I looked at the script. The scene was with Helen Mirren's character. The casting agent was reading her part. Her name was Doreen Jones, big pair of bangers and big glasses on. I walked in the room and I just felt a vibe off of her. I wasn't very good at small talk. I just wanted to get on with it. They do say you can lose the job as soon as you walk in by just saying the wrong thing, which I've always found to be a lot of bollocks because for my money, it's about the performance. The reason I'm there is to show them I'm better than anyone else for this part. It's not about whether I'm articulate or dressed the right way. Doreen told me later that she felt something when I walked in, how raw I was, how real I was. The part was a rent boy. I was a glue sniffer and a down and out. I hadn't any experience of being a down and out but I was near enough on the glue sniffing because the first time I ever got off me nut it was sniffing aerosols. In that way I suppose I had the edge of kids who hadn't done such dedicated research into the skanky lifestyle.

The story was about paedophiles high up in the police force. It's about a kid who gets murdered. He was a friend of mine, and Helen's character's trying to get something out of me. It was a nice little speech, came out of my mouth very naturally. Doreen asked me to do it again. She tweaked me to make me do it a little bit different, change the pace a bit. I remember thinking, 'Fuck me, why didn't I think of that?' I obviously took to the direction very easily and she clocked that.

I left the audition feeling good about it, pleased with what

I'd done. By the time I got home my mum had had a call from Charlotte, asking me to give her a bell back. It turned out that I got offered the job the same day. I was elated but also confused. I didn't know what the next step was. Remember, here I am about to act with Helen Mirren and I haven't even been in a school play.

My mum was over the fucking moon but she was quite confused about where this acting talent came from. I'd suddenly dug out this little career for myself, doing something thousands of other kids would put their nuts in a blender to do. And it's just happened in a matter of days. My dad reacted to it like my mum did. He freaked out. He couldn't believe I'd sorted the whole thing out for myself. Maybe if I hadn't have got the job I'd have thought I was kidding myself and it wasn't for me. But I did get the job, didn't I?

I got £1,500 for five days' filming – an unbelievable wedge that I managed to spend in about ten minutes. The biggest thing wasn't how much I got paid but that the filming was in Manchester and my mum or dad had to chaperone me. They'd be paid fifty quid a day. So I was giving them money, which was a brilliant feeling. I was especially proud to be able to put some money in my mum's purse because she never had any. She was an old-school housewife. Ironing, washing, dinner on the table, get us up for school, pick us up, all that. She never had time to work so we were always skint.

We got the train up to Manchester. I'd never been that far out of London in my life and it was amazing to see the country rolling by, knowing I was on my way to something so exciting.

By that stage my mum knew that I smoked so we sat

together puffing away on the train. It was great, I felt really adult. The whole thing was like a holiday. I felt like I was floating around, like everything was as good as it could possibly be which, to be fair, it was. They sent someone to meet us at Manchester Piccadilly, which felt mental. A car, with a driver, waiting for me? And someone paying for us to stay in a hotel room – they put us up in a Holiday Inn! I'd never been in a hotel in my life. My mum couldn't believe that I'd got myself into a position where all this was happening for me.

She stayed up in Manchester for a couple of days and then my dad came up and took over. On the way down to the first morning of our shoot we got into the lift with David Thewlis, who was playing my pimp. I said 'Hello' and he totally blanked me; ignored me and my dad completely.

He's quite lucky my old man didn't put one on him right there for his attitude but Dad was mindful that this was a big thing for me, so he swallowed it. What I didn't know at the time is that Thewlis is method – that is, he's a method actor. Method is a school of acting where you get into your role well before you even get on the set and remain in character throughout the shoot. He was blanking us for a reason – it's what his character would do. To him, I'm his little rent boy, he controls me and he wanted me to be scared of him, which worked.

Later down the line, I could see what Thewlis had done, and I understood it once I'd had a bit of time as an actor. It's just the way he approached it. He was playing a horrible cunt, the nastiest fucker in it. He's setting these boys up to be raped by paedophiles – he's the lowest of the fucking low. So that's how he acts around the set.

At the time, though, I thought, 'Prick.' He was rude and could have made me feel at home a bit more. Saying that, I totally respect him as an actor, he's brilliant. After it finished he acknowledged me a bit more, though I wouldn't say we were mates.

Him being so nasty could have had the reverse effect on me. I could have gone into my shell and thought, 'The reason he don't like me is that I'm shit, I shouldn't be an actor.' All that could have gone on in my head. Luckily it didn't.

We bowled up at the set and straight away I was just bouncing around looking at the hustle and bustle of it. Everyone's busy on the set, everyone's doing something. It was a bit like being on a building site but one on which everyone gave a fuck and was actually trying hard – laying down wires, rushing from place to place, calling weird instructions out, wheeling big racks of clothes past, meeting in little groups to weigh things up. People were sizing things up, pointing and gesturing and I'd no idea what they're trying to say but I knew it must be important. There were kinds of people I'd never seen before, wearing different clothes to what I was used to – arty types in open-necked shirts, blokes with long floppy hair, women talking in incredibly posh accents of a sort I'd only ever heard on the telly before. I think there were a few cravats going on. People were a bit dishevelled too. Where I come from it's all about gleaming white trainers and ironed shirts. Here people wore old stuff. 'Bohemian' is the word people use for the look. I obviously looked like the odd one out but it didn't bother me. The place was buzzing and I was raring to go.

The first scene was underneath a railway bridge. Thewlis was my pimp and was chasing me.

What he'd said to the director, which I didn't know, was, 'I want to chase him and when I get him I'm going to kiss him on the mouth to show power, that he to me is just a plaything.' So we do the chase and it's great to film because it's a long tracking shot. I'm jumping over things, I'm knocking things over, boxes going flying. Then he gets me, throws me up against this corrugated iron and I think it's the end of the scene. He says his line and he grabs my mouth and then his wet lips and his stubble are all over my mouth. I'm like, 'What the fuck was that?'

They cut the kiss out in the end. We only did it twice. I remember thinking, 'I want to do it again!' It was brilliant fun. Not the kiss bit – I'd have sooner nutted the cunt the way I felt about him right then – but just the chase bit.

The whole process was magical to me. I was listening to the crew's conversations about the scene, about what they were trying to do, listening about lenses and shots and everything. I'd found my calling. This was what I wanted to do. I thought, 'This is me just doing what I do and there's people paying me to be here. Ridiculous.'

I have to say that I completely fell in love with Helen Mirren, as did my dad. He got on really well with her. They met in the bar, pissed up and he was flirting with her. All the crew would be there and I remember her sitting on my dad's lap asking him about his tattoos. My dad was wide-eyed, couldn't fucking believe his luck.

Helen Mirren's one of the classiest people I've ever met. She's out of Essex and she's just amazing. My dad first met her in the Holiday Inn bar the night before we were due to start. He said, 'My boy's in it' and she was really lovely to me. She spoke to me and was really kind. She said, 'We've got a little scene together.' When I came to do the scene our little chat made me completely at ease and relaxed me with her. It was a fucking joy to be around people like that, to be out of the estate doing something constructive, feeling part of something bigger.

In the scene I did with Helen's character, DCI Tennison, she was interviewing me, trying to get information about Connie who was the kid who got killed. She feels sorry for me at the end of the scene but the next time she sees me I've overdosed on glue and died. She sees me dead in this graveyard and there's quite a powerful scene as she looks at the body.

I wanted to do that interview again and again and again. Helen leaned into me after we'd finished filming it and said, 'You're very good, you know that, don't you?' I'll never forget that. It made me very shy, to be honest. I've got to say I fancied the pants off her, her legs seemed to go on for ever and she had an amazing pair of tits. What I found most attractive about her, though, was her talent, how easy she made it look, how much charisma came from every pore in her body. She had an energy to her, an aura, and I really wanted to be like that myself.

This was a terrific education. I think the best way to learn is practically, on the job under a bit of pressure. You can learn techniques, do the posh stuff – work on Chekhov's plays, all that sort of bollocks – but you don't really know if you're going to be able to pull it out of the bag until you're there in front of eighty crew, people running around with cameras telling you what mark to hit, where your light is. You can get a bit bogged down with all that. It can be a bit intimidating if you think about it too much. If you're on the job, you're in there and you just have to deal with it that's the way to learn.

Years later, I did a film called *Greenfingers* with Helen. I hadn't seen her since I was fourteen and on *Greenfingers* I was twenty-three. I knew Helen was doing it; it was with Clive Owen too.

Clive's fascinating and he's a good actor but a bit of a drip for me. He's got something about him, though, no two ways about that. He's the romantic lead and women love him. Men don't get him as much. I didn't have nothing in common with him, he's not a man's man, but he's a decent geezer for all that.

I saw Helen coming out of the make-up truck and she said, 'Here he is, my Danny!' I couldn't believe it because I was a bit nervous at the thought of going up to her saying, 'Do you remember me?' You don't want to be a bollockhead, really. I'm sure she gets that all the time but she remembered me, came over and gave me a cuddle and set me up nicely for the job. That just shows the grace of that woman, something everyone should aspire to. I'm so glad she's won an Oscar and done it her own way. And a great pair of tits. You can't knock that.

Walking off the set of *Prime Suspect* I was buzzing. Life was brilliant. But then something happened that changed all that in a second, something I would have thrown the whole *Prime Suspect* thing away for, if only I thought I could stop it. But I couldn't and I was about to experience proper grief for the first time in my life.

5

TILL DEATH US DO PART

Prime Suspect seemed to take an age to come out. It was such a positive thing for me. But back at home a very negative thing was happening.

My granddad was the force of the family. He had six kids – four sons, two daughters, including my mum. He'd been in the navy and he'd been a boxer when he was younger. He was like Popeye, this man. He was only little but his arms were fucking massive, and tatted up. Around where I grew up, he was known. All the women loved him and all the men wanted to be him. He was old school, no teeth, drank rum. My dad, his son-in-law, was obsessed with talking about him, everything about him. Granddad got my dad into the painting and decorating business. He was the kind of bloke other blokes would tell stories about. He was a hard man and a fucking grafter. But that's not all he was. At home he would change nappies and look after the kids, do his bit as a father. He had a real sensitive side to him. He was soft and gentle and yet he could be a fucking man at the same time. When he was younger he was driving his van and he hit a kid. He didn't kill him but he hit him hard and hurt him pretty bad and after that Granddad refused to ever drive again. It had made too big an impression on him.

Around the time I got the *Prime Suspect* job, he got prostate cancer and, him being the old-school bloke he was, he didn't address it, didn't go to the doctor's. By the time we all found out about it, it was too late and it was terminal. He accepted that he was going to die. It was so fucking frustrating because if he'd gone to the doctor's early on he could have been treated. If only men would go to the doctor's a little bit more – but his generation just didn't do it.

We all watched him slowly get ill, turning from the force that he was to someone who couldn't go to the toilet. He had to piss in a commode. By the end he couldn't get up the stairs any more.

I moved in with my nan when I was about fourteen to help look after him. I loved it, to be honest. He used to call me 'Weedy' because I liked a joint. We'd sit watching telly together sharing a joint, watching Laurel and Hardy and laughing our bollocks off. If he needed a piss I'd help him piss, that sort of thing.

I was around him all day every day. He slowly got thinner and thinner. He was embarrassed by it, more than anything. He went from being such a force to having his wife getting out his cock to piss. It wasn't a good thing to see.

I looked after him for about a year. He fucking held on. He was in the London hospital in Whitechapel when he died, which was a cunthole by the way. The last moment I had with him was in the little room in that hospital watching England play San Marino. We had to win 7–0 to go through and we won 7–1. A lot of people have experienced this, waiting for the inevitable that a relative's going to die, but it really affected me. I had a moment and started to dabble with drugs. Not just weed.

Let me say a bit about drugs here. I don't condone taking them. If you can live your life without them then that's great. So if, God forbid, a kid should be reading this they should know that drugs can fuck you up, they can kill you, no question. You're swallowing something or sniffing it up your nose and you've got no idea what's in it, where it's come from, whether it's been transported up some fucker's arsehole and chopped up with a razor blade held in their shitty fingers.

Don't look on me as a role model because there are times when I've come within a gnat's bollock of chucking my entire career down the drain, losing my family, everything I love. And remember, you don't have to be an addict, you can drop dead on your first E, people have. Drugs can seriously fuck you up, and I've seen that happen to friends of mine.

Now, if you are a kid reading this, stop here. This next bit is adults only. What I'd say to any over eighteens is this – let's not be fucking hypocrites. Drugs can be dangerous but also – for a lot of us – great fun. People wouldn't take them if they weren't. OK, I see things differently now I'm older and my own kid is coming up to the age she might be exposed to that sort of thing. There's a lot more to life than being off your nut and it would kill me to think of my kids taking drugs. Drugs can do you in, no mistake. But when I was taking drugs back then I wasn't thinking about the downside at all.

I quite liked the idea of losing your mind a little bit. I've always been a bit nutty and I liked taking drugs that made you do all sorts of weird shit. I felt that way right since my first hit on an aerosol can, sitting up the park with a couple of skanky birds trying to cop a feel of their lils. Sometimes when I was round Granddad's house looking after him, I'd take speed and sit up watching him sleeping just wishing he'd be all right. He looked vulnerable lying there and I never thought of him like that. It made me feel very sad and angry that it was happening to him.

Speed is a nasty fucking drug, though, and eventually I had to knock it on the head. It leaves you shaking the next day, crying almost, and paranoid even when you're on it. There were a couple of incidents that made me question what I was doing and eventually stop taking it.

I'd gone to bed at nine or ten in the morning and I remember I'd finally just dropped off, into this weird sleep. My nan started screaming, 'Danny! Danny!' Her voice was drilling into my nut. It snapped me out of it. I jumped up out of bed and I remember my ring falling off my finger. I was obviously caning it far too much and had lost that much weight.

I went downstairs to see that my granddad had collapsed on the floor of the toilet. My nan couldn't pick him up, so I helped her. I could hardly lift him because I was so fucked.

I remember my nan's face, disappointed in herself and frustrated with my granddad. Unsurprisingly it had started to get her down. There was a tension in the house, you could feel it in the air, my nan was annoyed at him for being weak and annoyed at herself for being annoyed. This is the thing when someone's ill – part of you wonders why they can't just get up and be like they were. You know they can't of course but you have this big mix of emotions going on, anger that the person's dying, fear, resentment and, above that, just the grind of getting through the day to day. It wasn't a happy time and I wanted to forget about it so I'd just take a load of drugs and fuck off out of the house, lose myself hanging around with my mates.

I was doing too much speed. I hated the taste of it so I'd put a gram in half a lager and see what happened. Well, what does happen is that you start to get edgy, you talk your bollocks off, you brim with nervous energy – that's why it's called speed. When it makes you feel good you feel fucking invincible, like you could run through walls. There's a downside sometimes though and it can spark a bit of paranoia – particularly on the comedowns. If you don't sleep for a couple of days, what do you expect? You can end up with that feeling that the world's out to get you. I was taking a lot of it and it was doing me no favours.

The real final straw, though, was when I ended up lying on the floor of the khazi myself. When you take a lot of speed, if you get up quickly you get a big headrush. Anyway, I'm in bed at about eleven in the morning and I go downstairs for a piss and I get this big headrush. The next thing I know, I'm lying on the floor exactly where my granddad had been, curled around the toilet. My nan hears the crash and comes running, her voice 'Danny! Danny!' drilling into my head.

I was having a piss one minute, the next my nan is standing over me going, 'What the hell have you been taking?'

I got myself up on my feet and I felt disgusted with myself. I said to her, 'Oh, Nan, I just got really drunk last night.' She's not fucking stupid, though, she could see it was more than that. What had really done her was seeing me lying there just like my granddad was.

It was a moment when I thought, 'Fuck it, Dan, time to turn it in.' It wasn't doing me any good and it wasn't fair on my nan.

My nan's great, she's like Peggy out of *EastEnders* – four foot ten with her hair lacquered up. She runs around in Reebok Classics and tracksuits. She worked up until the age of seventy-nine or eighty as a cleaner for sixty-odd years, fuelled on forty Lambert and Butler a day. She'd get up at quarter to five every morning, out of that fucking door, on the graft. She's a massive part of my career. I was living with her when I was having auditions and stuff when I was fourteen and fifteen and I couldn't afford to get to where they were. She'd buy me my travel card to get there and she'd also give me my fag money for my ten Bensons. My nan loves a fag and couldn't bear to think of me going without. She'd make sure I got to my audition even if she had to give me the last quid in her purse. I love taking her to premieres and swanky dos now because she loves it, and I like being able to give something back for all those years she looked after me.

Knowing my nan has made me think about the way we treat our old people. She was a cleaner in a school and when she got older, they fucked her off and got someone younger. She was gutted. She needs something to do with herself, she can't sit there watching *Jeremy Kyle* all day. She needs to be able to do something. But as far as the school was concerned that was it – she was over the age of retirement so she had to go.

My nan has a massive heart. Losing her husband was a huge thing for her to deal with. She kept breaking down. It took her about five years to stop crying when she talked about him.

My granddad died on his son Gary's birthday. My dad adored my granddad, his father-in law, worshipped the ground he walked on, but he'd refused to go to the hospital to see him. I'd always go, 'Come on, Dad, come and see him.' He'd say, 'No, boy, I can't do it. It's not the image I want of him.' I'd say, 'That's fucking bollocks, this is the reality, you should come and say goodbye.' He never did and he regrets it to this day.

I was doing a show called *Speakeasy* when I found out my granddad had died. It was a talkshow presented by Emma Forbes, a debate show for kids. It was about how kids deal with their mum and dad splitting up. I got back in and everyone was round my nan's house, some of them with a drink in their hands. My uncle Gary told me to come outside and then he told me. I remember thinking, 'How can they all be drinking in there?' and I kicked the shed and stormed off. My uncle just followed me for twenty minutes to make sure I was all right. I couldn't believe it, I was thinking, 'people like Ian Brady are alive and my granddad and Bobby Moore have to be dead. How is that fair?'

When I first got told I was all right in terms of grief. I was more angry than anything. It was only in the days after the reality of his death hit me. I just wasn't there. I went to see him in the morgue and touched his head, freezing cold. I'd drawn him a picture of Laurel and Hardy and put it in the coffin with him. That was my last moment with him. It's a massive thing, something like that, for the whole family.

The Saturday get-togethers stopped. It was a different house when he died. My nan wasn't in the mood for banging out thirty dinners. People would turn up still but it petered out. Nowadays it's only my mum, my sister, my uncle Mark, sometimes my cousin Leigh.

My granddad never got to see me in *Prime Suspect*. Our family counted the days and hours until it was on. We watched it with my mum, brother and sister round our house, all crammed onto the sofa with fags and tea waiting for it to begin. I was fascinated by it, particularly as I hadn't read the whole script so I didn't know what the outcome was. Then it started and I was saying, 'I remember that actor in the bar!' I was so into it. Such a moment.

I'd have given anything if Granddad could have seen it because I know he would have been so proud. I do believe he's up there looking down on me, though.

He was gone and I felt empty but, the grief aside, things were about to become brilliant for me as I got success in a way that most child actors can only dream about.

6

BOY DONE GOOD

It was weird after *Prime Suspect* was shown on the TV. I walked out of the house and round the streets feeling very odd that so many people in our neighbourhood would know I'd been on the telly.

I got my first fan mail from twins in America. I remember the opening line: 'We are two green-eyed monsters from America.' I thought it was magic.

After *Prime Suspect* I went for lots of auditions and seemed to get everything I was up for: *Cadfael, The Bill* – inevitably – and *A Touch of Frost*.

In *Cadfael* I worked with Derek Jacobi, a brilliant actor. I remember him mincing around in his leather trousers with his boyfriend, not because it meant anything to me but for my dad's reaction. My old man came with me to where it was being filmed in Budapest and he wasn't all that impressed by him. Derek would be walking past and Dad would be saying, 'Look at that gay bastard, who does he think he fucking is?' I suppose the answer to that might be 'the lead actor on this set, the most important person here and one of the finest actors of his generation'. Wouldn't have meant much to my old man, though.

I can see why. You'd last about ten seconds acting like that where I grew up. That was the thing about my area; some people there were very homophobic, very racist. Times have changed a bit now, thank God. I never really got all that 'us and them' stuff. It was always around me but with a mum like mine I could never think like that. Before Dad left it actually caused a lot of rows at home.

A black bloke would come on the telly and Dad would say something – nothing over the top, just typical of a bloke of his generation and background – and then Mum would come back at him, 'How can you judge someone just on the colour of his skin?' Then my dad would say that he'd judge people however he chose and Mum would say, 'Just shows your fucking ignorance then, don't it?' and a row would start.

Meeting Derek was the first time I'd become aware of how many gay people are in the business. It didn't bother me at all. In a way it fascinated me, because I'd never really met many gay people at that early age, though my mum had a gay friend, her best friend Philip. He was East London through and through. He was a tough bastard and didn't give a fuck what he said to anyone. Him and Derek couldn't have been more different, which I guess goes to show you that assumptions about someone based on things like their sexuality or race don't work.

While the whole idea of how common being gay is was opened up to me, for me, though, it was more about Derek Jacobi as an actor. I loved to watch him because you can learn so much off a bloke like that; he's one of the greatest actors this country has ever produced.

He was also a bit of a strange cat but, then again, as an

actor you have to be strange. I'm a weirdo myself. To want to pretend to be someone else for a living is a weird thing. It's like being back in school in many ways but you get treated like royalty wherever you go.

After *Cadfael* it was *A Touch Of Frost*, which pleased my dad because we were working with David 'Del Boy' Jason. I didn't see that much of David on the set but I did see a guy called Craig Kelly.

I'd watched a film called *Young Americans* with Harvey Keitel and Craig. Craig was the lead boy in it. It was the role of all roles for a young actor, big budget, and a major marketing push when it came out. It looked like it was going to guarantee stardom to whoever got the part. Everybody auditioned for it, it was massive and he got it.

Craig Kelly was brilliant in that film. I thought he was going to be really big. A couple of years later he's in *A Touch of Frost* and I'm sharing my trailer with him. I was amazed. I plucked up the courage and said, 'Listen, I hope you don't mind me saying this but I'm surprised to see you here. I thought you had a massive Hollywood career in front of you.' He said, 'Do you know what, Dan? People kept telling me to turn everything down. I went through a period of six months saying "won't do that, won't do that" and I missed the boat over there.'

From what he had in that movie to sharing a trailer with me must have made him feel bitter, I would have thought. I took what he said on board and thought, 'Whatever happens, don't get too big for your fucking boots, boy.'

This is the thing about acting. You can't plan it. All you

can do is what's put in front of you. This is what fucks me off about being stereotyped as a hard man. I'm not a director, I'm not a producer. I can only do the films that are put in front of me. If they are sometimes similar then that's what I have to do.

As long as I shine in it, I don't see any more that I can do. I'm thirty-three. It's difficult for me to go in the other direction and be the romantic lead. I know I've got the talent to do it, and I'd love to do it, but I'm known as a certain thing. I'm a brand, whether I like it or not.

I've had to sit down with my agent recently. She wants me to go in another direction but I don't think it's going to happen. I don't get seen at auditions for period dramas; I'm the last person to be considered for roles like that. For a role that's a bit gritty and a bit dark then I'm the first on the list. I appreciate that. I'd do the period thing like a shot, though. I love a challenge. There's nothing I wouldn't play other than a nonce. I couldn't go there.

Around this time I was getting most things I auditioned for. One thing I didn't get was a play with Alan Rickman as director. He saw me but didn't want me. He did, though, write me a very nice letter saying why he'd rejected me. The part was Scottish and he didn't think I had the accent quite right. He didn't think I was quite ready for it yet. My agent told me it was very unusual for directors to write letters like that to actors and that I should feel flattered.

A play I did get was one called *Not Gods But Giants*. I was about sixteen years old then, I think. This was a play about domestic violence. It was about a drunk dad who bashes his missus up. I was the kid and this bad home pushes me into a relationship with the next-door neighbour, an older woman.

The star was a geezer called Paul McNeilly, who also wrote it. As soon as I walked in the room he wanted me. I was honest about my background and he could see that it had been a good preparation for the role. It was profit paid. This means you only get any money if it does well. The money meant fuck all to me, though. I just wanted to act.

It was put on in the White Bear, a shithole of the highest order in Kennington that was full of crusties, a real weird crowd. You had to walk through them all to get to the theatre at the back. You always felt you might get mugged on your way to the stage, or catch fleas off one of the dirty fuckers.

I loved it, though. It was the first time I met Neil Maskell, a chap I'd go on to work with in future. He played the comedy part.

It was a real experience for me because it was about working in an environment where you had to have total concentration or you'd lose it. It held about forty people but all you could hear was the pub and people fighting, the dogs out the back. Sometimes people would mistake the theatre for the toilet, come in and go, 'Oh, sorry,' and go out again. It was this idea of having to be completely focused. You'd walk out there, blank everything out including the audience. That's the thing about doing a play, you have to blank 'em but at the same time play up to 'em, let them feel like they're onstage with you. It's getting that balance right.

It was during this run that I got the letter from Alan Rickman. I wrote back and told him I was doing this play and I'd love for him to come down and see it. And he fucking came, especially to see me! I told the rest of the cast and they couldn't believe it.

He waited around after and said plenty of nice things about my performance. He made a point to me, which I took on when I became famous. I was introducing him to the cast but he was with a friend and I didn't introduce the friend. He told me that he was with someone and I should have introduced her too. He was right to say it and I never forgot that.

He has that really distinctive voice and I could hear his laugh bellowing out during the play. It was a real moment. I felt so flattered he was there and I thought I'd love to be able to make people feel that way by just showing up to something.

The play went up to the Edinburgh Festival but I couldn't go because I had paid work on a film called *Loving* – a drama for BBC Two. It was here that I began to learn a lot more about what it takes to be a good actor.

Anyone can be an actor. I'm not undermining what I do but every day as a human being you talk to people, you interact with them. You do come across some people who are as boring as fuck – one tone to their voice. There are many people I've met who have nothing about them at all. What surprises me is that they can't see that themselves and they don't make the effort. I don't even think it's a personality thing. Some people just like to talk and take for ever to tell a story, long words with big spaces between them in a monotone. What we as actors do is the opposite of that. You don't want to go too far, be hammy and overact but you want to be interesting, have a presence about you, have some sort of charisma, make people want to listen to you. You can even make a boring story interesting, if you put enough into it. Words are actors' fucking ammo. That's something I've learned from certain actors and one in particular on *Loving*. I didn't need to go to drama school because I worked with someone on *Loving* who has been my drama school. I feel truly blessed that I met him – an actor called Mark Rylance. He later became head of the Shakespeare Globe. There was a terrific cast on *Loving* – Georgina Cates, who was in *An Awfully Big Adventure* with Hugh Grant – she was fucking brilliant in it – Lucy Cohu, who went on to play Princess Margaret in the biopic *The Queen's Sister*.

Mark Rylance was fucking unbelievable. What he had, which was the opposite of someone like David Thewlis, was that he could snap in and out of the role. He'd be fucking around with me before a take – he was very funny and nutty as a squirrel's arse – but when he heard the word 'action' he'd snap into this whole different character, from the way he walked, the faces he'd give, the looks.

I was fascinated by the idea he could do that and it helped me with my role because in the drama, which is all about servants in a big manor house, I love him as my mentor and a father figure but I also hate him because the lead female character loves him and not me, so I have to fight with my demons a little bit.

He was just amazing. He would have a Dictaphone with people talking on it. He'd lived with butlers and visited butlers, which again I found fascinating. I was thinking why would you go to them extremes? How would you go about that? Do you just ring up butlers and go 'Here, mate, I'm doing a film and would you mind if I come and live with you for a few days?' I could never understand it but it worked. You'd listen to this butler talking on this Dictaphone, talking complete nonsense really, but it obviously helped Mark to get under the skin of the character he was playing.

Mark was a real friend to me, on the set and afterwards and I really listened to what he had to say about acting. He taught me an awful lot.

Loving is set during the Second World War, and it's about the goings on behind the scenes in a big manor house out in the sticks. Even though there's a big war kicking off all around us, us servants are living in this house in the middle of nowhere, away from it all but very aware of what's happening in the outside world. I play a pantry boy in it – a butler's assistant.

It's a love story. Looking back at it, it's hilarious. I'm in love with Georgina Cates's character, she's in love with Mark Rylance's character, who's the butler. There's a sort of love triangle thing going on. She's already got a boyfriend, an officer, too.

This was my first time as an adult on a film set, the first time that I had been to Dublin and the first time I was on set without a chaperone. It was daunting. When you go on a film set you all get thrown in together, complete strangers, six weeks right up each other's arses day and night, so you've got to bond as a team and make this thing work. That for me is always the hardest thing, having to go on the set, get on with everybody and be creative with them.

You spend all your time with them, you live out of each other's pockets, you eat together every night, you're around each other all day. That was always the toughest part for me. The acting came together very naturally but the socialising side of things was never so easy.

You have people from such different backgrounds, not just with me being from East London. There would be other people from other working-class areas there – the crew mainly. But it would be quite rare to come across someone from the same background as me as an actor. That didn't happen until much later on, really.

I was always acting with drama school people and I have to admit I did feel competitive with them; I wanted to show them just how good I was. Everything came together to help me do that, including something that allowed me to dig a little deeper into myself.

Up to that point I'd played little Jack-the-Laddy type roles but the one emotion I'd never got to express was sadness. Even in *Prime Suspect*, you can tell I'm a sad character but I don't get to express that in any of my dialogue, I'm always running from the police and when they do finally see a sensitive side to me, I've topped myself.

In *Loving* I have a crying scene because I had got down on one knee and proposed to Kate. She rejects me and I think it's because I haven't been to war and she doesn't respect me, so I need to go and sign up.

I was really looking forward to this scene because I knew I had a lot to give in it.

Just before we were going to shoot, I found out that my

dog, Sam, who I had had since the age of five had died. I'd thought he would live for ever, but he must have been fifteen or so, old for a dog. He'd been run over three times, survived it, been attacked by a pit bull, survived it, had an operation, survived it. But he got ill, just through old age, really. He went blind in one eye. Before I left home for *Loving* I remember he was shivering and I lay with him in the hall, wrapping him in towels to keep him warm. But I had to go away and do this job. I didn't want to leave him but I had to.

By then I had moved back to my mum's and she rang me and told me they'd had to have him put down. I broke up. I felt so far from home. All of a sudden I thought, 'Fuck this job, I don't give a fuck about acting, I just need to be at home.'

Mum said it was like Sam knew he was ready to die. They had to leave him in the vet's to have the injection. My dad had gone with Mum and even he was sobbing his heart out. I've said before that he don't show emotion but he did then. Mum said he got into the van in bits. This dog was a massive part of our lives, it was like he was one of the kids.

I had no one to talk to about it. I could have spoken to Mark but I didn't. The film was set in a castle and we were surrounded by lakes and gardens, beautiful really. I just walked off on my own.

Slowly, though, I began to channel this energy. I knew I had this scene coming up and I started to think about the dog's death in quite an adult way. I thought, 'OK, this is sadness, deal with it. It was inevitable he had to go. I'm glad I wasn't there because I would have refused to have had him put down, I couldn't have actually done it.'

So I used this well of grief for the scene. I remember crying in front of a whole crew, really sobbing. Then the scene ends and you switch it off. Not totally off, but more like a tap. The water's there but it doesn't always come out.

It was one more thing in my locker as an actor. I had the ability to do that because of something sad that had happened in my life. It felt like a gift from the dog. I could have tried to do that with my granddad's death but that never felt right. I wanted to remember him the way he was, not like he was when he was dying.

Things were going well for me at this time of my life. I was young, carefree, was earning a bit and all I had to do was sit around at home smoking dope waiting for the phone to ring for another job.

All that changed overnight and for two reasons. The first was that I changed physically. I'd always been very boyish. I didn't get hair round my bollocks until I was sixteen and I was the last one in the school showers to hit puberty, I remember that. I was having sex a long time before I had hair on my nuts. Then suddenly I went from being a youth to being a young man. The parts started to dry up. I went up for jobs and wasn't getting them, kept on getting told I wasn't quite right.

The second thing emerged when Joanne asked me to come upstairs with her at my mum's house one night. We'd been together since we were fourteen and now I was eighteen. I could tell by her manner something was up. She looked at me straight and told me. 'I'm pregnant and I'm having it.' This was a shock. Joanne was on the Pill but she had been taking some antibiotics and they'd stopped it working.

Joanne was quite calm and said that she didn't expect me to stay with her. If I did go, though, I should know there would be no coming back. She'd bring up the baby on her own and I'd have nothing to do with it. For about ten seconds I thought I should walk away. And then I looked at her and realised how much I loved her. How could I leave her?

Joanne was my childhood sweetheart, the girl I'd been with since I was fourteen. She was the one everyone fancied at school, really good-looking, the first to have tits. Her dad's Spanish and she has that look to her, exotic really. She was brought up in Custom House as well. Her mum's a proper old-school cockney who went on holiday to Spain and met this guy in Mallorca. He gave up everything for her and came over to move to East London to a council estate. It was like something out of Mills and Boon. He hardly spoke a word of English but he decided to bring up his kids here, which was lucky for me because I'd never have met his beautiful daughter if he hadn't.

So Joanne was the sort of girl you looked at from afar – you might wank over her but you'd never dare to speak to her.

Then one day she started looking at me a little bit and I noticed it. I didn't know what to do about it. I thought it was a wind-up. We're complete opposites, me and Joanne. She was really good at school, almost on first-name terms with the teachers, which was unheard of. I was a fucker. I couldn't get my head round the lessons. Nothing interested me, other than drama.

It seemed surreal, her sending her mate over to me and asking me for a date. A date in East London when you're fourteen is over the park with a bottle of Lambrini having a little lips up on a bench. She took me to fucking Pizza Hut. A proper sit-down meal. She was quite adult for her age. She paid for it. I knew from that minute that I'd scored out of my league and I think she knew it too, she certainly always held the whip hand in the relationship until we were in our twenties. Still, she liked me, so that was that.

It had only ever been her for me, really. We had our first snog in the rubbish room at the Shipman Youth Centre and it was there I'd felt my first pair of tits, which is what I'd say if I was describing it to the lads. Another way of looking at it is that it was the best day of my life because I met the girl who would become my lifelong friend and the mother to my kids.

I'd had girlfriends before her but she was so much part of me that I just couldn't imagine life without her.

So when Joanne told me she was pregnant, after the initial shock I thought, 'Stand up and be counted.' So I said 'Fuck it, OK, let's do it.'

There I was, eighteen, a dad to be, no work, no nothing. Standing in that bedroom, listening to Joanne, I thought it was all over, that I had to earn a living somehow and that living would be in one of the dead-end jobs the teachers had always thought I was destined for.

I went downstairs, picked up the phone and got on to my dad to ask him if he had any work going with him. The dream, I thought, was over. I didn't know that sitting in Cardiff a beautiful man was scribbling out a film script that could well have been the story of my life. It had a part in it that could have been made for me. The man was called Justin Kerrigan and the film was *Human Traffic*. It would capture the imagination of young people everywhere and propel me towards being the poster boy for the chemical generation.

7

ES ARE GOOD

Joanne's mum and dad weren't very happy about her being pregnant and they were right not to be. We always knew it was going to be tricky telling them, that it would turn out to be a right fucker, and so it did.

Joanne insisted on doing it on her own, for the good of my health more than anything. I think she wanted her old man to hear it while I wasn't in nutting distance. Joanne's dad Tolo – short for Bartholemew – is a real character. He's a force in Joanne's life, no mistake and had I been there when she told him, no doubt he would have been a force in mine – most of that force delivered by a tasty left hook. Eventually when I did go round there it wasn't exactly comfortable. I got the silent treatment. His attitude was 'I've had my doubts about you, now let's see what you're made of. Prove to me you're worthy of being a partner to my daughter and a proper dad.'

I had to sympathise. It was a big shock for her mum and dad. I'm not sure they even knew we were having sex – or I think they liked to kid themselves that we weren't. I was never allowed to stay round her house, never even allowed in her bedroom. My mother was the opposite to that. She's very liberal. She believes in the idea that you don't need money to get through life, you need love and a cuddle.

So Joanne would be allowed in my bedroom. She'd stay round sometimes and we'd be allowed to sleep in the same bed together from fourteen onwards. Joanne was very adult about it, I couldn't wait to get things moving along with her, like any teenage kid would, but she held back from all that and I think my mum saw the maturity in her.

After Joanne had given her parents the news, and Tolo had calmed down, I could start coming round again. I wouldn't say he greeted me with open arms, but though we've had our moments, we're sweet now.

Her parents were right to have the hump about Joanne being pregnant. Any idea that she might have gone into further education or fulfilled her potential in a career ended right fucking there. To be fair, if my Dani came back at that age and told me she was up the duff, I'd go mental too. As much as I love my Dani, and of course I'm overjoyed we had her, I would advise anyone to have a child later on in life.

You should live your life first. There are benefits to having kids early, for sure. I'm thirty-three, I've got a fourteen-year-old. By the time she's eighteen we can go out together, grow old together even. But you lose a lot of your own childhood and self-discovery.

When you have a child, that's the only thing you can think about. Your whole motivation in life changes to looking after this defenceless little thing in a crib that has to be clothed and fed and nurtured and loved. That's all there is, as I found out smartish.

It was a twenty-four-hour-a-day thing, me and Joanne

around the crib in her tiny little house. We'd moved into a little flat in Custom House with a sofa we got from Joanne's mum and a tumble dryer my dad had dug out of a skip.

The baby and the lack of cash put a lot of stress on our relationship. All we could talk about was how much sleep we were having, shitty nappies, and where the next pound note was coming from. Sex goes out of the window for a bit and you have to start earning properly, no fucking about anymore. It's a major shift and at the time I was afraid it was going to have a bad effect on my acting career. I needed a regular wage and, sod's law being what it is, this was exactly the time when my work dried up.

Any young people who want to become actors should know the hardest thing is the rejection. People saying, 'No, we don't want you, we want him. You're not good enough. You're not right.'

Up to that point I hadn't experienced it, because I had a result in almost every job I went for as a child. Almost overnight, it seemed, that changed and I started to get the nos. And, fuck me, did that fuck up my head; I'm a Leo, I'm a winner, a bad loser. I started to get really humpy. When I got rejected I wanted to know exactly why they didn't want me. My agent told me I just had to accept it but I couldn't. I wanted details. 'Why, exactly, have I been turned town, tell me their fucking precise reason. Tell me why the guy they did pick is better than me.' Of course Charlotte didn't bother ringing the casting directors to ask because there's no point in asking. If they don't want you, they don't want you. End of. And I had to earn, didn't I, because of the kid.

I became a bitter fucker; looking at things I'd gone for and seeing other actors in them I'd say, 'He's shit! Why would they go with that over me?' I'd drive myself mad trying to work out what I was doing wrong.

I was learning something that every adult actor knows: rejection is the biggest part of the game. Even now when I guarantee an audience for a film, for every one job I get, I lose out on twenty. It doesn't matter who you are. De Niro's lost out on parts, Pacino's lost out on parts. It's part of the process you have to learn to live with.

Still, you can't say to a baby, 'I'm sorry, darlin', this is a bit of a shit period for me. If you can just wait for your clothes, your bottles and your crib until it picks up in two or three years, that would be cushty.'

So, no fucking about, when the baby arrived I had to go and work with my dad painting and decorating. It was disgusting and I hated every fucking minute of it. I respect people who get up at 5.30 every morning in the freezing cold to get picked up to work on a fucking building site, slaving their bollocks off, but I can't say I enjoyed it. It wasn't so much the work itself as the fact I'd had a taste of something else, something I was really good at, and I'd had it taken away from me for what seemed like no reason.

It didn't help that my dad wouldn't let me paint nothing. Instead of a brush, he gave me a broom. I had to do all the shitty jobs – sweeping up, loading the skip. He wouldn't even let me paint a fucking fence. I thought, 'If I'm here I might as well learn something. I'm not learning anything by sweeping up fucking sawdust.' Of course, I hadn't given up on acting,

I'd never do that and, in fact, the bullshit work made me a lot more determined.

But things got worse before they got better. My dad didn't give me work for long so I had to join up to a temping agency. They would ferry me out to different places all over London where I'd work as a labourer. I would sometimes talk about the acting, but not much. I felt like a melt for talking about it really but it was hard not to because it was always on my mind.

Every time I was putting the dustman's gloves on, throwing things in the skip, I'd be thinking, 'I can't wait for my next audition, I don't care what it is, I just can't wait.' Still, I wasn't getting many auditions, maybe one every two weeks, and even they were costing me. To go to an audition meant an afternoon off loading the skip, an afternoon off being paid, less money for Joanne and less money for Dani. I had to keep the faith but I had to persuade Joanne to keep the faith too. The pressure indoors was intense, as Joanne needed me to keep earning. It should have been the time of my life, shacked up with a new baby, but I was under a lot of stress. I'd keep getting rejected, keep getting angry and my missus started saying to me, 'Look, Dan, maybe acting ain't for you.' I couldn't let that be true.

Looking back on it, this was always going to happen. When you move up from being a child actor to the bracket of a young man then you're up against fiercer competition. You always see child actors who do well and then disappear off the face of the earth or top themselves. It was easier for me because I wasn't a massive star like Macaulay Culkin or Corey Feldman.

I was just a working child actor, who was now getting used to a life on the sites.

It gave me this aggression, which wasn't healthy. I'd look at every audition as my last and I would despise whoever I was going up against. I'd be sitting waiting, thinking about taking the afternoon off earning, which was always going to give me the hump. I'd be looking at the competition across the waiting room with seething bitterness, thinking, 'You cunts, you're going to take the food out of my baby's mouth.' It's a good way to get your mettle up but you have to channel it in the right way. It gives you an adrenalin boost but that's not always helpful. If you're a boxer, you can get yourself all worked up like that because you're going to be battering some fucker as soon as the bell goes. But you can't be seething like Tyson in a grudge fight and then go into an audition for a bit of light comedy where you're meant to be playing a lovestruck fucking florist. It doesn't play.

It might not have done me any favours but I always told the truth in the auditions. I would sit there and they would say, 'What have you been doing?' And I would say, 'I'll tell you what I've been fucking doing, I've been loading fucking skips and it's fucking killing me. I need a job.' Soon as I'd say it, I'd feel a tension enter the room. The casting people don't want to hear that. It's not a life they understand and why should they? It wasn't the right type of energy to come into the room with. You're meant to say 'It's been non-stop, darling, I'm up for some really big roles,' giving them the nod that you're in demand and they'd be lucky to have you. It's bull-shit and everyone knows it's bullshit, so why pretend?

Hearing 'Sorry, but no' was shit on its own but having to relay it to Joanne was terrible. It was almost worse telling her that I hadn't got a job than it was hearing it myself. The waiting was agony. It was bad enough with a TV audition, where you might hear the same day. With a film they whittle it down and whittle it down which keeps you there waiting at the phone for weeks on end. I don't think I got past the second stage audition for anything at that point. I went for *Band of Brothers*, and that was massive because it was Spielberg's thing, but they elbowed me from the first round.

This was a tough, tough time but it shaped me. I like to think it gave me a bit of character. Even when everything was really shit, and money was tighter than a gnat's chuff, I never thought of quitting for a second. It made me want to work harder, learn more and really not take it for granted if I ever became successful.

So I was in a bad place when I was given the script for *Human Traffic* but it was like a light in the darkness to me. Right from the first page I could tell it was quality. It excited me so much because it was basically a description of my life. I thought, 'Oh my God! This is me!' I loved the fucking raw honesty of it. It was a script about living for the weekend. People getting off their heads Friday and Saturday nights because they work in a shit job all week earning a pittance. It was so true, undeniable. That life was all around me. I could see my mates living it, I was living it, everyone I knew was living it.

The film was brilliantly honest. It said that if your life is as boring as shit, on the weekend why not spend what little money you earn on losing your mind for a few hours and talking shit with your mates? Then you have your comedown, go back to work on the Monday and put up with the daily grind until you can do it all again the next weekend. From Monday to Friday you're fucking depressed, a wage slave, getting it up the arse from your boss who's making you work your nuts off, turning you into a nothing. So, come the weekends and it's your time, why not take some E?

I'm not condoning E but millions of people take it. They're not fucking idiots, they do it because they like losing the plot a little bit. And, while I'm truly sorry for anyone who's lost someone through the drug, let's get a sense of perspective. As many people die of drinking in an hour as die in a week from taking ecstasy.

That's what the film was saying. There's no big moral to it. No one dies, no one gets raped or murdered. The film was also quite subtle. You never see anyone doing any drugs; you just take it as read that drugs have been boshed. The important thing about E is the friendships it helps form. It removes your inhibitions, makes you open and friendly. It doesn't make you nasty, doesn't get you angry or raged out. The worst I've ever seen anyone on E do was talk ninety-nine shades of shit. And that's what the film was about.

I read the script virtually drooling. I thought, 'This is the final straw for me. If I don't get this job then I'm not bothering no more. I can't stand the rejection. It's starting to do my head in.' I said in the extras on the DVD that if I hadn't got the job I'd have slit my wrists. That wasn't quite true but it wasn't far off. It would have been a class A kick in the bollocks if I'd missed out on it.

There was no way I was going to fuck up this audition so I went about learning my lines like a maniac. I lived with that script, I ate with it, went to the bog with it, went out and stayed in with it, slept with it and woke up with it.

Given that I wasn't exactly fucking Einstein at school, you might think I find learning lines difficult. Not at all. Learning lines is fuck all. You just have to keep reading it and reading it and reading it again. You read that script over and over and over. When it's embedded in your skull and it's all you can think about, then you can play with it. Learning the script inside and out gives you the freedom to fuck around.

I'd been for a few other auditions and got close but this one was all or nothing, shit or bust for me. The only fucker for me was that the character – Moff – was Welsh, because the whole thing was set in Cardiff.

Faced with that, you have to get creative. I read the script and thought, 'This guy doesn't have to be Welsh.' I could see what this character was about, what he represents. He, out of the bunch of mates, was the nutty fucker, the one that just canes it. He's got no bird, sells a bit of puff to earn the money to buy his own drugs. He's a nice kid – a peace-to-all-nations sort – from a really square family. Everyone knows someone like Moff, that kind of character. There was a lot of myself in him.

I tried the accent again and again on my own but I just couldn't do it. I ended up sounding like someone pissed in an Indian restaurant doing a bad impression of the waiter. I didn't have the money to get a voice coach so I walked into the audition shitting myself. My nerves were off the charts. For the first time in my life the thought that I wasn't actually going to be able to do it crossed my mind.

I immediately sat down opposite Justin Kerrigan, who wrote it. It wasn't a good start when he opened his mouth because he was as Welsh as a fucking leek. I liked him straight away, though, he was a real bundle of energy. Before I'd even turned the page to start reading for the audition he said, 'Do you take drugs?'

For a second it occurred to me to lie. In an audition room, drugs are a no-no. No one speaks about them. I looked at him, took a deep breath and heard myself say: 'Yeah, I fucking love drugs.'

This big grin cracked all over his face. He went, 'Wicked, let's start reading.' Again, I felt myself getting nervous. I couldn't start reading straight away and come over sounding like something from *Goodness Gracious Me*. So before I began reading I said, 'Look, man, I love this script, I love everything about it, I love the honesty, the vibe, everything, but does this guy really need to be Welsh?' Justin kind of went, 'Errr, I hadn't really thought about it.'

That was all I needed to hear. 'I'm going to do the speech as me then,' I said. He said, 'Yeah, do what you want.' I started to read and this energy seemed to come bursting out of me. Justin gave such a positive vibe, the script was brilliant, and I was reading as myself. I fucking smashed it. It was the taxi driver speech, me off my nut on speed, talking to a taxi driver about whether he's seen *Taxi Driver* or not, going on a rant about Peter Andre, how I hate him and really want to hurt him.

I remember Justin's face, it lit up. He was pissing himself with laughter too. He didn't offer it to me right there but I thought, 'I've nailed that. I couldn't have done it any better.'

Still it was by no means certain I'd get the part. Justin saw virtually every actor in the country for that one. I think he saw actresses like Anna Friel, people like that. He turned down a lot of big names for the role because they all denied taking drugs – and he was right to. It's hard enough trying to play a drunk. Trying to recreate being on ecstasy is impossible unless you've taken it. The only guy in the main cast who hadn't taken E was the young kid in it, which was right for the part because it's his first experience of the whole thing.

When I heard I'd got the part I was so pleased I nearly hit the fucking ceiling. The money wasn't great – we were all on five hundred quid a week – but it didn't matter. I'd just had a baby, been working in jobs I hated and I just needed to get back into the acting side of things. And this was a feature film, not TV. This was a fucking movie, which was exactly where I wanted to be.

Theatre's great but it pays worse than the temping agency, TV's great too but there's a pressure to produce. You might do six pages of a script a day on a movie. On a soap you'll do twenty. That doesn't give you time to fine-tune your performance, to really do you your best. You say the line and, if it comes out of your mouth without you stumbling then it's a wrap. There's no 'try it with a bit more warmth' or thinking about using your eyes a little more. TV's a production line.

Movies give you a chance to really express yourself. Plus, it's the premier league of acting, where the big money is, where everyone wants to be.

I didn't have to do much acting when it came to drugs, though. I've dug out the whole method acting thing but I can say that on this film I had no problem going method at all – for the six-week shoot I was Moff, right on it twenty-four fucking seven. In fact, I ended up being him for some time after too, but that's for later.

Human Traffic was the maddest job I've ever done. I don't think I'll ever get a job like it again. It was a break from family life, a return to the mad existence I'd had before Dani had come along. Joanne stayed at home with the baby. She's never been one for caning it anyway, she's a straight goer. I, however, ripped the living arse out of it. It was a complete six weeks of debauchery and we managed to make a film in between. I hardly slept. I think I blinked twice.

Unfortunately this didn't do a lot for my financial situation. My wages for the six-week shoot were £3000. My bar bill was about £3250. I ended up owing the film company money rather than getting paid. These things happen, though I have to admit it was pretty irresponsible. The trouble was, everyone on the fucking film was right at it as well. You're in this little pod when you're filming and it's easy to get caught up in that and forget the outside world exists.

These days I would never take drugs during a shoot and I wouldn't advise people to take drugs and try and make a film at all, unless you are playing a complete raving lunatic. Luckily, or unluckily for my bank account, I was.

A lot of the scenes were improvised as well, the stuff in the clubs, all that. A lot of actors shit their pants at the idea of improvisation – they like structure, the whole thing laid out for them. So do I, up to a point. However, on this one I had a lot of freedom to make things up as we went along. Owing to the drugs, a lot of the stuff I was doing was rubbish, but now and again I would come up with something that would be pretty exciting and right on the money. It was a mad thing, being off your head but still being creative. I was so eager to please and hungry to do something decent after struggling to get work for a while. Having no money, sitting in the back of the transit with my Tupperware box and a cup of tea, stinking of sweat, it wasn't the life for me.

Acting on *Human Traffic* was about being completely left field and being weird. I wish I could remember more of what I improvised but it's such a blur that film. The mad thing about it was that in the original script there was so much more going on. But because we only made it for £300,000 we had to cut about ten scenes a day. On the back of the call sheet – the notes on how the next day's filming's going to pan out – there would be a list of all the scenes that had been cut and you'd pray it wasn't one of yours. Luckily with my character, I got away with it. All my stuff stayed in.

It was one of those sets that you'd turn up to and see people skinning up. It was a mad way to make a film and I've never had that experience again. Like I said, drugs are a no-no on set. They fuck with your mind and as an actor your brain comes in pretty handy. I lost the fucking plot and just totally went for it – as did most of the other people making the film.

I was only nineteen, but I made some lifelong friends there, Shaun Parkes and John Simm, both great geezers and great actors.

The film captured the whole clubbing thing perfectly, largely because we were all clubbers and, during the shoot, we were all clubbing like mental in Cardiff every night. Cardiff is a buzzing town and we took full advantage of that. We were in a hotel right near the train station and no one really went to sleep. We all felt part of something really special. Nothing had ever been done like this before. There had been *Trainspotting* but that was dark and about heroin and a smaller number of people could identify with that. *Trainspotting* had all these shots of needles going in arms, junkies crawling around in shit-ridden crack dens, all that. The brilliant thing about *Human Traffic* is that you never see anyone take a pill. Usually in films about drug culture you see the obligatory shot of the geezer with the E in his mouth, putting it in his bird's mouth. It's all bullshit, that. There's only one real drugs scene in *Human Traffic*, the one where Shaun and John are cutting up a line of coke. It wasn't a real line or it might not have survived the retakes. Someone would have hoovered it up.

There were scenes in that movie that could only have been written by someone who'd taken a lot of drugs – take the mad wanking scene I had to do.

Now I can't say I was looking forward to that scene. Sex scenes are really uncomfortable but at least there's two of you. When you're just pulling one off on your own in front of forty people, it does seem a bit odd. In the original script I'm reading a porn mag and I have a dream, a fantasy, and these two women come to life out of the pages of the mag. They start kissing my body and it cuts to me wanking and then back to what I'm thinking about. I thought that would make it easier because it was a fantasy, and at least I'd have a couple of birds kissing me. Great.

So it gets to the day and, because we had no money, we couldn't get any actresses. Nobody was willing to get their tits out for the money we could pay them so they sent out for a couple of prostitutes, real rough old brass, thirty quid-a-go Cardiff girls.

They turned up and they were a right state. I was afraid I might catch something just from standing next to them. I think you can get a picture of what they were like when I tell you they were willing to do the whole scene for a bottle of Bell's each. The idea of it being a fantasy just didn't work because they were too fucking rough. I don't like blokes who dig women out over their looks but there comes a point when you have to call a minger a minger. So my dream sequence wasn't going to work. It would have been more like a nightmare. I had a look at them, Justin had a look at them and he said, 'Dan, you're just going to have to wank on your own, mate.' So I just had to get on with it.

I didn't exactly go for it for real but how do you recreate wanking? I can only wank how I wank. So I near enough had my cock in my hand. Justin's note to me was, 'Remember, you've been taking E all night, so it's a fucking disgusting wank. I want to see veins popping out of your head, I want to hear you slurp.' I was like, 'Oh my fucking God!' When you're going into these things, you have to give it 100 per cent. You can't hold back or you look a complete twat. I had about three or four hours of that scene, tugging one off for a whole afternoon while the crew stood about drinking coffee and scratching their arses. Not sexy. It won't surprise you to read that, when the shot cuts away and reveals I've got a hard on, that is in fact a prosthetic they had to put down my pants.

Still, I'm glad I did the scene. It broke a few barriers for me because it was a weird thing to do, a personal thing to do. I wasn't so glad at the premiere with my mum and my nan sitting beside me watching me, sixteen feet tall on the screen, tugging one off. I've had more comfortable evenings at the cinema, let me tell you.

Some good did come out of it though. I'd lied about taking hard drugs to my family and it was a way of letting them know that this was part of the person I was. As much as they were proud of me, they were also freaked out that I took drugs and I clearly had been taking them for most of my youth. I can't stand dishonesty, though, and this was my way of showing them that side of my life.

Human Traffic put me on the map, but it took what seemed like decades to come out. We made it in '97 and it was a weird feeling for me because I'd made a movie, was raring to get my film career going, but it took nearly three years before it hit the screen. Leah Betts, who went into a coma after taking E and never woke up, was still very much in the minds of the media, which made everything very sensitive. Ecstasy is a weird drug. I think if you're going to come unstuck it will be on your first one; you'll have some sort of bad reaction to it.

Everyone I knew was gutted about Leah, and really felt for her parents. She was terribly unlucky.

The film was huge but Justin didn't make much money on it because he'd signed away all the rights. He hadn't had any choice. Because of the subject, no one wanted to touch it and he had real problems getting someone to front the cash to back it. But eventually, some producers bought the rights to it in a 'take it or leave it' deal and gave Justin £300,000 to get it made.

That would have been fine but, from where I was standing, it looked as though the producers then started to take over on the set. I'm not saying they did, but that's how it looked to me. It ended up in scenes being cut, which started to do Justin's head in. As far as I know he was never consulted about what was going to make the final cut, but we just had to get on with it.

On the shoot there was a lot of arguing between Justin and the producers. Justin didn't want anyone else's input on that film, and he was right not to because the bloke is a genius. It was his idea, his script and he really wanted to make it his way. This was his life, his movie, his baby. All the roles are based on himself. His dad was in a mental home for a while so he based bits of it on that. The fact he couldn't get it up for a while is fed into John Simm's character. The fact he went on through a really insecure stage with his girlfriend and he was really jealous is reflected in Shaun Parkes's character. He once got caught wanking, just like my character did. It was all him. And he was a canehead, the biggest canehead out of all his mates. Every character in it reflects a different aspect of his life.

The core of the film – me, John, Lorraine, Shaun, Nicola and Justin – began to feel like we were battling the elements. The producers felt like outsiders to me, enemies almost. And Justin didn't have a leg to stand on because he'd signed away the rights to the film.

The film was like a trip in itself – a massive high followed by a comedown. Justin's high had been the biggest, so his comedown was the worst. It hit a low point when the movie was rereleased under a new title, *Human Traffic – The Remix*. It had been recut, with different music on it, and with added scenes that Justin had cut. That absolutely killed Justin. Justin got no money out of it as far as I know. That said, the producers had taken a big risk on the film, so some might think they were entitled to a bit of payback. At first no one wanted to distribute it and, if no one had, then they could have been caught for £300,000. Eventually the distributors Metrodome did put it out and it was a huge success. It took millions and millions of pounds, though Justin saw none of that cash and the producers claimed it never made a profit.

The real sadness for me was that Justin didn't make another film for ten years. A guy that talented, with the film world at his feet, and he just stopped working. I think it was because he felt fucked over by the whole experience. He pretty much lost all faith in the film world.

I saw him two or three years ago and he was directing a pop video for a band called The Twang, which I agreed to appear in. The song was called 'Two Lovers'. I was just thrilled to hear his voice again when he asked me to do it.

Just to be around him again was brilliant. It was great to

see he'd got his energy back. He's just made a new film, so hopefully he's back working again for good now. He's been away ten years and the British film industry has been the poorer for his absence.

Despite the fact that I got paid bollocks all for *Human Traffic*, it turned out to be a watershed moment for me. It really did put me on the map, though it didn't all happen straight away. I had to go through my own comedown first.

When I finished the job, Joanne was understandably fucked off that I'd spunked all the money I'd earned. She came down for the last couple of days of filming and I didn't break the news to her until we got back to London. I wanted somewhere with a bit of cover that I could duck behind in case she started throwing stuff.

It meant I had to go straight back to work loading skips. I was back on the graft again. Luckily another job was round the corner for me with a cast of some of the top British talent of its generation – including a future James Bond. But first, it was off to the theatre and a very challenging role, not only for me but for my family. Given my dad's views on homosexuals, I suppose it was inevitable that my first really big break onstage should be playing a gay man.

8

UNCERTAIN YOUNG MAN

My agent Charlotte rang me shouting down the phone as if her tits were on fire. I'd been asked to audition for a play – *Certain Young Men* – with one of the leading directors of the theatre, Peter Gill. He's very well respected in the business but I didn't have a clue who he was. She said he'd already cast Jeremy Northam in it. I'd not heard of him either, and didn't know he'd already bagged an Olivier award – one of theatre's Oscars – for the most promising newcomer. No bother, though, it was a job and I was well up for the audition. I asked her if they'd be sending a script over but she said, 'Peter Gill doesn't work like that.' This seemed a bit odd to me but I thought 'whatever' and went along anyway. So I went in and had a chat with him, which was really boring to be honest. We had nothing in common whatsoever. And like I said, I'm not very good at talking bollocks in auditions. It's just not me. I sat there while he rabbitted on. He was a tiny guy with pure white hair, quite a jolly little face, but I could see he was a powerful man, and very gay. He was a bit like my dad's stereotype of a gay man really, as camp as a row of chiffon tents, as they say.

We spoke a bit about the character and he asked me what I thought of gay men and I said, 'Whatever, you know. Each to their own.' He said, 'I'm looking for a gay young lad, not camp, not feminine, a wide boy but who knows how to manipulate older gay men. A young man who wouldn't be afraid to sit there and say, "Are you going to suck my cock or what?"' I thought, 'It's a job. I can do that.' He offered me the job right there – a six-week run at the Almeida, a proper old theatre behind a very classy pub in Islington.

We started rehearsals and I didn't know whether I was coming or going. This was my introduction to a very weird way of working indeed. I got to the audition and there was no script. Peter only writes the script after he's cast. He knows what he's going to do, he even gets funding beforehand, but not a word goes down on paper until he's met the actors, formed a view of them and talked their fucking ears off in the process.

For weeks we were just sitting around the table talking, which is my worst nightmare. I just went into my shell while everyone else was bollocking on. We all knew what character we were playing but we didn't know in what context, where each of us would come in to it – the beginning or the end of the play – or what sort of journey our character was on.

So there was six of us, three different couples – an old gay couple, a younger couple where one's cheating on the other and my relationship where my character runs around fucking men and robbing them.

We had to sit about and talk. I had no script to refer to so I was just sinking into my seat. This Peter Gill cat would just talk and talk and talk. There were days when I'd walk out having learned nothing. He talked about how all men have a gay side to them. Weirdly, for someone who was so keen on gay issues, as far as I'm aware, there wasn't one gay man in the play, so no one else really had the experience to argue with him either.

After about two weeks of yak he gave us all a piece of paper with about four sentences of dialogue on it. These would be our opening lines. Then we'd stand up and do a little bit. It was such a weird way of working. The other actors were much more comfortable with gassing on and they pretty much blanked me. When I did say something, no one would take any notice of me. I just started to get bored with the whole thing and could hardly keep my eyes open.

Actually, there was a bit of method to Peter's madness. It was a strange process but I eventually realised how brilliant Peter Gill was and how important he was for me at that time. It was clever what he did, watching us and writing the next bit of script based on his observations. He builds the character up around the actors that he casts, which is a rare thing.

We finally got up to do the lines and he gave me a real opportunity to express myself. When I started doing my bit, I noticed the whole cast changed towards me. They got some respect for me. I could see it was a shock to them because they had me down as being shit, with me not saying anything for a fortnight.

The majority of actors have to really work at the job, analyse it, break it down. For me it's not like that. It's fun. Hopefully, it means that rubs off on others and makes it fun for them. That's not me being big-headed; it's just the way it is. And for me to be able to sit there with these older actors, people who have been to drama school, was great. The way they changed towards me in an instant was a moment of power for me, I suppose, and I loved it.

Respect from your peers is what you crave as an actor. You want that. You get a fan base, you get people in the street recognising you, but what you really want is people in the same game as you to look at you and say, 'He's good.'

We did the play and Mum came to see it, though my dad gave it a swerve. The reviews for *Certain Young Men* were OK – they praised our acting but weren't so sure about the content of the play. I could see why, really. Some of the films I've done have been aimed very much at a certain audience. *The Football Factory*, for instance, is a bloke's film. It's not one to sit down and watch with your bird. This, in its way, was similar. It was a play for gay men, I think, about gay relationships and how they're similar to heterosexual relationships, the only difference being there's two cocks involved. It wasn't going to interest a straight critic. Gay men, though, loved it.

Around this time I also got a job on a film called *The Trench*. It was about the First World War and was directed by the writer William Boyd. The cast on this shoot was incredible. It had someone who would become a great pal of mine – Paul Nicholls who was massive at the time from his role as Joe Wicks in *EastEnders*. It also had Julian Rhind-Tutt, Dr Mac in *Green Wing*, and Daniel Craig, who would later go into another fucking stratosphere as James Bond.

I knew Daniel a little bit and I knew he was a terrific actor. Years later, it surprised me when he was getting a backlash over the Bond thing, people saying he couldn't play it. I thought, 'You wait and see what he's going to do.' All the other actors who played that role couldn't lace his boots, even Sean Connery. He looked the part but I found him quite irritating. I was brought up in the eighties with Mr Slick himself, Roger Moore, so maybe I was biased, but Sean's Bond didn't do it for me. I knew Daniel Craig would be brilliant and I was proved right. For me, he's the best Bond so far.

In *The Trench* I played a character called Del, who was a lance corporal, but secretly a coward. I give it the big one, how we're all going over the top and I'm going to be a hero. But inside I'm shaking. Then I get sent on the rum ration – which is what the army call fetching the rum. Apparently, before they went over the top they got a shot of rum. I get the rum, and I sit there and I drink it, get completely off my nut. And then a bomb lands and smashes everything up, so I come back with no rum and Daniel Craig gets me and he holds my head in a puddle and is about to drown me, but he doesn't he just throws me back in the line and says, 'You're fucked now, boy.'

It was brilliant working with Daniel on that. I felt a real energy coming off him and that helped me to lift my own performance. It was perhaps a bit strange we hit it off so well as actors because, though we got on, I wouldn't say we became mates.

Daniel was a joy to work with, though. Little did I know what he was going to go on to do. He's a national treasure now, can't fucking go nowhere without paparazzi following him about. I know that he's never been into the fame side of things but how can you turn down a role like James Bond? You know that signing up will change your life for ever. You become part of history but then you wave goodbye to your private life, you'll be known throughout the world internationally, recognised wherever you go. I know he struggles with that, as anyone would.

It was a lot of fun making the film and I really liked William, the director. It was the first film he'd directed and what I loved about him was his attention to detail, the fact he was so obsessed with the First World War. He really helped me along because I didn't know that much about the war. He'd give us little speeches about it, or read out poems from the trenches, so it helped me understand what I was supposed to be portraying.

However, at one point he did push things a little too far with the whole realism thing. He organised for us to go to Southend to do a night in a trench to get a sense of what it was all like. Now I wasn't happy about that; I was never going to get a sense of the horror and terror of trench warfare from sitting in a hole in Southend. I wasn't the only one who thought the idea was arseholes; there were grumblings from the rest of the cast too.

Anyway, William was paying the wages so we had to go along with it.

We went down there, all in full uniform, accompanied by these weirdos who re-enact all that for fun. We had to wear the uniforms throughout the rehearsals to get used to the feel of them and march around with the guns and stuff like that. We had to eat this rancid stew every day, just like the troops would have done.

Me at the *Dead Man Running* premiere. Armani treated me to a whistle, but don't be fooled, I had to give it back!

Mum and Dad on their wedding day.

The legends that are my grandad and nan.

Mum and Dad, semi-happy times.

Carol, Tolo and my sister.

Joanne's mum and dad.
What a romantic
love story!

Me and Joanne at 13.

Me and pals
having a
cheeky lager
after school.

Me and Jo loved up
to the eyeballs.

Having it large with the *Human Traffic* crew (1997).

Joanna with the lovely John Simm and Lorraine Pilkington.

Me and the old man before
the *Football Factory* premiere
(posing in Custom House).

My little bruv and
best mate Tony.

My mum and sister Kayleigh.
How beautiful are they!

Working hard in Thailand.

So this trench was set up and they started setting off fireworks to try and recreate the terror of the whole thing. To be honest, I started to get the pox with it. I appreciated what William was trying to do but it wasn't doing nothing for me. Me and Paul Nicholls, who were quite pally at the time, said to each other, 'Listen, shall we fuck off?'

We decided to check with some of the others and went to see Julian Rhind-Tutt. He played the officer and he was all right because he had his own little dugout, his own bed, nice and snug. So we went to see him but he wasn't there. He'd put a note on his bed saying 'Sorry, boys, couldn't deal with it, gone back to Blighty. This bloody war.'

He'd fucked off out of it! There was no way I was staying in a freezing trench after that. So me and Paul decided, in our First World War outfits, still with our bayonets strapped to our legs, to jump on a train and go to Paul's house in North London.

Now Paul was really famous at the time. He had been in *EastEnders* and all the girls loved him. We walked across this field and found the train station. We had no money on us so we had to blag it. Obviously me being quite good at bunking fares and slipping behind people, I did it no problem; I'd had the practice. Paul wasn't so good at it. We got off at Kilburn. It's a bit tricky trying not to get noticed jumping a fare when you're walking around in a First World War uniform with a bayonet and everything. And Paul got caught at the barriers. There was a moment at which I thought, 'Fuck it, just run.' But I waited, so we both got collared. He had to fill out all these forms, which confirmed to the Old

Bill that he was the bloke out of *EastEnders*. It made the press of course.

We got bollocked by William for bunking off. He wasn't happy about it at all, but I explained to him that trench life wasn't doing nothing for me and I promised I wouldn't let him down on the job. 'You watch. I'll come through for you,' I said.

It was a tough old job, and it gave me a shitload of respect for the people who fought in that war. They built these trenches at Bray Studios and it was hard enough being stuck in them all day without some cunt shooting at you, never mind the cold and the mud of the real thing. Actually, I think one of the problems of the film was that we looked a bit too clean in it. They could have done with making us all look a bit more lice-ridden. It was a good job, though, and I loved it. I met some good people on it – especially Paul, who's one of the nicest blokes I've known.

It was the first time I bonded with Paul really. I really respected and liked him a lot; he's a good kid and a good actor. There was one actor on *The Trench* who it seemed to me didn't get on with Paul from the get go. Perhaps it was the fact that Paul was the lead role and the fact that he came from *EastEnders*. Actors can be quite bitter towards each other because a lot of the time we are competing for the same roles. If you go into a soap then you get a lot of admiration from the public, from the blue rinse lot, from mums and kids, but your peers tend to look down their snouts at you a little bit. I don't. Listen, I respect anybody who can make a living in this game, TV or not.

So this actor was a bit of a prick with Paul, I thought, and I felt sorry for him a little bit so I backed him up on *The Trench*. I told the actor straight: 'Let his acting do the talking.' And that cooled things off.

I could see Paul was a bit of a vulnerable kid – he was only around nineteen at the time. He's from a similar kind of background to me, though he's from up north. He's from Bolton, from a single parent family and he comes from fuck all himself. He came down to London at an early age, landed the *EastEnders* part and it was all a bit much for him. He's got Hollywood looks and I don't think he could deal with the fame and attention they brought. I wasn't famous at all at the time. I used to go out in town with him and people would go mad to see him, especially the girls. They'd be screaming and chasing him down the street. He didn't like what that did to his freedom.

He was only a kid, and yet he was living down in London on his own. Fair play to the BBC, they got a nice flat for him in Kilburn and he had a few quid about him, but he didn't know quite how to deal with the fame side of it.

We stayed in touch, me and Paul – he was the only one I struck up a lasting friendship with.

After *The Trench* I did another film – *Borstal Boy*. This was the first film I was offered exclusively. I didn't have to audition. I got a phone call direct, not through my agent, from Jim Sheridan who made *My Left Foot*. He's a big-time Irish director. He left a message on my answer machine at home, saying he'd seen *Human Traffic* and he had a part for me.

I was so excited; I immediately thought I was going to be in a film like *Scum*, that I was going to play this nutty little bastard, who gets to put snooker balls in a sock and bash people up with them.

Not for the first time in my life, I was wide of the mark. I got sent the script and it was about the poet Brendan Behan. I play Charlie Millwall, an openly gay prisoner, and a sailor as well. *Borstal Boy* was set during the Second World War and, as far as I know, it's a true story. Apparently Brendan Behan had a bit of a gay love affair in borstal, though he never claimed to be homosexual. It was more of a friendship between two men; they became very close, had a bit of a fiddle and that was it.

I was a bit disappointed with the script because I'd had images of me running around like the young Ray Winstone. But then it gave me the opportunity for me to do something completely different. I was very flattered that Jim would offer me a role like this. So I flew out to Dublin and prepared myself to play another gay role.

It was a bit like *Certain Young Men*, I suppose. It was the same sort of character. I'm a sailor and a bit of a rough sort but I'm so in love with Brendan Behan and I just feel that we are meant to be together. The whole thing for me is that I'm trying to win him over. It's a love story between two men, one more in love than the other.

Brendan Behan was played by an actor called Shawn Hatosy, an American actor. I was surprised that they'd get an American to come in and play the poet, considering he's a massive Irish hero. I didn't really get on with Shawn, but that might have been less to do with his personality than the way I was supposed to fawn over him, which made me resentful. My character loves Behan so much, and he doesn't really feel the same about Charlie, so maybe I was feeling angry on my character's behalf. I said I don't go method but sometimes the role does leak into your ordinary life.

Dublin is a beautiful place and we had a real laugh. It was the first time I got to work with an actor called Lee Ingleby. He's a great young actor who plays my enemy in it but we bonded.

Still, there was something hanging over the whole shoot. I had to do a kissing scene with Shawn. I knew that in the script I finally win him over and I get to kiss him on the mouth. Now remember, I'm not too fond of this bloke so it's a bit difficult for me. All the time I see him on the set, on the dining bus, in make-up, I'm thinking, 'I'm going to be snogging that before long.' It didn't do a lot for my appetite, I can tell you.

My character's the one who's pulling all the strings, trying to snog Behan. So for my character it's a massive moment. Brendan Behan's not so sure. For the bloke I'm playing, the idea of his mouth on mine is the ultimate thing. That has to come through in the scene. I was dreading it, man, really dreading it, not just for the kiss but because of the acting challenge. I had to look like I was enjoying something that in reality was going to make me heave.

You can call on all your resources, but I don't care who you are, if it doesn't float your boat, you're not going to be able to enjoy that moment. We had to do it about six or seven times. I'll never forget his mouth coming towards mine and me having to suck on it like it was some sort of sweet toffee apple, when actually the whole thing was just horrendous. But I did it, made it look good, and I was proud of myself. There's also a scene where I get gang raped, which was quite horrible to film. I get held down by the boys and they're just about to rip my pants down when Brendan comes in and saves me.

I was a bit worried about how my dad was going to react to *Borstal Boy*. In the end, he was all right. It was never going to be his favourite film, was it? I think he respected me for putting myself up for such a big role. I was proud of my performance, on the whole. I took the role seriously and I think it shows in the finished product. I managed to push my acting to another level.

I didn't know I still had some way to go – in terms of performance and also, for good and for bad, in terms of fame. When I got back from Dublin I met someone who would have a massive effect on my career – and on my personal life – the director, nutter and genius Nick Love.

9

LOVIN' IT

I didn't know it at the time, but I was on a slippery slope with the drugs. I needed someone to sit me down and give me some straight talking about it. Well, they don't come any more straight talking than Nick Love. He's a man who calls a cunt a 'fucking cunt', if you see what I mean.

Paul Nicholls knew him and said to me, 'Listen, I think you should meet this guy Nick Love, you would love him, you really remind me of him.'

I was like, 'Oh, I've heard of Nick Love.' It wasn't for his work, though. I'd only heard of him because I'd seen him splattered all over the front of the newspapers when he married Patsy Palmer, Bianca out of *EastEnders*, and then left her because he couldn't deal with the whole fame thing. He was known as a love rat, all that sort of stuff. Even then I knew that the way someone appears in the papers can have no relation what-so-fucking-ever to the person they actually are, so I didn't set too much store by it.

That said, I thought he looked like a right flash bastard. Some of the clothes he wore were real bling. He had a gold tooth in front of his mouth and I thought he really fancied himself. Never mind, Paul thought he was all right so that was good enough for me.

Nick had a film he was going to make which was called *Goodbye Charlie Bright*. Paul got me in the door to meet him.

As soon as I shook his hand I could see Nick had something about him. He was as cockney as fuck and I loved the slang that he used – haddock for car (haddock of bloater = motor); kettle for watch, which is one I've used my whole life without ever knowing where it comes from. Some he just made up: 'Give us a glass of Janet' – Janet Street Porter = water. This guy's knowledge of movies and his charisma absolutely blew me away. I hadn't come across anyone like him in the business. On the surface, it looked like we were peas out of the same pod. In fact, we had next to nothing in common. He's a straight goer, very intense and normally in bed by eight in the evening. Not much like me then.

Nick was big into drugs years ago. It's a well-known fact he had to turn his life around because he was on the verge of death. So at sixteen or seventeen he went into rehab to sort himself out, came out, and went straight to film school.

I wanted the lead role in *Goodbye Charlie Bright* even though he'd given it to Paul, who was one of my very good friends. Paul had to play a cockney in it, and the way I saw it, he was never going to be as good as me, who's the real thing. Nick sat me down immediately and said, 'I can't give you the lead role. I think you are great actor, I want to put you in my film, but you'll be playing a smaller role. Paul is a bigger actor than you and I have to give it to him. He's going to sell the film.' I was sweet with that and I totally understood it. It's all about arses on seats in this game.

The cast was pretty good. Roland Manookian, who I'd do

a lot of work with later on, was in it – a proper cockney kid and a real diamond. There were people like Dani Behr in it too. I wasn't very sure of her first but she done the job, I think. She was adequate – quite sexy, which was lucky because she was playing a sexy role. Like all the birds, she quite fancied Paul but he was petrified of her for some reason. He didn't want to know. A lot of blokes on the set were quite envious of him.

The film's about a kid from the flats, played by Paul, who wants to leave the life of crime, drugs and casual sex. I play a member of a firm who goes after a local nutter when he discovers he's shagging his girlfriend. I end up getting run over.

Goodbye Charlie Bright had a nice budget on it and so they had some cash to spend on the acting talent. Phil Daniels was in it, and he was a bit of a hero of mine. I always respected Phil, being a massive fan of *Quadrophenia* and *Scum*. It was good seeing a guy with the same kind of background as me having done so well in the film world. I loved being around him, and I loved the way he approached his part. He played a right nasty fucker. I have a bit of a face-off with him because he ends up shagging my bird, Nicola Stapleton, who played my girlfriend in it. And when we started the job, it turned out that she was a fan of mine from *Human Traffic*. It was a beautiful thing. There was mutual respect between us. We worked really well together.

It was the first time I'd met Frank Harper as well, who I would work with later on. I loved Frank – he had something about him. He was a great actor and he was from my manor. Or rather, though he was South London, he had my mentality.

I was starting to meet people who were quite similar to me. I hadn't come across them in the business until then. I'd done theatre and worked with some respected actors but I had nothing in common with them away from the acting. It was great to work with people who were just so similar to me, who I could go for a beer with after the day's work on set. It was such a buzz for me.

Up until that point I'd been the odd one out and always felt a bit tongue tied around some of the other actors, a bit 'I'll get me coat' if I swore like you swear if you've grown up where I did, or if I mentioned some programme I liked that they looked down on. With these blokes they didn't blink if you swore and, if you mentioned an episode of *Only Fools and Horses*, like as not they'd seen it and would laugh along with you rather than saying some shit about David Jason's mastery of the form.

It was great being around Nick too. I loved his energy and the way he directed the movie, ruling with an iron fist. He did it in a way that you totally trusted him. I felt relaxed around him because he was from my background and he used the word 'cunt' as much as me. He had a sexiness about him, a real magnetism. You just wanted to be around him.

It was unusual for me to pay so much attention to a director at that stage of my career. There are some actors who absolutely hang on the director's every word, who will get their number and ring them of a nighttime and talk about the film. I'm not like that at all. I'm very instinctive. I like to trust myself and my performance. I'm not very good at taking notes from a director – when we talk about 'notes' it's just jargon for taking direction, they don't actually give you a note. If the direction is absolutely bang on, then I'll take it in my stride and say, 'Fuck me. You're right, let's do it that way.'

That used to happen quite rarely when I was younger. I was a know-all who thought he knew the game back to front. I'd take it as a bit of an insult if someone had an opinion on the way I was doing things. I've had to lose that as I've got older. Back then, most directors were nonentities for me. I did my thing as I thought I should do it and didn't really listen to them. Not that I'm an intimidating character or a diva, but there's a way of dealing with me and most of the time the directors I'd worked with trusted me because I was getting it right. But there's a way of getting into my head and getting my creative juices flowing and Nick certainly found it.

I don't think this would work for everyone but it worked for me. Like I say, his approach might be best described as 'straightforward'. 'Unambiguous' is a word I heard used about him and, once I'd looked it up, I had to agree with it. He doesn't leave you in any doubt about what he thinks. One of his regular notes would be, 'What's that, you cunt? Go again,' which is fucking unheard of in the film business. I loved it, though. I can't have these directors pussyfooting around me saying, 'It was perfect, but . . .' Just tell it to me straight.

Paul was right on my nut on this job because all he kept saying to me was, 'You should be playing this part. I'm not good enough, I'm shit, I'm shit.' At first I tried to put my arm around him and say, 'Listen, kid, you've got an opportunity here, you're leading the movie, you've done well to come out of a soap, you've got a good career in front of you, stop pissing about. You've got the talent to be here. So trust your fucking self.' But he went on and on and it was driving me mad.

I wasn't the only one. There were times when Nick wanted to lose it with him. But he needed him to do the job and we didn't have the technology in them days to do the whole CGI bit and finish the film by animating Paul's corpse. If we had, I'm not sure he would have survived the job.

Anyway, Paul did a bang-up job in the end, really pulled it off. And I was really pleased because at the end of the shoot Nick turned to me and said 'Listen, man, I think you're fucking great. I love what you're about and the next movie that I make, you'll be the lead.' And I was like, 'Fucking sweet as.' It rang all the bells for me.

I totally believed Nick and I totally trusted him that he was going to put me as the lead in his next movie. But unfortunately, *Charlie Bright* died a death at the cinema. It got great reviews: the *Sun* said it was 'Hilarious, terrifying, tender, an awesome rollercoaster ride you won't want to get off.' Made no difference. It made me realise that there's a lot more to the success of a movie than just being a good film.

There are lots of reasons a film can fail and one of them is just dumb fucking bad luck. *Charlie Bright* came out on 11 May 2001, one of the hottest weekends in twenty years. No one wants to go and sit in the cinema in weather like that. It's a ruthless business and it's all about that opening weekend. If it doesn't earn £200,000 the distributors will take it off and put it on a shelf. Unfortunately, because it didn't perform,

Nick wasn't given any money to make anything else for while. It wasn't a good start for him. So I didn't hear anything from him for while and I was cracking on doing my thing, which was mostly looking after little Dani and occasionally getting bollocked by Joanne for trying to live the life of Jack-the-Lad and leaving her to care for the kid. I did my fair share of childcare, don't get me wrong, but I was also out on one quite a lot, which was unfair to the family. You can't roll in at ten in the morning and expect to go to bed and sleep it off while your missus gets on with taking the kid to the park. Not if you live with Joanne, anyway.

It was around that sort of time when *Human Traffic* was starting to become a cult movie. I was going off to do my Ibiza thing acting in *Is Harry On The Boat?* – cockney rhyming slang that you'll have to work out for yourself.

It was bad timing. *Human Traffic* was a creeper – a word-of-mouth film. The longer it was out, the more successful it became and, as I flew off to film *Is Harry On The Boat?*, interest in it was coming to the boil. Try being one of the best-loved characters in a film about E-heads in the party capital of the world and staying focused on the job in hand. If I opened my mouth to speak, someone would shove a pill in it.

It's a weird thing, fame. It isn't the case that you make a film, promote it, it comes out on 2 June and you're famous on 3 June. It doesn't work like that. Six months later, after it's come out on DVD, that's when people start to recognise you. *Human Traffic* was becoming a cult at just about the time I landed in Ibiza. Oh, fucking dear.

If I needed evidence that my level of fame had gone up, I

even got a stalker. Not that the melt lasted long after I had a word with him.

His name was Chris and, unbelievably, he followed me out to Ibiza. I remember I was out one night, obviously sloshed off my nut, on the top floor of this massive nightclub in Leicester Square, and I gave him my number because he was a massive *Human Traffic* fan. And then he kept ringing me and texting me all the time. I told him straight, 'I shouldn't have given you my number, mate, now kindly fuck off.' He didn't get the message, though, and kept turning up everywhere I went. When he turned up in Ibiza, that was the final fucking straw.

I was working, filming round the pool in the hotel. The rich bird off the soap opera was out there with me and he knocked on my door. He'd obviously been studying my movements because he knew where I was staying.

I wasn't around but she let him in and he said he had nothing for the sunshine, so he borrowed a pair of my shorts. I couldn't believe my fucking eyes when he appeared at the side of the pool. There he was, this fat weird fucker, crammed into my shorts! The front of it! Not only is he stalking me, but he's wearing my fucking shorts! The fat cunt could only just get them on. I totally give it to him, and I nearly punched him out there and then, to be honest with you. He was waving at me going, 'All right, Dan?' as if I'm going to say, 'All right, mate, you look good in my shorts.' I told him to take the fuckers off there and then. He fucked off in his boxer shorts.

I did feel a bit bad afterwards, because I started shouting at him, saying, 'What are you doing, following me out here?

Get away from me, you weird bastard.' I remember him sloping off all depressed. I never came across him again. I didn't have to call the police or nothing like that, because I could have dealt with it myself if he'd come back.

Is Harry On The Boat? was my first lead role. I was in every scene. I didn't embrace it, though. I got wrapped up in the whole Ibiza thing, which wasn't a good idea. They wanted us to go out there two weeks early to get a suntan. But because I was getting off my nut all night and sleeping all day, I was as white as a sheet by the time the shoot started. This fucked me up because then I had to get rubbed down with St Tropez bright and early every morning, which, ironically, meant I had to come in first thing to get it done. It was painful getting up that early. If I'd just got a tan I would have saved all that bollocks. As we started shooting I could already tell the producers were questioning why they put me in it.

It was the first time in my life I started to struggle. I couldn't remember my lines because I was off my nut. I was living off MDMA powder, staying up all night. Because I'm the lead role, I'm being called at seven in the morning to do a twelve-hour shoot. So I would turn up on the set with a vodka and fucking orange in my hand, still battered from the night before. Before then I'd never experienced acting to be tricky or difficult but I really did then.

I was fresh off the success of *Human Traffic* and was maybe a little bit up myself, quietly arrogant. I was surrounded by ex-soap stars and I got a bit too big for my boots. This is why I thought I could get away with taking all those drugs and still do the job, because I thought I was better than the job.

Bad attitude, childish, really. It was physically and mentally impossible to put in a good performance and party like a wild fucking animal.

The producers took me aside and bollocked me but I didn't give a fuck because I knew they couldn't sack me. My attitude was, 'Well, you shouldn't have brought me to Ibiza, what did you fucking expect?' We were filming it in the closing party season – September time. I was in a place where I'd never been recognised so much in my life. It was the end of season parties and we were ripping the arse out of it at Manumission, Space, Eden, all over really. I was so run down by the end of the job I got an ulcer on my eye. To cover it up, they had to shoot me from one side. I was walking around with a weeping eye, looking like the monster out of a horror movie. The producers were shaking their heads clearly thinking, 'You'll never work in this business again.'

As I've said, I was fucking around with someone on the set – an ex-soap girl who I'm not going to name out of respect to Joanne and also because I'm not trying to do some kiss and tell.

My missus found out. It came out in the *Sun* not long before I came home. It was awful for Joanne to read. I'd been away for six weeks, and she'd been waiting for me to come home. She'd bought me all my favourite shopping, a bit of sushi for the fridge, got the lagers in – all nice and cold.

I'll say this about Joanne: you don't want to get on her wrong side. The woman is a force. I wanted to explain things to her, or at least to offer some excuses, but I couldn't contact her. She changed her number on me. We had a joint account at that time and she took all the money out of it, which I totally agreed with and understood. So, as I said at the start of the book, I moved straight in with this other bird when I came back from Ibiza. It was a terrible time for me really. I wasn't myself, I had no direction, drugs were controlling my life. But I was with a girl who was a multimillionaire, so money was no object.

The whole thing went in a blur. I can't remember one occasion that we sat down and had a meal together or anything like that – it was just one long drug-fuelled party.

Weirdly, none of this seemed to affect me when it came to getting jobs. Around that time, I did *High Heels and Low Lifes* with Mel Smith who is fucking brilliant, funny as fuck.

Minnie Driver was in the film, along with Mary McCormack, who's fucking great in it, and Kevin McNally who's probably best known now for being Joshamee Gibbs in *Pirates of the Caribbean*. Kevin's great, I loved him, loved being around him. He likes a little booze, I'll tell you that.

Mel Smith was on pills for his heart but he didn't give a fuck. He's a mad character, always dashing about and full of energy. Minnie was on some sort of apples-and-cheese diet that she had to eat at eleven o'clock every day, so we had to halt filming while she went back to her trailer. I don't know whether it was just a ruse, because I did sense some tension between her and Mel, so maybe she just wanted to fuck him off. Maybe, maybe not.

I'd been back in the country a bit after *Is Harry On The Boat?* when Paul Nicholls phoned me up talking like he'd banged about fifteen tonnes of sulphate, mad with excitement.

He'd been called to an audition at the Almeida theatre. 'What's the big deal?' I asked him, 'I've been called for that too.'

I'm not sure Paul wanted to hear that because we were mates and the idea of going for the same role was always going to be a bit tricky. But, like they say in *The Godfather*, 'it's business' and you just get on with it.

'It's with Harold Pinter,' he said, 'don't you know who he is?'

I told him I'd never heard of the geezer, and I was telling the truth. I didn't know at the time that he would have an enormous effect on my life, professionally and personally. I was about to receive an honour greater than any award or review could ever give me. Harold Pinter is to theatre what Elvis is to music, Pele to football. If he was a horse he'd be Desert Orchid; if he was a boxer he'd be Muhammad Ali. In theatre, he's the mutt's nuts, the numero uno. If you stuck all the awards he'd won on one shelf then the fucker would fall off the wall.

He had an aura about him. For instance, most playwrights are scared of critics. But Harold, he shat the life out of them; you could see it in their eyes when they met him. If they didn't like one of his plays it showed there was something wrong with them, not him. They were scared that if they slag him off they'd look stupid.

So I was about to go to work with the greatest playwright this country has produced since Shakespeare and, more than that, become one of his go-to actors. As Paul raved on the phone, though, I just cocked a deaf 'un. To me it was just another job. Fuck, was I wrong about that.

10

THE BIG LEAGUE

It was around this time, the beginning of 2000, that things went nuts for me. I was desperately unhappy to be parted from Joanne and Dani. In fact, I've never been lower in my life and the fact that I was entirely to blame for the split just made me feel worse. I was with a girl who liked to party so it was easy to just pile a load of drugs up my nose or down my neck and try to forget about it. I couldn't though. I'd hang about outside our old flat waiting for a glimpse of Dani and Joanne but, when Joanne did show up, she'd just usher Dani inside without speaking to me. I was heartbroken not to see Joanne and more down than I can even describe about not seeing Dani. I think that's the worst thing on earth, being separated from your kid. Anything I've been through, all the bollocks the press has thrown at me over the years, all the years of having no money, being misquoted, misrepresented, nothing even comes close to losing your kid from your life. I'd take all the crap that has come my way a million times over rather than go through that again.

So my personal life was a disaster but my professional life was about to move up another gear.

If my agent had been excited when I was called for the Peter Gill audition, she was on another planet when she told me about Harold Pinter. I genuinely thought she was having some sort of asthma attack when she phoned me up. By this time I'd moved agencies – to the biggest one in the world, ICM. They'd courted me, really, getting my numbers and ringing me up to explain that Charlotte's was a small agency, whereas they had loads of directors on their books and could offer me a first look at all sorts of juicy scripts. In the end they sold themselves to me and, feeling very guilty, I dropped Charlotte. She was great about it. She said she always thought it would happen and wished me the best of luck.

I didn't understand what the fuss was about with Pinter, but Claire from ICM told me there was no bigger name in theatre and it was a once-in-a-lifetime chance. She said: 'He hasn't written a play in fifteen years. This is a new play, this is a massive opportunity for you, I really need you to learn the dialogue.' I was like, 'Whatever, I'll go and do it.'

It was slowly penetrating my brain that this was a little bit above the level of anything I'd done before so I got my shit in gear, took it seriously and learned the lines well.

Paul was up for the job too and we went to the audition as mates, although secretly we were both really keen to get it. Mind you, he was keener than me because he knew who Harold Pinter was and what the gig meant.

Sitting in the Almeida bar waiting to go in, I was a bit nervous, but a good kind of nervous. I fancied a cheeky lager, but I didn't out of respect to the job. The tension in the room from the other actors was unbelievable. The Almeida's an old-fashioned boozer – all mirrors, brass and deep brown colours but you could have been forgiven for thinking it was a den of speed freaks for the nervous energy in there. It rubbed off on me a bit, but I didn't feel it as much as they did because to me it was just another job.

That said, I could tell that the script they'd sent me – *Celebration* – was a fair cut above some of the other stuff I'd done. It was a great monologue, really musical in the way the words are used. I loved it and that made it easy to learn.

The play is set in a restaurant, and it's two different tables, really arrogant snotty-nosed people sitting round being horrible to the staff. My part is the waiter, I'm bringing food in and I have these amazing speeches. I interject, I say, 'Were you just talking about Gary Cooper?' and then I get this big rant about my granddad, how he used to knock around with the old western actor Gary Cooper and the film gangster Edward G Robinson. Of course, he's a complete bullshitter this waiter, although he has massive speeches.

Paul went in first, did his speeches and came out. From the look on his face he wasn't too pleased with the way it had gone. I didn't have time to talk to him about it because I was keying myself up for my own audition. I felt confident. I thought 'OK, sweet. Let's do it.'

So I walked in the room, and there was this old boy there, a big unit though, and he was flanked by all these people – PAs, agents, whatever. I walked straight up to him and said, 'All right, son, how you doing?' I felt the room go 'Fuck!' He loved it, though. He said, 'Oh, I've never been called "son" before. I'm very well, how are you?'

People just stood around and no one asked me to go up onstage. I think I was meant to chat to him or something but

I'm fucking useless at that so I said, 'Listen, mate, can I just crack on? I'm not really here for the small talk.' This is how I prefer to do it; I'm there for the job, not to talk about what I've had for breakfast.

I got right on that stage, and I smashed it first time. It really did flow for me. I was at total ease with it. This is because of the dialogue. You always know a good writer, because the words roll off the tongue like you wouldn't believe. You don't have to play with it that much; the music of it, the sounds just carry you. It happened for me on the first time. He said to me, 'OK, will you do it again, but just slow it down?' I did exactly what he asked me to do. I thought it was better the first time but I slowed it the fuck down anyway. I finished the speech and he said, 'Thank you, lovely to meet you.' That was it, I was out of there.

Paul was waiting in the bar and he asked how it went. I said it went OK. I wasn't too excited about it anyway. I was up for some films at the time and that was the way I wanted to go. Films excited me that bit more.

I got a call the same day and they offered me the job. I had my agent almost screaming down the phone at me. I'm not joking. It was the same tone people use when they're calling 999 because their house is on fire.

My immediate thing was to think about it because of the money. Not that I'm driven by the dollar, I'm not, but I needed to earn. You do a play, it's three hundred and fifty quid a week, which is never going to break the bank. This is the weird thing about theatre – it's acting in its purest form, the kind of thing lots of actors get fucking excited about, but it pays fuck all. You do eight shows a week and that needs real dedication. It's a real test of you as a human being and as an actor but you get fuck-all money for it. You go and swan about on a film and get ten grand a day, but you sweat your bollocks off doing eight shows a week you get three hundred and fifty. And you have to give your agent 12 per cent of that. It's fag and beer money, no more.

Some actors go from play to play to play and they're skint throughout their entire career. They're brilliant actors, win Olivier awards, all that, but they haven't got a pot to piss in. I could never understand that. As a young actor, I never thought for a second about the cash but actually, bollocks to that, fuck it. I want to earn a pound note. You've got all these two-bob no-talent actors earning all the money. I want some of that.

By the time I got the call, though, it had sunk in that Pinter was big fucking banana. I thought, 'Sweet, this is it, Pinter, let's go work.' I was working with Lindsay Duncan, Lia Williams and Keith Allen. This was the first time I met Keith, who's become a very good friend of mine. I was in awe of him a bit, because of who he was and the stories I'd heard about him on the grapevine. He's got a reputation for being a fucking lunatic, putting it politely. I felt like a kid around him but I didn't realise how much of a good actor he was until I started working with him.

He'd worked with Harold before and I could see he was in awe of him. When you spent time with Harold you realised the clout he had. When he walks in a room, people go quiet and wait. They fear him because he can snap at any point about anything. Keith, who's a pretty scary character himself, was fucking petrified of him. As for the girls, Lia and Lindsay, they were scared to death. He could flip on women – men as well, but I've seen him really turn on a couple of birds and reduce them to tears. He didn't like being interrupted and if you spoke out of turn he'd give it to you straight. I slowly realised who he was, how big he was, and I started to be wary around him. You pick up on everyone else's attitude to him. That said, the atmosphere was intense but it wasn't nasty. I had a good time working on his plays because you're with top actors and a top director, not some planks out of a soap. It's 'Welcome to the Premier League' and if you can't cut it we've got a thousand like you waiting in the wings who think they can.

We rehearsed in the Almeida's rooms, which is on Upper Street in Islington. This table would be set out in the front of the stage with a bottle of wine and a glass for him. He'd turn up with his briefcase and come and sit down and start pouring his wine and you'd get on with it. He doesn't give you that much direction because the play's all set around tables and there isn't that much moving around. He trusts the actors – he hires you for a reason and that's your acting skills. He gives you little tweaks here and there but nothing major.

I got on with Harold and I really liked him. He was from Hackney, an East London boy and a West Ham fan, though he'd lost the accent by the time I met him. I don't think nothing of that. In his day, if you wanted to get on you had to talk like a posh fucker or no one would take you seriously.

I think he liked me too. I think he saw how raw I was and how much I wanted to learn.

I understood *Celebration*, which is more than I can say for some of the others of his that I acted in. Later he'd cast me in a play of his called *No Man's Land*. I did six months of that and I still can't tell you what it's about. Not a fucking clue.

I didn't feel I had to ask too many questions on this, though. There would be moments where you'd ask him questions about why your character was saying something and he'd just say, 'Ask the fucking author.' He was dry, Harold.

So, that would just cut you dead, and you'd just laugh it off. He didn't need to explain anything, because it's all on the page, that was his point. The rehearsals were fun, as they should be with such a great part. I had some top-quality speeches in it.

It was never going to be that me and a lunatic like Keith would work together and not get on it at least once. Keith had bought himself a black cab so he could park it up Soho. One night he said to me, 'Do you fancy coming to the Groucho?' For anybody who's been living in a hole for the last twenty years, the Groucho is the club in Soho where lots of famous people go. There are no cameras allowed in, no press. It was all my dreams come true.

So we went out and we had it and we both turned up a little bit worse for wear the next day. Me and Keith were having this thing about who was going to get bollocked first by Harold, and as it turned out it was me, because I was the muppet who turned up late. Harold tore me out in front of everyone and said to me, 'Danny, if ever this was an ensemble piece, this is it.' What he meant was that they couldn't rehearse without me there. An ensemble piece means that all the actors are required all the time, throughout all the rehearsals. Keith was sniggering up his sleeve while all this was happening. And then the next day Keith turned up late. So he took a bollocking off of Harold too. Which was nice.

It's not a pleasant experience being on the receiving end of Harold's anger. When Pinter gives you a bollocking he doesn't shout, he talks slow and doesn't really raise his voice, but there's a look that he gives that's scarier than buggery.

We rehearsed the arse out of that play and then we started to do a few run-throughs. During this time Harold gets more involved with giving you notes on your performance. He watches the whole thing through and at the end he gets this tiny little black notebook out. When he looks down at it you dread him looking up because he could be pretty fucking brutal with his comments. You think, 'Please don't look at me, please don't look at me.' To be fair, he took pity on me and didn't give it to me that hard. He was quite rough on the girls though. I don't think he exactly had a problem with women, but he was an old-school gent, and he found them irritating at times. We rehearsed the play so much that I got the pox with being in a rehearsal room, and I was really ready to get it done in front of an audience.

It was 16 March 2000, the first night, and it was rammed, a real buzz in the air. I'd been at the Almeida before, but this was much more of a production – Peter Gill had hardly had a stage set – and also it was a Harold Pinter play, which was always massive in the world of theatre. It didn't get any better. We smashed it with some great fucking reviews and then we had the opportunity to do it in New York at the Lincoln centre, on Broadway, which is another level above.

I started getting on really well with Harold. It helped that he liked a drink and I liked a drink. On top of that, he was one of the most interesting blokes I've ever met. I just felt intelligent standing next to him.

In the play, I talk about all these poets. I'd never heard of any of them so he invited me to his house – a fucking massive roost in Notting Hill – for a little education. In this house, he had a book-lined study like something out of a professor's house in a film, which is my idea of heaven. I love the thought of having wall-to-wall books in my gaff, even if I might never read the fuckers. Probably goes back to my time at the boot sales with my dad. I love having all those old things about me, it gives a real sense of time and place.

Anyway, we sat there in the corner next to the fireplace. He had a bottle of wine but he showed a thoughtful touch by getting in four lagers for me. While we drank he explained to me who were all the people that I mention in the play, W H Auden and all that sort of mob. He just wanted me to feel at ease with all these names. I met Lady Antonia, his wife. She was lovely. I got on really well with her. I remember walking out of his house in Notting Hill and thinking I was part of something special. It set me up very nicely for the run in London. I didn't fuck up once during it, which wasn't the case – unfortunately – when I got to New York when the play went on to Broadway. The drug thing was really getting a grip of me by then and it was about to cost me big style.

I went to New York with the Supernova Heights girl. Harold seemed to really dislike her, I have to say. He gave it to her one night and really upset her, made her cry. In general, he didn't like people coming up to him with compliments, didn't believe in all that bollocks, and that was exactly what she did.

He turned on her and told her straight: she was some small time actress out of a soap. He really upset her. I remember her sobbing her heart out to me. I challenged Harold about it, told him he was out of order.

He wrote me this amazing letter apologising to me about it, not apologising to her at all. I guess he could see that her lifestyle wasn't good for me. He wasn't some sort of fucking Cupid or anything like that, he wasn't going to try to run my life, but he was right. I was about to fuck up in grand style, and it was all down to the life I was leading. Like I said, I was not handling the separation from Dani and Joanne particularly well and I'd found myself overdoing it big style with drugs. I was still whacking a load of gear up my nose every night at the twenty-four-hour party at Supernova Heights and banging down a load of sleeping pills to get to sleep, drinking a lot too. I was young so I was getting away with it. If I drank or took drugs like that now I'd look like Bernard Manning in pretty short order which isn't a good look for a bloke trying to make a living playing the fresh-faced young lad.

When we went to New York I fell in with a real canehead crowd and started to hit the crack pipe. I was forgetting why I was in New York in the first place. One night we went to this massive apartment that was in Soho, in Manhattan, above a meat market. It was a rich kid's sesh pad: big sparse studio flat, huge setee, glass table covered in weed and God knows what else. Crack is like coke times twenty, you get a massive rush and feel you could take on the world; it's like your blood's been removed and replaced by electricity. I took to it like a duck to water, which should have been the warning I needed to leave it alone. I was sucking back on a crack pipe and I sat back in the chair, looked up at the clock and it was eleven o'clock in the morning. I thought, 'Fuck, I've got to be at the theatre at six. I've got to go home and sleep.'

I got back to the hotel where all the cast were staying, sneaking in, all the time thinking, 'Please don't bump into Harold.' Let me tell you, after sucking on a crack pipe, sleep's not really going to happen. I smashed a couple of Valium and finally dropped off into some sort of haze.

I didn't feel too bad when I woke up, just a bit bleary-eyed, but I walked onstage a few hours later to one of the worst nights of my life – coincidentally, my birthday. My character doesn't come on until about half an hour into the play. I come in at the beginning with plates of food but don't speak. I got that out of the way, God knows how because I was shaking like fuck. Then I had to hang around for ages.

The really annoying thing was that the play was going beautifully. The audience were laughing. We'd got them. You would know within about ten minutes of a comedy whether it's working or not, whether it's just one or two people laughing or if the whole audience feels confident enough to laugh. You always find with theatre that it's you against the audience. If you do a play for a long time you start to hate the audience, you hate it if they cough or if they mutter to each other. It drives you wild. At the beginning of my theatre career I couldn't understand that. I thought, 'Hold on a minute, they're paying forty pounds a ticket, we're expecting them to believe that they're watching something going on in a restaurant, and it's all real, so they're entitled to cough now and again.' But I started to get like that too, to think, 'Who keeps fucking sneezing?' and all that.

So I came onstage and I started interrupting the diners' conversation like I'm meant to do. I'd done this play for six weeks and I knew it like the back of my fucking hand. So I interrupted, started speaking and bang! My mind went blank. I always thought I'd be confident enough to improvise my way out of it but my brain had nothing in it, nothing at all. I was shot to fuck on the crack and all the other shit I'd been putting inside myself.

The blood rushed from my head to my feet. I had this overwhelming feeling that I was in the wrong business. Right at that moment, I thought, 'What am I doing here?' The worst thing about it was that I was looking down at the other actors and they all started to shrink into their seats and look at me as if to say, 'Oh my God. Please don't do this to us.' I was putting them right in the shit.

I could see the fear in their eyes. I was right on the verge of crying on the stage, I could feel my bottom lip going. It was Andy De La Tour who shouted the line out. I was just about to walk off the stage, and he said 'Oh, I bet your granddad knows W H Auden doesn't he?' I suddenly snapped back out of it. I finished the speech, got offstage and sobbed my heart out.

That was going to be my way of dealing with it, sobbing like a melt. I felt I'd let myself down, I'd let the other actors down and I'd let Harold down. But I got through it, got off the stage, and waited in the wings, dreading the next time I had to come back on. I came backstage, and I remember that an actress called Indira, a brilliant actress and a real sweetheart, came up to me and said, 'Look, Dan, you'll be all right.' She was trying to build my confidence but if anything that was making me feel worse. Then the play finished and everyone was backstage pussyfooting around me, trying not to catch what I had.

Harold came up to me and said, 'Don't worry, Danny. It happens to the best of us,' unaware that I had just spent the whole night before sucking on a crack pipe. Keith, who is a bit more switched on about that sort of thing, came up to me and said, 'What are you doing, you cunt? You've got to sort yourself out.' I needed to hear that, I needed a man-to-man conversation. I needed someone to say, 'Sort yourself out, you soppy cunt, liven yourself up.' But the rest of them were just crawling around me saying, 'It's all right, you'll be fine.'

Because me and Keith were good friends and I felt close to him, he could say what needed to be said. It was my birthday so I tried to get pissed up that night but I wasn't into it. I kept thinking about all the hard work that goes into the play – everything from the set design to the costumes to the hot food that needs to be warmed up for the waiter to serve onstage – and how I'd ruined it. All that effort and I'd just fucked it all up and broken the spell for everybody.

Harold's famous for leaving long silences in his plays and people think that because you've got that Pinter pause, you can get away with it. It don't work like that, believe you fucking me. It was a major lesson in my life as an actor and I will never ever put myself in that position again.

I cleaned up my act and did the rest of the run but I didn't enjoy it. The reviews in New York were great, though. It was a Pinter festival. I was out there with Ian Hart, who was a good friend of mine, and he was doing *The Homecoming*. Ian's probably most famous these days for playing Professor Quirrell in *Harry Potter and the Philosopher's Stone* but he's done a whole bunch of other good stuff.

He told me not to bother about drying up onstage and told me a story to make me feel better. He said he was doing Pinter's *The Homecoming* with Sir Ian Holm. Sir Ian's a fucking major player in the UK theatre scene and also the bloke who played Bilbo Baggins in *The Lord of the Rings*. He is a top actor who deserves all the recognition that's come his way. Ian Hart said that the older Sir Ian gets, the more he suffers with stage fright. There was one moment where Sir Ian forgot his lines, and it was onstage with Ian Hart, just the two of them. Sir Ian got up and walked off the stage and left Ian on his own. Hart didn't know what to do so he's walking about the stage opening drawers and trying to look busy. Sir Ian Holm goes backstage, takes a look at the dialogue, gets his head together and comes back onstage. Then he looks at the audience and says, 'Sorry, just been for a piss,' and cracks on. This is a very well-respected actor – a great actor – who's been in millions of plays and he still gets stage fight. Ian Hart would've punched anyone else in the mouth, but because of who it was he swallowed it down. That's not exaggerating things with Hart. Apparently he once went to chin an audience member he thought was talking too much, just jumped right off the stage and came at him, so he's been known to take his work pretty seriously.

I was afraid that I'd get a mental block after forgetting my lines. It's a well-known fact that it can happen, the fear of forgetting begins to paralyse you. It doesn't get any easier the older you get either. The more you think about it, the harder it gets, I suppose. The younger you are as an actor the more invincible you feel. For me, after that moment, that feeling of invincibility had disappeared.

So when I finished *Celebration*, I said to myself that I wouldn't be doing any more plays and putting myself through that. I had a bit of a complex about it. I thought, 'I can't do it, I'll just go through that again and I don't want to be found out, I don't want to be exposed.'

And then, right at my lowest ebb, right when I thought there was no way I was going to carry on with theatre, there was a voice at the end of the phone. Who was it? Harold fucking Pinter. He rang me and said he wanted me again in *No Man's Land* for a six-month run at the National, one of the best theatres in the world.

The prestige that comes with doing Pinter again, directed by Pinter, with Corin Redgrave, John Wood and Andy De La Tour was enormous. But I was scared. I pondered on it and my agent said, 'You have to do it, Dan, for many reasons, really.'

I sat down and had a long think. I thought that I'd never get over that fear of failure, that stage fright, unless I did it. I had to do it. It was a little bit more money, not much, and it was six months of my life, but I made up my mind to fucking go for it.

I have to confess I found it a very strange play, not one I could really understand. It was a play about a rich old drunk at a house and the two servants who look after him. I was playing one of the servants. The rich bloke brings home random people to this big manor house and one day he brings back an old friend played by John Wood. We don't like this geezer because we feel threatened by him. It's a mad fucking play. I never quite knew where we stood, to be honest, or what the story was supposed to be about. That said, I was working with some real top actors.

Sometimes when I think of some of the shit actors I've been forced to work with it can nearly make me heave. Not so here. This lot were top fucking drawer, no mistake.

Take Corin Redgrave – he's just died, which is a real shame. He was a member of the famous acting family and a very accomplished actor. I had nothing in common with the man. At all. I remember we went on tour and I had to get the train with him to Newcastle and we sat there for four and a half hours and didn't say a word to each other. Not one thing. I think I went to get a sandwich and asked him if he wanted anything and he said he wanted a cup of coffee. That was it for conversation.

We didn't dislike each other. We just didn't have any point of mutual interest – until it came to acting. I watched this man like a fucking hawk. He was unbelievable. Some of the speeches he did were works of art, how he used the rhythm of the language and brought out the music of it. Listening to him every night, I could recite his whole speeches by heart because they were so well delivered they sunk into me.

It was a long run of rehearsals and we went over the play again and again. At the time I had this dopey voicemail on my phone, which said something like, 'Hello, this is Danny. I'm not about at the moment. I'm either in bed or I'm off my tree, so leave a message and I'll get back to you.' Then I got a message from Harold. I can still remember his voice – slow, almost embarrassed. It said something like, 'Hello, Danny. This is Harold. I hope you're out of bed or you've come down from your tree, but unfortunately I have cancer. This means I won't be able to direct the rest of the play, but don't worry. I'm going to fight it.' I nearly dropped the fucking phone.

It was a horrendous feeling when I thought about the struggle he had in front of him. I really liked Harold, I worshipped him, really. I loved how he didn't conform to anything. I loved the fact that all these poncey critics were frightened of him.

It's going to sound selfish but I'll say what he did for me. This is independent of my respect for the bloke, which was fucking massive, but I think it's worth saying what his approval did for an actor. He opened me up to a whole new audience, and he brought me credibility.

All these people out there who do doubt me and think I'm some two-bit actor, some moody cockney who just does gangster films, have to think again when they know I had Harold's respect. I've done Pinter at the fucking National, I've done Pinter on Broadway. For as actor, it doesn't get any better than that. I remember Jude Law coming up to me in a nightclub going, 'Dan, fucking hell, you're so lucky. What I'd give to be in your shoes and work with him.' I was looking at a multi-millionaire actor who was at the height of his fame and he was on me, asking me about Harold and envying me, basically. I knew how lucky I was to be around Harold, make no mistake.

Harold told me about his illness a couple of weeks before opening night, and it was a big blow. His assistant, a guy called Gary, took over the reins. I was trying to do the play, but all I was thinking about was Harold. The run went well but – like I said – I never understood the play. It was almost like doing Shakespeare just because there were these lines in it that I didn't find funny at all, but the audience would be pissing themselves.

They were a snotty crowd, the National lot, and I never had anything in common with them. They'd be giving me compliments and everything, but I couldn't stand being with them for too long. I had to fuck off after one drink in the bar.

When Harold came back to watch the first night, his hair was gone, he was frail and he had a walking stick. You can imagine the amount of pressure that night knowing he's out there, wanting to do well for him. And we did smash it. He gave his notes afterwards; he got his black book out. He was in good spirits and he was right to be. He was a tough old fucker and he fought against his throat cancer all the way to the end.

The whole way through the run of *No Man's Land*, I was still getting off my nut at Supernova Heights, and everywhere else, to be honest. I'd promised myself after the balls up in New York to try calming down and taking better care of myself, but I was finding it tough to pack it in. What I did do was to get off the crack. I had to give that a swerve, it's nasty stuff.

Anyway, I badly fucked up again on New Year's Day, though nowhere near as badly as before. The mad thing is they expect you to do the play on New Year's Day at the National. You have understudies there, though. I'd never experienced that before, because you don't have understudies at the Almeida.

I liked my understudy, he was a nice kid and I felt a little sorry for him, so I said to him, 'Listen, tell your mum and dad and your family to come New Year's Day, because you're doing it. I'm going out to get off my fucking nut on New Year's Eve and I refuse to get up and work on New Year's Day.' Who the fuck goes to watch a play on New Year's Day? It doesn't make sense. I thought I was doing a good deed for my understudy, but more truthfully it was for selfish reasons.

So I phoned up the next day and said I wasn't coming in. It was obvious I was ducking it because of New Year's Eve but there was nothing they could do. I mean, I've got an understudy so why not use the geezer? Anyway, I do my thing, and the understudy does his on New Year's Day. I was a bit worried because there was a part of me that was thinking that maybe this understudy might be better than me. That was all I was afraid of.

What I didn't realise was how much I was going to upset the rest of the company. Any relationship I had with Corin, with John Wood and with Andy disappeared right then and there. I didn't realise how uncool it was to use your understudy for no good reason. If you're not ill, you go onstage, end of. The others didn't use theirs at any point during the six-month run.

The thing was that if it was coming to the end of the job it would have been fine, but we had to go on tour afterwards. That was a bit of a tester, particularly as the audiences weren't always up to scratch. Try putting on Pinter in Newcastle. We had about ten people in the audience. It was really horrible, such a dent to the ego after playing to packed houses at the National. I'm not saying they're not a cultured bunch in Newcastle. They are and they do go to the theatre. I don't think Pinter was their cup of tea. Gary Wilmot was up there the week after us in a pantomime, and that completely sold out, so that shows you.

The other actors were tricky around me. I had no relationship with them, no common ground. I found myself going to lap-dancing clubs on my own. I was the youngest in the play by about thirty years. They'd all go for a nice meal or something afterwards, and I'd be stuck on my own in one of these clubs, watching birds taking off their clothes, feeling like a loser, like it was all getting away from me.

My life was just spiralling into another dark place again. My relationship with the girl from Supernova Heights was almost over and I was headed down the bottom of a bottle. I wasn't enjoying the play and I was just starting to question myself a little bit. And even though I was doing Pinter it didn't feel the same without the man himself. When he was part of the company, I felt strong; without him I felt weak.

Still, I was working with quality actors. All that was about to change though, as I got a part in a film called *The Mean Machine*. From working with Corin Redgrave I was suddenly opposite Vinnie Jones. The pay was better, and it was a good job too, because to take a step down like that it needed to be.

11

ME AND MR JONES

A lot of people would have expected me and Vinnie to get on, and I was one of them. I was really excited about working with him but he turned out to be a major disappointment.

Again, they offered the job to me without me having to audition. The producers came to me and asked me to be in it – because of *Human Traffic*, maybe. They gave me the option to talk about the part, how I wanted to play it, and I was quite proud of myself about that.

I'm sure plenty of you reading this have seen it, but for those of you who haven't, *The Mean Machine* is a remake of an American football film called *The Longest Yard*, only this is about real football, not the silly American sort. Vinnie plays the England captain who's been banged up for assaulting two police officers. He's mistreated by the screws and the prisoners until he gets a chance to redeem himself by organising a prisoners' football team to take on the guards.

When I read the script, my character was really aggressive, nutty, a bit backwards in the head. That's why Vinnie puts me in the team, because he's frightened of me. It might surprise a few people who think I'm always busting to play hard men that I said, 'I think it'd be better if I'm a fan of his and I'm really sweet and he feels sorry for me, and that's why he puts me in the team.' Believe it or not it had never occurred to me to play a hard man at this stage of my career and I had no ambitions to do so. People imagine actors control what they appear in. Most of the time they're just grateful to be paid and take what's put in front of them. This, though, was a chance to have some influence about what I did and I jumped at it. They rewrote the script and that's how the part came out how it did.

I had the idea that my character would do anything for Vinnie's, that I just wanted him to look at me, to acknowledge me. However, that was the part, not real life. If someone cuts me dead for real they can go fuck themselves; I don't go crawling round no one. When I first met Vinnie he didn't know who I was and he totally blanked me.

It was a Guy Ritchie produced film and the whole *Lock, Stock* mob were there, Jason Statham, people like that. They'd play cards at lunchtime, I'd just get blanked and sit in my little trailer. I thought, 'Fuck it, whatever.' Then I did the scene with Vinnie and he started sucking round me because he could see I could act.

He obviously thought – wrongly – he was a top actor and I don't blame him for it. Everyone is blowing smoke up his arse and he was winning awards left, right and centre, but he soon found out where he stood.

That's the one thing I loved about doing that film was seeing the fear in his eyes whenever we had a scene together. He just could not keep up with the pace. I could see him struggling. He'd be waiting for his cue, thinking, 'Oh, now I speak' and I'd fuck about, wait a little bit, do something a bit odd, a bit left field, chuck that in the fucking mix. I'd just hesitate a little bit on the line I was meant to be speaking or bend me nut, forcing him to react instead of just reading out his line like a robot.

When I first meet him, I'm on the prison wing and I slide up to him and I'm holding on to a bar. And because I'm supposed to be star struck, I thought I'd just bend back on the bar like a kid who's really embarrassed. I could see he had no idea of what to make of it.

He clearly thought, 'This geezer's quite good' and he started to want to be my mate a little bit, but he could fuck himself by then. It's shallow to only want to know someone if you rate them at what they do. There are plenty of people I've worked with who are fucking rubbish, but as people they're still all right. I would never start giving it the 'big I am' on a set. I take as I find, from the extras and the crew to the major stars. I couldn't look at myself in the mirror if I didn't.

I got eleven grand for that job and he got a quarter of a million. I thought, 'Why the fuck is he getting that sort of money?'

I remember seeing Vinnie out on set and I thought that he was trying it on with the crew a bit much. He didn't try it on with me because as soon as I open my mouth and go, 'All right, mate, how you doing?' he knows I'd tell him straight if he did.

I've learned to stand up to bullies in my adult life. In the acting circle no one fucks with me because of where I'm from. You see these big-shot fucking actors and they're careful round me. Vinnie's got the myth around him, he's a tough guy and, to be fair, he did hand it out on the football pitch and people used to fear him. He never did like getting it back, though, did he?

I remember him coming round West Ham and Julian Dicks – who is a real hard man – marked him. Jones was like a little kid round him. Julian Dicks put his nut on his and they squared up and Vinnie walked away. I fucking love Julian Dicks.

Also, Vinnie makes out like he's had this hard life but it wasn't that bad. All right, he was a fucking hod carrier for a few years, so what?

If he'd been a bit more humble I might have liked him more. He was decent in *Lock, Stock* but it was a brilliant film and he was lucky to be part of it. He had a good look in it, was on the cover with his two shotguns, so it couldn't go wrong for him, really. He's not a leading man in my opinion. He's not even really a supporting actor.

His lack of acting nous really showed on *The Mean Machine*. There's a real poignant moment where he explains to all these other prisoners how he's fucked up his life. You read the script and he's meant to cry. When he came to do it, I wanted to put my head in my pocket. It was abysmal. He looked more like he was about to take a shit.

The hardest thing for me on *The Mean Machine* was that my character adores him; I'm his biggest fan in the film. I'd sit there and watch him acting up round people and my character's got his name on my shirt. I was playing a role of a kid who really looked up to him so in the film I had to follow him round like a lap dog. That was a tough thing to do, I had to draw on everything to make that believable, I can tell you.

I love the fact he did *Big Brother*. Lots of people on that commented that he was a bully there too. I can't see myself doing something like that unless I was fucking desperate for cash. Once you've gone on that show you can't be taken seriously, I think. Do you reckon you'd have ever seen anyone whose career was going very well on there? Of course not.

I've heard Vinnie's got a problem with me, that producers have gone to him and offered him a film and he's gone. 'I won't do that, them parts are for Danny Dyer.' They've come back and told me that and I've thought, 'This fucker couldn't lace my boots.'

I'd never walk around demanding this, that and the other. I've still got the passion for acting I had when I was a kid, the idea of wanting to learn. Vinnie wants to take a bit of that on board – it's about delivering a good performance, not being some famous star and having people look up to you. I'm happy with myself; I don't need no other fucker to suck up to me to make me feel that way.

They filmed two endings to *The Mean Machine* and I didn't know which one had made the final cut until I went to the premiere. They'd gone with the one I hoped they would. In one version Vinnie scores the winning goal but in the final cut it's me. I was happy with that.

This was the first time I met Guy Ritchie – Mr Madonna at the time and the director of *Lock, Stock and Two Smoking Barrels*, which, like I've said, was a great film. He was producer on *The Mean Machine*, the geezer charged with getting all the money for the film, appointing the director, all that. To be honest, we didn't really see eye to eye when we first came across each other and after the film I did an interview with *Loaded* saying so. A stupid move really, and one I regret.

A few years later, Guy summoned me up to his office, when he was casting for *RocknRolla*. I read the script and I thought there was nothing in it for me, but he really wanted to see me so I fetched up at his office in South Ken, near to the Natural History Museum. I walked in and he was sitting there with his feet up on the desk, his shoes and socks off, watching the film *Smokin' Aces*. As soon as I came in he said, 'Look, sit down, you've got to watch this scene.' So I sat there and thought, 'The last time I saw you we was clicky as fuck.' He was sitting there laughing at the scene, the one with the spunk on the bodyguard's coat.

The scene finished and he turned to me and said, 'Look, let's let bygones be bygones. The thing is, you're a good actor, and we will work together one day. There's only a few of us making British films, and we all need to go through each other and to stick together.' I said, 'What about the script, there's nothing in it for me, is there?' He said, 'No, unfortunately. But I just wanted to get you in to say my piece.' And that was it.

I walked out of there feeling good about the situation and thinking it was classy of him to bury the hatchet. As a young actor you're supposed to suck round these people's arses because they're the ones who'll give you a job. I've never been good at all the schmoozing. It makes me ill, if I'm honest. I want to get the job on my own right, not because I bought some cunt dinner. I don't believe in all that, although from some of the stories I've heard (none I can tell you here) you can get far in this business doing it. Far as I can tell, that's the only reason for events like the Cannes Film Festival.

I could tell it was a new beginning for Guy. He did have a point, actually. Over in Britain, where the money's tight and there's not that much funding about, we are all fighting the same battle and we should look after each other. I watched *RocknRolla* when it came out but it wasn't really for me. A personal opinion but, like I said, there's no point lying. Actually, maybe there is a point lying because you'll get more work that way, but the downside is that, next time you see yourself in the shaving mirror, you have to say, 'You are a bullshitter.' But I did see his *Sherlock Holmes* movie the other day and was blown away. He did an amazing job on it.

So, anyway, I regret that *Loaded* interview about Guy. He manned up enough to ask me to come and see him and I respect that.

The Mean Machine ended and I was glad to get Vinnie out of my sight. Unfortunately it wouldn't be the last thing I had to do with him and, believe me, our relationship would get no fucking better. In the meantime, I had more to think about than him.

My relationship with her out of the soap was over by the time I did this film. I was spending all my days working, she wasn't, and she never appreciated what I was doing at all. She had no idea about the commitment that goes into being a proper actor. Added to the mix, I was off my nut most of the time as well, not healthy.

When it inevitably came to an end, I just called a cab, got in and went back to my nan's in Stratford. I sobbed my heart out all the way home. I don't think I was upset about losing her, I was just upset about the mess I'd made out of my life. It was another big kick up the bollocks.

Joanne was with someone else by this point, as she should have been. We were getting on again though. It was civil; I think she almost felt sorry for me a little bit, which made me love her even more. I went back to my nan's settee. It was a dark time for me. I had about five or six grand to my name and that was it. It was a big fucking shock to end up on my nan's settee in Stratford, though I still had my nan's love, obviously.

That was when the breakdown started really, around 2002. Going back to live with my nan, I went on the rampage. I was living out of a vodka bottle for about eight months, drinking heavily. At the height of it, I actually got a job called *Second Generation*. It was an Asian drama with Parminder Nagra out of *Bend It Like Beckham*.

I was having it large with my pals – we'd picked up where we'd left off a year before. The brilliant thing about blokes is that you can do that. You phone your mate up after a year and he says, 'All right, Dan', like you saw him yesterday. I was smashing it all night, every night. I'd get the car to pick me up and get straight in with a bottle of vodka and go to the set. The make-up girls really looked after me, bless 'em. They'd usher me straight into my trailer, give me mints and put some drops in my eyes to try to make me look normal.

I'm embarrassed when I think of how I behaved on that set

and the way I treated people. There was one time I turned up on set with a couple of mates. I sent the runner around the corner to get me a crate of lager and I left my two mates in the trailer. I'd go and do my scene, and come back to the trailer to find my mates all curled up, rushing off their heads on E, drinking beer, smoking snouts. I'd drop in and do a line with them and go back out. It makes me heave to think about it now. Again, I knew I couldn't be sacked. I'd got the job, had already shot a lot of it, so the way I saw it, they had to suffer it.

I know from watching it which scenes I'm off my nut in and which ones I'm not. I was quite good at reining it in, composing myself for short bursts, doing the scene and then crawling back to the trailer to recover. It was bloody difficult remembering lines, though, and that normally comes very easily to me. My mind, fried on all kinds of different shit, would go completely blank. That should have been a warning sign.

Second Generation was a critical hit but a ratings flop – it won some awards and made the 'Top Ten TV' of the year in one of the papers. Obviously this made me feel I could get away with doing what I liked. That is no way to conduct yourself. I feel truly sorry about the way I treated people back then but I wasn't myself. I would never disrespect the other actors, the crew and the viewers like that nowadays. The only explanation I can give is that I was dying inside without my family around me.

However, it seemed I could do no wrong at that point and everything I touched turned to gold. I was about to resume a really big professional relationship for me, the one that would see me do the best film work of my career, push my level of fame through the roof – for good and for bad – and eventually get it through my thick fucking skull that acting and drugs don't mix. I was about to undergo some rehab therapy – Nick Love style.

12

THE FOOTBALL FACTORY

I hadn't seen Nick Love in about two years, when I got a call from my agent saying he wanted to see me. It was quite strange he didn't ring me direct as we'd always got on very well. He chose to do it in a professional way. It struck me as weird at the time but I didn't know why he'd taken this approach until I met him later on at the Groucho Club.

I was excited about seeing him again, to reminisce a little bit, excited about talking about the projects he had coming up. Also, to be honest, it was always a laugh going to the Groucho. Nick wouldn't have wanted to get on it, but I was sure someone in there would.

I bounced in and I could immediately see that he didn't look happy. I went to cuddle him and he was so standoffish. He had this look on his face like he was going to nut me. He said, 'Sit down, I have to tell you something.' I asked him what the matter was.

He went in his bag and pulled out a script and slammed it down and said, 'Look at that, will you? I wrote that fucking script for you, as the lead, but because you are fucking running around acting like a cunt I can't offer you the part.'

I was knocked back. I said, 'What do you mean?'

He said, 'You know what I'm talking about. You've become

a fucking liability with drink and drugs – no one will touch you with a fucking bargepole. The producers I've got do not want you in it. Now I'm fighting your fucking battles. I want you to take that fucking script, take it home, read it and you're going to audition like everyone else. Sort yourself out, you cunt.'

That was it. I was stunned. He got up and left. I was expecting to have a beer and a good chat. Now this wasn't exactly Sigmund fucking Freud but it got through to me. No one had had the arsehole to tell me I was acting like a twat. I was behaving like a character out of one of films, in a way. I was going into clubs and people were just giving me Es, wanting to get off their nut with Moff out of *Human Traffic*. And I wasn't saying no.

I would go out with a couple of my pals and end up going off with complete strangers who were fans of mine. I'd end up in some madhouse in Barnet or wherever and because I was Moff I never had to put my hand in my pocket. I'd be round their house, complete fucking strangers, people I'd known for a couple of hours, and they'd chuck *Human Traffic* on, and then we'd all sit round agreeing what a diamond geezer I was. I was starting to creep up my own arse.

It had to come from Nick. If it had come from anyone else I would have told them to fuck off and probably put the nut on them. But I liked Nick and I respected him and I knew that he spoke from the heart. His words hit me like a thousand razorblades. My life was fucked and Nick had just pointed that out to me in the only language I could understand.

I went back to my nan's house in Stratford, and I remember

crying all the way back on the Central Line on the Tube. I think a few people recognised me, but they didn't dare come talk to me in the state I was in. I didn't dare open the script on the train. I just couldn't. I was frightened of opening it for some reason, and so I waited until I got home. I went upstairs to my little room at Nan's, lay on my bed, and started to read the script. This was *The Football Factory*.

As I read it my hands started to shake. I could see immediately it was the script of my dreams. I saw myself in the lead role, what I was going to do and how I was going to do it. I started to buzz off of it, off of acting again, and the idea of me doing this film. The opportunity was massive. In the days before the audition, I'd start daydreaming about doing the film but snap myself out of that by thinking, 'I haven't got the part yet. I have to audition. I've got to get it, I've got to get it.'

By the time the audition came round, I'd read the script over and over again. I almost wore the print off the page. My God, I was so nervous going into that room. You've always got to have a bit of nerves, it's worrying if you haven't, but this was almost a paralysing fear. You've got to remember at this point I'd done quite a bit of film work, but this time round, it felt like my first-ever job. I was scared there would be someone out there better than me. That wasn't the way I normally thought.

I went in to the audition room in the film company's studios in Kentish Town. It was with Vertigo. Nowadays when I go in there my face is plastered all over their walls on posters and pictures, but back then I was unknown to them. Nick had calmed down by then and he was rooting for me. But I needed to prove to the producers that I was capable of doing it. I know Nick saw a few people for it, and it was down to me and a geezer called Tom Hardy, who at the time was an up-and-coming actor. He's done a few things now. I've never met the geezer but he's obviously someone who's not from the flats. He's not someone who is posh, but he has to play up the working-class thing. For me it comes naturally. So I knew I had the edge over on that, but I also knew he was a good actor and there was a real buzz about him at the time.

I just pulled on all my resources, really gave it my best shot. I think I had the advantage because I'd worked with Nick before, and Nick doesn't like to see people 'act'. One of his favourite notes is 'stop acting', which is strange considering the whole thing's one big performance. Anyway, he had his own style and I was lucky to have seen it before.

What I learned from Nick was to rein it all in, to be subtle, to use the eyes. It's all about your mince pies at the end of the day, especially when you make movies. Theatre is a different thing. In theatre, you have to be big, project, use diction. But in a movie it's a close-up shot on your fucking face projected onto a sixty-foot wide screen, so the slightest move of an eyebrow or frown can make up for a thousand words. That's what I learned from him, the subtlety of it, to bring it all down.

We went round to the pub afterwards, all of us. Nick didn't drink but, thank God, it didn't stop him going in a boozer. This was when I first met Tamer Hassan, who'd go on to appear with me in a number of films. Tamer is a bit of a nutter but

I liked him straight away. He sat down and said, 'Dan, pleasure to meet you. I'm a big fan of yours. What are you doing here?' I said, 'I'm auditioning for the lead role.' He asked me why I was auditioning and said he would have expected I'd be offered it straight. I said, 'I've got to earn my place, son.' He said that was fucking bollocks and that I had to be in it.

So me and Tamer hit it off right from the start, and not just because he said flattering things. He had a bit of banter with Nick. Tamer had a suit on, and Nick was saying, 'What, you've just been up in court, you cunt?' And then Frank Harper, who plays Billy Bright in the film, joined us and it made me want to be part of the film even more. These were all people like me, from my background, and I felt right at home with them.

I was trying to gauge how I'd got on, but Nick didn't give nothing away. Clearly I didn't want to start acting like a melt and ask him how I'd done in the audition. So I told myself that I just had to wait and see what happened. If it didn't happen, which was an unbearable thought, I'd have to cross that bridge when I came to it. I went home and it was a couple of days before I got the call from Nick. I picked up the phone and the first thing he said to me was, 'You're in, boy.' The feeling was overwhelming, I felt this tension I'd been carrying around for days disappear from me. I knew it was a second chance and I was lucky to have been given it. Nick had one further Yoda-like statement: 'You fucking dare turn up late once, or pissed, and I will punch you in the mouth.'

It wasn't the punch in the mouth I was worried about – I'll take a punch in the mouth all day long if I'm due one – it was the idea that I would let him down. I knew that I'd done well enough in the audition, but the producers' argument would be 'Is he going to turn up? Is he going to fuck us over?'

I was still living at my nan's but I ditched the drink and drugs and I totally embraced this job. It's strange really: this was one of the nuttiest films I'd done by then but it was also the start of me getting myself sorted out. *The Football Factory* was a searing film, a film about lads being lads. The genius of Nick was that he got real football hooligans in as extras, the real deal, in which gave the whole thing its authenticity. They've got a look to them that you wouldn't have got with normal extras. They look very unfit, with their beer guts poking over their trousers and a coked-up paleness to them, but I wouldn't have told them that. That lot are hard as nails. The sort of hard you can't learn; you've either got it or you ain't. It's an inner aggression that seeps from their every pore. They were dangerous geezers, by and large. Some of them were on tag, some of them had just got out of the nick, some of them were on banning orders, some of them were up in court. They were mostly Millwall as well, with a few Chelsea boys dotted about, and I was West Ham, which gave a nice edge to proceedings.

There was no money on this film, we made it for half a million quid, which sounds like a lot but in the film industry is shit all.

I'm the lead role. I've got all the dialogue, but at the same time, I've got to mix it with the lads. Like I said before, I try not to put a barrier between me and the rest of the crew, but here it had to be more than that. My bond with the boys in the film has to look natural, so I have to get in with all the extras so it comes out looking like a real firm in the final thing.

I can't turn up as some poncey actor or these fuckers would eat me alive. So I'd turn up in the morning and most of the extras, the firm, would be drinking lagers. They'd be sitting in my little trailer with a joint on the go. They'd say, 'Here, Dan, have a fucking lager.' Now, normally I'd have been only too pleased with that. But this film was a new start for me. I didn't want to take the piss anymore, not that Nick would have let me.

So I had to get the balance right between being the lead actor and getting on with them. So I'd take the lager and nip round the corner and empty it out, or I'd have couple of puffs on a joint just to keep them sweet, so they would say, 'He's all right, that Danny, he's as sweet as a nut.'

But at the same time, my focus was totally on the job, on getting it right. No distractions could be allowed to get in my way. It was a tough gig in that respect.

There was a firm from Chelsea there along with some of the Millwall boys. It was funny to see them all sitting about having a drink, reminiscing about how they used to kick the shit out of each other in the eighties. Nick had control over them for most of the time, though not always.

When we did the fighting scenes, Nick had a whistle to start and end it. It was like being back in school. It did go off a couple of times, which is only to be expected with the crew we had on board. One geezer broke his arm, a couple of people lost teeth. There were minders on set that were proper old-school villains though, who kept everyone in check, and they managed to calm things down fairly quick when it was looking like getting nasty.

There was a stuntman there who would normally coordinate all the fighting scenes but Nick didn't want it too technical, he wanted it messy. He wanted to see fat blokes with their bellies hanging out, blowing out of their arse within about thirty seconds of swinging punches, because that's what happens when it kicks off for real.

As much as some men like to fight, not every man has it in them. Not everyone wants to go round swinging punches at people. Despite what people might think of me, despite the way I'm portrayed in some parts of the media, I'm not like that myself. If someone brings it to me I'll be right back at them, but I don't think I've ever started a fight in my life. I'm an easy-going bloke and I'm proud of that. I'm not a hard man, and I've never wanted to be one.

I had to bring the audience with me on my journey. And that's why I love what Nick did with the script because within quarter of an hour I'm questioning the idea of being a hooligan – is this the life for me? This is why I have these psychic dreams going on. I keep dreaming I'm going to die and I keep seeing this kid with bandages round his face, wondering who it was. But I don't turn it in and return to a normal life because once you're in that world it's hard to pull yourself out. I had to make the audience believe I could have a tear up, but also that I was just a normal bloke who doesn't really want to get involved in all the brouhaha.

Nick's so good about writing about the male mind. *The*

Football Factory gave you three different generations of men and Nick did them all justice on the screen. The old boys were in it, representing the old-school man who fought for this country – that is, someone who had a genuine reason to fight. Then you got the middle-aged men, aged forty-odd, who's still running around on the terraces swinging punches at people for no reason, the racist type. Then you've got the younger generation who are coming up in the ranks who are a bit lost and don't know their arse from their elbow. They're part of this army, but they don't have a clue what they stand for or why they want to go up to Burnley and kick off and stamp all over people's heads. They just go. Nick was trying to get the essence of that and I think he succeeded. The film was a complete joy for me. I jumped out of bed every morning just to get on set.

This was a rare film, a bit like *Human Traffic* in the way it dealt with youth, but in a different kind of way. Where *Human Traffic* was quite a hippie film where everyone was chilled out and loved up just like they were in the movie, *The Football Factory* was about men coming together to have tear ups and kick the shit out of each other. And, like I said, those fights did become real on some occasions, just like the drug taking was real in *Human Traffic*.

Also, like *Human Traffic*, the pay was bollocks. It was five hundred quid a week, Equity minimum. Didn't matter. I'd have done it for nothing because it was an opportunity for me to put myself back on the map and to work with Nick as his leading man. I felt this was a winner from the get go, and I wasn't wrong.

The result of doing *The Football Factory* and *Human Traffic*, probably the two films I'm best known for, is that I've got a very strange fan base. I've got my *Human Traffic* fans, my peace-to-all-nations posse. And then I've got my *Football Factory* mob, all these little hard nuts running around, the Burberry boys. They're a totally different audience.

I love 'em both, but it's a lot easier to get on with the *Human Traffic* mob, I'll tell you that now. If I walk into a boozer with villains in it, they're going to cop for me straight away. And they're going to want to stand there and have a booze with me. Sometimes I'm not in the mood for it, sometimes I most definitely am, but the thing about fame is that people have a perception of you. They want you to be a certain thing and if you're not what they expect, they'll be disappointed. So what do you do? Are you honest to yourself or do you keep them sweet by giving them what they want? To tell these people they're mistaking you for your character is going to be more aggro than it's fucking worth. But who am I closer to as a person, Moff or Tommy Johnson the hooligan? Moff, all day long. I'm not a violent bloke. I can play one, but being one is something entirely different.

I came through that film, smashed it, and I still had a lot left in the tank as well. It taught me about bringing my performance down and being subtle with it. The bit I enjoy about being the star of a film is not the money – and on five hundred quid a week that was just as well – or the fame or anything like that. It's about being on the job and having a lead role, that responsibility of being on camera for 90 per cent of the film, having the story revolve around you, carrying the whole movie. It's a massive responsibility but it's what every actor worth their salt should crave. You have wave after wave of dialogue, you do a twelve-hour day, you get home, you're fucked, you get up again at 5.30 and you're back at it again. It's knackering, but ultimately, it's fucking rewarding.

Luckily, I don't suffer much with anxiety about how the shoot's going to pan out. The way I work is I take each day as it comes. I don't look too far ahead and I give that day 150 fucking per cent and then go home and concentrate on the next day.

I never learn the whole script. That would be a ridiculous idea. You film it all back to front anyway. Of course, you need to know where you are in the story so maybe you'll all read a couple of scenes that come before the one you're doing, just to see where the story's going, but a good day's filming is six pages – six minutes of screen time. That's a twelve-hour day. A lot of people don't realise that.

With a twelve-hour day, you've got to keep your wits about you. All the concentration, the jumping about in the script, you need to know right from left, up from down, so when I was filming *The Football Factory*, I got right off the hard stuff. I didn't go anywhere near it. That was made easier by being around Nick who's as clean as your nan's front step. I've been out to a couple of nightclubs with him but he stands in the corner with a can of Red Bull and he can't deal with it. He's useless in a club around that wildness. He's obsessed with the idea of it, and I think he enjoys the wild side to my character, but at the same time he hates it and thinks it's unfocused.

I've got nothing in common with him away from filming

and being creative together. We don't have a lot to talk about, because he goes to bed at eight o'clock every night, and he doesn't watch telly. He's a mad, driven character like that.

I bonded with Tamer at that time as well. I also caught up with Roland Manookian, a great young actor who played Zebedee. Roland plays a right miserable little shit in the film – a sneaky little chav and a brain donor. Roland's nothing like that in real life. He's peace to all nations, loves his bit of gardening. He's a real spiritual kid. I met him on *Charlie Bright* but on that film we were enemies. We did have a bond up then, but we got to know each other better on *The Football Factory*.

I loved Roland because he was from the same background as me, though he was out of Bermondsey. He came to acting quite late and he just loved everything about it. He was brilliant in *Charlie Bright*. It's strange how his career developed from then on – he was selling Christmas trees last year. It's a tragedy, he's a great actor. One I'd really like to work with again. I'm sure he'll be on the up soon. There aren't many actors who don't have to do something else to earn their crust once in a while. People imagine that I'm fucking minted, for instance. Not so. I've made a decent wedge in the last couple of years but right up until then – 2007, maybe 2008, I've been skint for most of my life.

Tamer was very good in *The Football Factory*, a natural talent. He plays a right hard bastard from South London, so he didn't have to go very method on it, being a right hard bastard from South London himself. He came into acting very, very late after a varied life. He was a boxer for years, but then something happened to his eye and he couldn't carry it on. Afterwards, he ran nightclubs and restaurants and was a big success at that. But he liked the idea of acting and came into it wet behind the ears. At the start he just wanted to learn more about it.

One of the reasons he got a part in *The Football Factory*, other than being a natural, was that he lent his football club's ground for us to film some scenes. He owns Greenwich Borough FC. The scene where he collars me in the toilet was set in his football club. He had an ingenious way into acting. He bought his own agency, and an agent with it, and got her to represent him. Now that right there is a smart move. But he's definitely got the talent about him, no two ways about it. He came into it at thirty-four, thirty-five which is late to start. However, one of the reasons he's good is that you need a bit of life experience to get the emotions right up there on-screen. You do need to be in touch with your emotional side as well, which Tamer is.

When it came out, we couldn't believe the success of it, really. We did work hard to spread the good word, though. We did a tour around the country, Tamer, Nick and me. We went to Leeds, Cardiff, London, Birmingham, Bristol – about ten places in all – and, through our contacts, we'd get hold of the firms – proper firms, like the Zulus in Birmingham. We'd tell them we wanted them to see this movie and let them watch it for free. A lot of them thought the offer was bollocks and that it was the Old Bill playing a crafty one to get them to the cinema and nick them, so in some places the turn out wasn't much to write home about.

But when they did come, we would show the film and then do a Q&A with them afterwards. There's no better way to find if you've got it right than doing it in front of the real thing. And they fucking loved it.

We weren't glamorising hooliganism, particularly if you're following my character. There's nothing glamorous about it. I basically get battered in a tunnel for most of it. What they liked about it was that it was real and it was honest. This stuff went on, still does, as the firms knew full well. I think they saw a lot of truth in the way we'd portrayed the life.

How is it that some men who live normal lives can turn into complete lunatics on a Saturday afternoon, go and punch the bollocks out of someone they don't know, then go home to their wives and kids, have a bit of dinner and go to bed? That's what the film was asking.

It's not as bad now, but through the eighties and nineties it was front-page news every day. I think I do understand what causes the hooliganism. It's about territory and about the feeling that you belong to something, belong to the unit of an army, that you're fighting for your area. That's a fascinating subject, men being men, expressing themselves through their fists. It's not something I'm into but I think it's just a raw male aggression that people have, seeking any sort of outlet. All men have it a bit but it normally only comes out defensively, when someone has a go at your missus or mum, something like that. Other blokes have it with every waking breath.

We got a great reception wherever we went. There was only one cunt who got a bit lairy in Manchester, because we don't mention Old Trafford, but someone took him out the back and gave him a bit of a clump. There was a few other firms, mainly up north, who got the hump because they didn't get a mention, but you couldn't include the whole lot. It was about Chelsea and Millwall, London firms, so some of the other firms around the rest of the country would be, 'Where are we?' We had to explain that Nick's a cockney and so he's going to write about cockneys, just like the director Shane Meadows is from the Midlands, so he writes about people from the Midlands.

Cardiff got a little shout and they were over the moon with it. That was the most worrying for me, Cardiff – the Soul Crew – now they are a proper firm. They're Welsh and we're English so we thought we might get an interesting time down there, but they were sweet with it. There aren't many of them but they can all hold their hands up and they're a powerful crew. Every other geezer has a Mars Bar – a scar – on his face. A few of them took us all out afterwards and we went on a mad night out. Nick slipped off quite early. They were a bit disappointed he didn't drink. I did his drinking for him and I think he was happy with that. Nick said, 'Go on, boy, go and enjoy yourself,' and I certainly fucking did. You're always a bit edgy around hard bastards like that, particularly given the Welsh–English thing because they could do the turn on you at any second. None of them did though, and they were really good to me.

I didn't feel so guilty about going out and having a line of gear up my hooter again because the film was over. This is what I've learned: you don't mix business and pleasure. By all means go out and let your hair down now and again but, when the camera starts rolling, you need to be sharp as arseholes.

The Football Factory was a massive success – it took £1 million at the box office and only cost half that to make. And with the DVDs and everything, the profits went through the roof.

I think it's the best hooligan film ever made, and it started the influx of them that came afterwards. Straight after that you had *Green Street*, which in my humble opinion was a pile of shit. They put Elijah Wood in it and it had a £9 million budget, but it wasn't convincing. On the one hand I was disappointed because it was about West Ham, but on the other I was relieved that it was so shit because it was potential competition for *The Football Factory* as the definitive hooligan film. The lead actor was supposed to be a West Ham boy, a local geezer, but he had about eighteen accents in it, like Dick Van Dyke in *Mary Poppins*. The actor who plays him had just got back from LA and it shows.

The Football Factory brought a bit of credibility back to me. People in the industry and out on the street started to take notice of me again and my level of fame went up tenfold after the movie – something I have mixed feelings about. I like the fact that people will turn up to see a film just because I'm in it, obviously. I'm less keen on not being able to go for a quiet drink any more.

I did start to notice that it was a different crowd who were saying hello to me, but I was buzzing off it. I was in a good place and not just professionally. I had love back in my life.

I went out with a couple of birds, big-time caners too. But I needed a steadying influence, a straight goer. If you're like me you can't go out with a buzzcat. You need a moderating influence in your life.

I found one in Joanne, the mother of my kid Dani. The way I got back with Joanne was a strange thing, because at the time both of us were seeing someone else. I was picking Dani up every Sunday from Joanne's house and bit by bit, we started to flirt with each other again. There was this weird thing going on. I started to look at her in a way that I hadn't looked at her since school.

Thinking back, maybe we both needed to see what other people were like, to experience something different and new. We'd been going out with each other since we were kids after all. We'd grown up together, had a kid at a young age and had never really known if the grass was greener.

I noticed the vibe from her and I loved flirting with her. I wasn't just looking forward to picking the kid up. I was actually making excuses to see Dani more, when I really wanted to see Joanne. That was a surprise to me, because at that point it was all about the kid. I didn't really even acknowledge Joanne for a time when I picked up Dani. Our relationship had gone completely dead. But then one thing led to another and we started to have an affair behind the backs of the people we were seeing. No disrespect to the girl I was with, but it felt right.

But this was something different. This was going back to my roots and it was all my dreams come true. Joanne had her own place by then, a gaff in Canning Town, but nice and cosy and perfect for her and Dani. I had started staying over, and putting the baby to bed again. I can't tell you how much I'd missed my family, having that rock at the centre of my life.

Dani, who was about four at this time, would ask, 'Are you staying tonight, Daddy?' And I would say, 'Yes, babe,' and I'd put her in her bed. I used to well up every time she asked me. It was everything I'd missed for so long. Piece by piece it felt as if I was getting my life back.

The acting was going well. I was passionate about it again and my daughter and Joanne were coming back into my life. We kept this affair going for a little while and then we sat down and said to each other, 'What are we doing? We have a beautiful kid together, why are we sneaking about doing this?'

So we elbowed the other two and I moved back in with her. It was like a whole new relationship again; we really appreciated each other. When you have a kid, you can take things for granted and your relationship can go on the back-burner. It's a twenty-four-hour, all-consuming job. You haven't got the time to talk about your relationship, or put in time with each other. It's about bringing this child up, nurturing her and making sure she's happy twenty-four hours a day.

All of a sudden we started to think about our relationship and we realised how much we loved each other. Although we've spent some time apart and seen other people, it's only ever been her for me, really.

So things were going well, very well. I was in a good mood,

so good that I agreed to take the lead role in a film that was being made for no money at all, because I liked the script. It must have been good karma because that film was called *Wasp* and it won an Oscar.

13

AN OSCAR

I'd just done *The Football Factory* and got chatting to the girl who cast the extras. She came to me and said a woman she knew was making a short film and she thought I'd be perfect for the role. Would I like to look at the script?

'No' is usually the short answer. I get a lot of these requests and most of the time the scripts turn out to be pony. Anyway, I liked and respected this girl, so I took a look at the script. Straight away I could see there was something about it.

It was set on a council estate and it's this love story about a young girl who's got four kids. She meets my character and I'm like her knight in shining armour. But she doesn't want me to know about her children. We arrange to meet at a pub one night but she's got no one to look after the kids so she brings them along and leaves them outside the pub. One of them's a baby. She keeps having to run out with crisps and drinks for them and say, 'just stay there' and then run back in and be all sexy with me.

The reason it's called *Wasp* is because a wasp flies into the baby's mouth and one of her older kids comes running into the pub saying, 'Mum, Mum, come quick.' She thinks I'm going to go the other way on her, do one out of the pub, but actually I come to the rescue. There's a horrible scene at the

—— 159 ——

start of it where her kids want something to eat and she has to give them a spoonful of sugar each out of an old bag. The last scene is quite simple, I take them all to the chippie and we're sitting in a car eating chips, having a little moment.

Like I said, I thought the script had something so I had to go and meet the director Andrea Arnold. I remember I quite fancied her. She was about forty, ginger hair, quite sexy. She had a different way of working though. She didn't believe in the idea of action and cut, and so she would just shoot and shoot and shoot. She also, which I liked, didn't want to cast kids from drama school, she wanted kids off council estates, raw, not the 'Do it for Mummy' types. She was a strange one because she'd just walk around council estates watching kids, which in our day and age could lead you into trouble, man or woman. Any kids she liked the look of, she'd just go to them and say, 'Can you take me to your house, because I'd like to see your mummy' and then explain to their mums who she was and what she wanted. We started shooting at night and I was a bit concerned because one of the kids was running around in a little tutu and it was freezing cold. I started to get a bit didgy around the whole thing, and the mums who brought their kids just wanted to go home and get the kids into bed.

But there was a method to Andrea's madness, because she caught this great moment. The kid was waiting outside, sitting there bored with a little tutu on, all dirty, and this moth flies in, really just randomly and it lands on her hand and the kid panics. It's an amazing moment of film-making, because you see how vulnerable the kid is outside the pub. Then it cuts back to the music of the pub, and I'm in there, getting all sexy round their mum as we're playing pool.

I did it for £250. I loved Andrea. I loved her energy. I didn't enjoy her methods that much, because I'm used to action and cut and know how it works, but she got good performances out of everyone so there's no complaining. The actress I was with was called Natalie Press – a good little actress, but she wasn't from my school. She wanted to analyse everything and break everything down, to find out her motiv-ation – all that malarkey. I went and had a fag while she did it.

I thought I'd do Andrea a favour and try to help her get her career off the ground. Then she went and won a fucking Academy Award! An Oscar! For best live short. I was in Thailand at the time doing a documentary about the tsunami. I couldn't believe we'd won it. It was good enough being part of something that was nominated, but to win it was incred-ible.

I remember them showing it, cutting to me on the big screen in front of the whole Oscar crowd. It was an incredible moment. Andrea's gone on to do some amazing things. She did a movie called *Red Road* and recently *Fish Tank*, which won two BAFTAs. The woman is amazing. I saw her again in Cannes recently and we had a right bond up and a good drink. And I'm very proud to be part of her success. It's a weird thing – you do a little job thinking you'll do it for the love of it, and it goes on to win a fucking Oscar. I love what she said when she picked up the Oscar. She got up to the podium and said, 'This is the dog's bollocks.' It went down like a lead balloon, but I loved it. I'm proud of that piece of work, it's a good little short.

The tsunami documentary was actually a life-changing experience, something that made me value what I had back in England. Even though at that time I didn't have a lot it was still a shedload more than anyone in the areas I visited in Thailand had.

I was skint at the time, I didn't have any work about me and MTV approached me about doing a documentary called *The Backpacker's Guide to Thailand*. The idea was that I would go to Thailand as a backpacker would, and see the devastation the tsunami had caused. The Thais were trying to get their economy back on track and wanted backpackers to return to the devastated areas, because tourists were treating them like a no-go zone.

I didn't take it that seriously. I thought I'd go out there on a bit of a jolly up. I had no idea just how bad the damage from that wave was so as I loved the idea of a freebie to Thailand I jumped at the chance. The tsunami happened on Boxing Day 2004, and I went out there the following February.

It's fair to say this whole experience made me grow up a lot and changed my outlook on certain things. This was before I'd done *The Real Football Factories* documentaries and it was my first taste of presenting and being followed around by a camera and crew. They broke me in gently: we saw the sights, I went on the little boats and all that and I was generally having a lovely time. All that changed when we got to the areas that had been smashed by the wave. Thailand is such a beautiful country, the people are lovely, the food is cheap and fucking tasty, it's sunny and the scenery is stunning. The only downside is it gets hit by this hundred-foot wave every century or so.

My first interview was with a Swedish guy on Phi Phi island. The problem they had was that, when the waves struck, if you were in your house, not only were you underwater but the walls had collapsed on top of you as well. This guy told me very matter-of-factly that he woke up, realised what had happened and looked across at his wife and saw she was dead. Completely gone.

So he makes the decision to leave her and goes to help people. He said it was the hardest decision of his life but his duty was to the living, not the dead. I was in love with the guy.

A tsunami kills his wife and he gets up and goes out to start helping people. Incredible. He's up to his waist in water and he's treading on drowned bodies. I found that image very difficult to get out of my head. While he's walking along trying to help people he sees others looting. He remembers picking up a stick and whacking people, telling them to stop, trying to get them to help him.

This happened to him two months before I met him and I could see the full impact of what he was telling me still hadn't hit him. I had to stop him at one point, because I couldn't take in what he was saying, I didn't know how to react; I just wanted to cuddle him.

After that, the documentary crew wanted me to go bone scavenging. There are people out there who can't find the bodies of their loved ones, so the bones that people find are collected in piles and taken away for DNA testing. People need to grieve, and even if you just have two bones of your relative, you can still bury them and feel that bit closer to them, instead of them disappearing off the face of the earth without a trace. But I couldn't believe what I was doing, I really couldn't believe it. I have these gloves on, because when you're looking through rubble, there are all these needles and sharp nails that can stab you if you're not careful. And with all the stagnant water around, they'd be carrying all sorts of diseases. I didn't find any bones, which I was pretty glad about. To be honest, I don't think I was mentally prepared for what the show was about. That's probably why they chose me. I'm a Jack-the-Lad sort, no worries and all that bollocks, and so when I come across all that destruction and all that death, you see the change come over me right on camera. By the end of it, I was a blubbering wreck.

What I found really fascinating was the animals. Just before the tsunami hit, every single animal on every island fucked off, just went. Cats, dogs, birds flying in the opposite direction towards the hills. Some people clocked that and followed them.

The last day I came up with the idea that I wanted to have something to remember Thailand by, which is why I have a tattoo on my hand. I'm not really all that big on tattoos, but I fancied having Dani, my daughter's name. I think it was having the experience of seeing so many people lose the people they love that made me want to have some physical sign of the love in my life. They took me to this seedy little gaff, the geezer had ball bearings in his arms, and long fucking fangs.

The tattoo fucking hurt, believe me. He didn't give me no Vaseline or cream to put on it. But every time I look at it now, it does remind me of Thailand – not that I need reminding because it's an experience that no one could ever forget.

14

MEMO TO SELF: BEFORE ACCEPTING ROLE, READ SCRIPT

I've done shorts for other people too. I did one called *Free Speech* for these two brothers I met who were film-makers. I had to sit in a bath with a bird. The idea was a couple sitting there, talking about their fantasies to turn each other on. She tells me I can go anywhere in my fantasy, say exactly what I want, and so I say to her I have a fantasy about her sister. That flips her out and she storms out and leaves me in the bath. I spent about eight hours in the bath with that bird. It was a weird day, because she didn't want to show her tits to anyone, so I had to keep my hands over her nipples.

Luckily, the missus doesn't really ask too much about what goes on on set. So I didn't feel I had to tell her I was sitting in a bath with a naked bird all day. You might think there would be a 'wood' situation going on there. Not at all. You've seen one pair of tits, you seen them all. Believe me, it's not a sexy situation sitting in cold water with an entire crew around you.

I do like to help people out and I feel flattered when people approach me to be in their shorts. So quite often, if I like the script, I'll do it for nothing. When I was very young I did one called *The Prince of Denmark Hill*. It didn't really go anywhere but it was a good little story, a gangster type thing with a lot of dialogue in it. I enjoyed it. There was a northern actor in it called Stephen Lord who I thought would go on to massive things. He went to do *EastEnders* recently, which ain't half bad.

However, my open and trusting nature (yeah, right) does get me into trouble occasionally, no more so than with a film I shoehorned in after *The Football Factory*.

It was called *The Great Ecstasy of Robert Carmichael* and is the only film I've ever done without looking at the script first. I really, really, wish I fucking had. I learned the hard way on that one, let me tell you that.

They wanted me for four days, not a bad wedge. I thought it was a piece of piss and I'd do it standing on my head. I knew it was about kids on an estate and I knew there was a rape scene in it, and that's all I knew. Never reading the script meant I didn't realise how graphic this rape scene was. Luckily it was nothing to do with my character so I did my bit, got paid and fucked off. Then, a few months later, I started to read things in the paper about how people had been sick at the Cannes film festival watching it. Obviously, because I was the biggest name in it, my name kept coming up. I'd only done four days on the fucking thing out of a six-week shoot. At this point I started to ask questions about what was in the film. It might seem strange that I agreed to a script without reading it but it was a short job, good money and I suppose I paid the price for being cocky.

In the end I went to see it. I was up at the Edinburgh film festival for something else and it was on. I sat through it and I literally couldn't believe my eyes.

The idea of the film is that there's this talented young violinist who gets involved with the wrong crowd. I play a proper villain in it, a violent criminal who gets out of prison and meets up with his cousin who thinks the world of him. We go back to someone's house and my character starts this gang rape on this girl, which you don't see as it's all shot through a crack in the door. You hear it, which is bad enough. My character rapes her, as does my cousin and his mates after. Then I get arrested and that's me done – I'm out of the film. But the other lot like the idea of rape so much that they break into their teacher's house with her husband and they tie her husband up. It's all done on this wide shot so you see everything. They strip the teacher naked, they stab him a few times – you see him lying there with a knife sticking out of him – and then they rape her. It's horrendous; they take it in turns, these young boys. And then, believe it or not, they start fucking her with a sword-fish. You see the whole lot. Honestly, my eyes were popping out of my head while I was watching it. There are ways of making films, ways of telling stories. In my book, some things you can imply without having to show in such detail. Swordfish fucking being one of them.

There was blood spurting everywhere and as I'm sitting there in the cinema, I start feeling ill. It was giving me a headache watching it. After they've finished, they light a cigarette, piss on her and then they walk down the road. And then the credits run.

I'm all up for making films that don't have happy endings, but fuck me! Don't leave that as the last taste in people's mouths. The last scene of the film is what people take with them out of the cinema, it's what they'll all remember. And in this case they'd remember a fish with its snout up someone's fanny. There was no explanation of why they were doing it – they're bored, they're young, they live in Eastbourne, on an estate, that's it. I've lived on an estate all my fucking life and I've never been bored enough to do some bird with a swordfish.

I felt like jumping under a bus when I left the cinema. There's a part of me that gives respect to the director because he doesn't give a fuck. But on the other hand there is a limit. I was embarrassed to be associated with it, to be honest.

Thank God that I was about to make a proper film with a bloke who limits the swordfish input to having a steak off a barbecue with a slice of lime. This was to be one of the most exciting and best films of my life, one that would push me to another level with my acting. I was about to make *The Business* with Nick Love.

15

DOING THE BUSINESS

The Business was written for me and Tamer. Because I did a good job on *The Football Factory* I didn't have to audition and was given it straight by Nick. That's always a lovely moment as an actor because for most of your career you have to audition. To have someone write something especially for you is really special. That moment when they hand you the script sends a tingle down your spine, especially when it comes from someone like Nick, because you know it's going to be right up your street.

It's like when you're a kid and it's Christmas Day. You've got loads of presents sitting there, but there's a big massive one and you don't know what it is. You can't wait to get to that big one. So you open all the little ones first and they're nice presents but your eye is always on that big one in the corner. It was the same with the feeling of the script for *The Business*, guessing what it might be, hoping it's what you want, ripping it open, and the reveal. As soon as I read it I thought, 'Oh my God I've rung the bell with this.'

It was a tale of villainy set on the Costa Del Sol in Spain. This used to be a haven for criminals because we wouldn't give the Rock of Gibraltar back to Spain and so relations between us cooled right off. British crims realised this and so villains who were on the run from the Old Bill over here would fuck off to Spain and live it up, knowing that the coppers couldn't touch them. Spain would refuse to arrest them or deport them, so all these gangsters were lounging around over there getting suntans, sticking their fingers up at Plod back home.

The Business was a true story of how the Costa Del Sol became a gangsters' paradise. I'd actually met one villain who used to be out there, back when I worked on *Human Traffic*. It was the drug smuggler Howard Marks. Howard's not exactly your typical drug lord, being educated at Oxford University and coming off as quite a gentle geezer, but he was the real deal, believe you me. At one point he was said to control 10 per cent of the world's trade in dope.

He was so chilled out, which wasn't that much of a surprise considering he appeared to smoke his own weight in weed every day. Howard had his own Rizlas, with his face on, and he gave me a pack. He walked around with a tin with all different types of weed in it and he'd skin up where ever he was. Because this was in Wales, and Howard was a Welshman, he was a local legend. They let him smoke weed openly in pubs. However, because he's a peaceful bloke and claims to have built up his drugs empire without ever using violence, I couldn't really use him as a model for the part.

I read the script and I thought, 'This is the role for me. This is going to put me on the map.' I hardly had any lines in it and that's one of the biggest challenges for an actor. This was an opportunity for me to really hone my craft. I'd have to react, react, react all the time and tell the story through the emotions on my face.

Acting is more about the reacting than it is about the speaking of lines. It's about listening to what the other actors are saying as if you're in character and have never heard it before. Too many actors wait for their cue and think that as long as they deliver their line all right, everything's fine. That's not acting, that's just remembering the words and reading them out. You have to drink in everything that's going on around you and then react. It's hard to do right, which is why a lot of people choose to hide behind just delivering their lines and hoping that'll stop them being found out.

I flew out to Spain with Geoff Bell, who was also in *The Business* with me. Geoff's done a bunch of good work, and we'd bumped into each other previously on *Mean Machine*. Our flight was delayed and, as me and Geoff were at Heathrow, we slipped off to a seafood bar. As you do, we had some champagne and got a bit pissed. Quite a lot pissed, actually. The trouble is that once you're on a roll, it's not that easy to stop and we carried on boozing on the plane as well.

Unfortunately Nick was waiting for us at the hotel in Spain. When he saw the state we were in, his face took on that look you see on Alex Ferguson's face with Man U losing to a dodgy goal at half-time – when he's boiling up so much inside that you can imagine the top of his head bobbling about like the lid on a pan of spuds. Not happy. In fact, he had the raving hump.

He actually had no right to have the hump, because we were out there to do a week's rehearsal first and we weren't going to be filming the next day. So it wasn't as if I was letting him down. I said, 'Hold on a minute, I'm entitled to have a drink. The flight was delayed, I'm with Geoff, we're having a bond up, what's wrong with that? Let's not get off on the wrong foot. If we start working and I let you down, then fair enough.' I can't say he looked very impressed by that, though I didn't get the smack in the mouth he'd promised me, thank God. I'm not saying Nick shat out, not at all. I think he was so angry he actually forgot he'd promised to hit me. I wasn't about to remind him.

It wasn't a nice feeling really because me and Geoff were on a real high, excited about everything, and we turned up and Nick tore a strip off us.

Nick was in a mad mood on this film, I don't know what was going on in his life at the time but he was very fucking aggressive on it. He suffers a little bit from Tourette's and one of his quirks is that he doesn't like people crunching around him. No crisps are allowed on the set, no sweets either, and he didn't like the sound of flip-flops, so no one was allowed to wear those. He was in a foul fucking mood for most of *The Business*. Still, it's a great film, one of the best I've done. It's a whole collection of different gangster stories that Nick's sewn together and done with cockney characters, all in a beautiful backdrop.

As much as *The Football Factory* was a beautiful thing, it was set in Bermondsey and Lewisham, grey and horrible, all pissing down and tobacco-stained. *The Business* was all bright colours, drenched in sunshine. I loved the clothes, the Fila stuff, the Bjorn Borg tennis shorts.

I was all tanned and I was fit as fuck during that film. Drugs weren't running my life any more, because I had something to live for – Joanne and my kid.

I was also buzzing because I was going to be working with Tamer, and it was his first big role. There was an energy coming off him on that film, no mistake. He was very nervous about his role and he wanted to get it spot on. He shouldn't have worried. This part was made for him – he's a playboy in it, and that's what he is in real life. He smashed it.

It's a three-way love story between me, Geoff and Tamer. Tamer and Geoff are best friends and then I come on the scene as a youngster and Tamer takes me under his wing. Geoff gets royally fucked off about that and ends up hating me.

We go on this whole trip of discovering cocaine, which is quite ironic, considering some of my previous recreational activities. *The Business* is set during the first time that cocaine really came into play in the UK, when the floodgates opened – in the eighties, the Thatcher years. Before that it had been around but it was pretty exclusive, something for rich people. It's not like today when everyone's right at it.

The change from innocence to experience is shown by my character. I start off as a young kid, very vulnerable, but go on to become this sexy character that's got a bit of clout. There's a change in the way I dress – fluffy haired at the start to wearing it all slicked back, my clothes much more fashionable and cooler than when I begin.

When Tamer turns on me, everybody turns on me and I've got to fight for survival. It was a massive journey for me and I needed to be right on my game – no drugs, concentrating from the start of the day to the end of it. I got some inspiration from an unexpected source. The TV out there was all in Spanish so I bought the box set of *The Godfather* and watched that, on Nick's suggestion more than anything. Nick said he wanted me to watch Al Pacino's character Michael because he's very understated in it and he wanted me to channel some of that into my character.

Although Pacino's brilliant in that film, it was Brando who took my eye. I took the photo of him from the DVD and put it on my mirror. I'd kiss it every morning before I went out to work. I've never had a ritual like that before but it felt right when I was doing this film. Now that's a big ask to take a genius like Brando and to try to put some of him into my performance, but it's what I tried to do.

It was a long shoot, and it did take a lot of concentration to keep my performance up to scratch – especially because Nick was barking at everyone and being a complete bastard, really, not necessarily to me but to the people on the crew. It was a weird working environment, but I knew that as long as I did my bit I'd be OK.

He did have a moment with Tamer and really gave it to him one day. I'd never seen him in that kind of mood. Tamer went right on the back foot. Nick was threatening to punch Tamer in the mouth, a move I would advise against considering he's a former professional boxer, built like a brick shithouse and was dragged up on some of the meanest streets in Britain.

Luckily Tamer is a gentle giant, so he was happy to avoid a little slap in the chops from Nick. I have seen him switch a few times, though, and when it happens, it's a scary fucking sight. I was in the back of a cab with him once and he was with his agent Camilla. They were always fucking around with each other, flirting in a harmless way. We were in this black cab and they were having a laugh with each other. Tamer reached across and got her around the head and said, 'Shut up, you little fucker,' just fucking about. They were always doing stuff like that with each other, just a bit of fun.

The next thing we know, the cab driver's stopped the cab. He got out and said to Tamer, 'Right. Get out, you cunt, get out of my fucking cab.' Tamer said, 'Look, mate, I'm only joking, I'm only fucking about.'

The cabbie went, 'No, you cunt, you bully, get out of my cab.'

I don't think he realised what a big unit Tamer was until he got out of the cab and said, 'See you, you little cunt, you better get back in and drive this motor. I told you, I was fucking about.'

And the cabbie went ,'I'm sorry, mate, it's my old man used to bash my mum about.'

Tamer said, 'Get in the cab and drop us where we want to go.'

The geezer jumped in the cab and started driving. I could see Tamer slowly seething.

I was trying to cool it down, telling Tamer, 'He's got it wrong, but you've got to respect the geezer.'

Tamer said, 'Yeah, yeah, yeah.' And then all of a sudden he started punching the window, shouting, 'Stop the cab, now!' I thought, 'Oh my fucking God.' The cab stopped, and at this point other cabs were pulling up, because cabbies help each other out like that. I noticed that there was a restaurant next to us and I said, 'Tamer, go and get in that fucking restaurant.'

Tamer was shouting, 'Cunt, cunt!' at the cabbie. I took out forty quid and I gave it to the cabbie. I went, 'Look, mate, you've had a touch.'

He said, 'Look, I've never lost a fare yet.'

I went, 'Just fuck off, take your bit to go and do yourself a favour.'

Which, thank fuck, he did.

About six months later, someone came up to me and said, 'Did you and Tamer bash up a cab driver?' I totally denied anything had happened, but somehow it'd got around and the truth had gone to fuck, as it often does. It's weird how that kind of thing gets back to you when you get a little bit of fame. I'm often asked about stupid, random things that never actually happened, things I'm supposed to have done.

I respect that cab driver, because if there was violence against a woman going on in the back, then fair play to him for trying to stop it. I'm aware that last line is going to sound like I put it in there just because of the incident that occurred with me and *Zoo* magazine. Believe me, this isn't the case. Growing up where I did, I've seen my fair share of violence against women and I despise it. Any bloke who raises his hands to a woman is among the lowest of the low in my opinion. So, now I've brought up the subject, I want to clear a few things up:

As some of you will know, I used to write a column for the lad mag *Zoo* – a jokey, sort of spoof thing where I'd generally take the piss and say stupid things in answer to readers' letters.

When I say 'write it', I didn't actually write it myself. One of their journalists would call me up once a week, I'd talk shit for ten minutes and he'd be relied on to edit that into something that people would want to read. Now I got on with this bloke really well, had a laugh with him, so I used to just bang on, saying the first thing that came into my head.

Someone had written in asking me for advice on what to do with his girlfriend. She'd dumped him and he couldn't bear to think of her going out with other blokes. Me and the journalist were trying to come up with something funny to say – it's not a serious column and the answers are supposed to be stupid. So after a while of not coming up with anything that funny, I said he should go on a rampage with the lads, get pissed up. As a joke – a bad joke – I said to the journalist, 'Maybe he should cut her face so no one would want her.' Why did I say that? Because it's a ridiculous thing to say. It was a rubbish and tasteless joke. Even as it came out of my mouth I wasn't proud of it. I was more embarrassed than anything. The journalist seemed to like it, though, so I said no more about it. But I never thought for a second that he would stick it in the magazine. In fact, the only reason I thought he'd find it funny is that it's precisely the sort of thing he could never stick in the magazine. It was a sick and outrageous suggestion. But then it was printed, and my world collapsed around me.

The journalist phoned me saying he'd had a 'brain malfunction'. Honestly, he sounded like he was nearly crying. When he told me he'd put the line in, I nearly fell on the floor. I live with three women, two of them my own daughters. All the most important people in my life have been women. I despise violence against women. And now, because I made an admittedly rubbish and stupid joke, I'm getting hung out to dry in the press and on Twitter. I was gutted. It totally misrepresented who I am. Look, call me what you like, a twat, an idiot, a gobshite, but I'm not a bloke who is violent to women, thinks violence to women is funny or who could ever have any respect for someone who was violent towards a woman.

So, the idea that I was seriously advising someone to cut his ex-girlfriend's face so no one would want her is ridiculous. I think it popped into my head because I'd done *Thieftakers* years before, and there's a line this pimp says to a rent boy: 'I'll cut your face, so that no one will want you!'

I asked the journalist what he was going to do about it and he said he was going to go away and make it right.

Basically, *Zoo* was going to take the blame because they printed it. But they didn't take the blame, did they? They put out a statement that muddied the waters. They put it down to a production error.

I had to make a statement and I said how devastated I was that it had gone in and completely disassociated myself from comment. This meant that *Zoo* got the hump, because I was passing the buck back to them. They sacked me from the column. I thought, 'You fucking snakes!' All this time the journalist I dealt with was texting me saying he was sorry, but the whole thing was out of his hands and he couldn't do anything about it. I could see he was just trying to save his own skin.

When you ask yourself who's to blame for my sick joke ending up in print, consider how a magazine works. I gob on to the journo for ten minutes, on the understanding he will edit what I say to fit in with what the magazine's readers want to see. The journo writes the piece. Then it's edited by a sub-editor who checks it for legality and taste, as well as writing headlines and knocking any mistakes out, then the editor reads every word of the whole thing before it goes out. Editors have to look at stuff because the tradition is that the buck stops with them if anything dodgy gets in their mag. So there were at least three people there who could have said, 'Hang on, do we really want to say this?' Or said, like they said afterwards, that it was outrageous. And none of them did. They looked at those words in the cold light of day – not off the cuff like I'd said them – and thought, 'That's fine, we'd like our magazine associated with that sort of sentiment.' Like I said, I'll hold my hand up and say I'm thoroughly ashamed of my part in the whole thing. I don't mind taking the blame because it was a horrible thing to say, a joke gone wrong. But is it right, considering they must have had days to drop that out of the magazine, that they should make me take the rap for the whole thing? Why won't they own up to their part in it? Because it would require some bollocks, and that's something they seem to be lacking in.

It's difficult to overstate the effect this had on me. I've had bad press before, but never like that. The thing is, if I'd been caught bashing a bird up, then fair enough, but I've never raised my hand to a woman in my life. I haven't got it in me. This hard man, tough guy image backfired on me. For people who don't like me out there, and there are some people who hate my guts, this was something for them to jump all over.

I was getting death threats. There are moments when I'm lying in bed, my kids are asleep, my missus is asleep, and you don't know if someone's going to come through the front door with an axe. If I was a single man, I'd deal with it but I hated having that kind of pressure on my kids or my missus.

The only bright spot in the whole episode was that my fans came to the front for me. I got bags of support, on the Internet and people coming up to me in the street. I have a very loyal fan base, and I love every one of them for sticking up for me. There are a lot of people who are stuck up who look down on my fan base, who think they're all thick as shit, that they're all chavs. But they're not, they've got a lot about them, and they see who I am and understood that I would never support violence against women. You've got to remember that my daughters are going to have boyfriends; am I going to be advising them to cut their faces?

This is the dark side of fame, though, and we all know it comes with the territory. However, it's not pleasant to feel your life isn't in your hands at all, that's it's in the hands of the media, lots of whom have already got their knives out, waiting for a slip up.

Frankie Boyle had a go at me about it in his column. He took a pop at me over this and said people should boycott my films. I can take a joke but when he's trying to take the bread and butter out of my family's mouths, it's a different thing entirely.

Frankie's the last person to have a go at anyone about sick jokes. On the same page he lays into me, he has a go at JLS, who are remaking *The Sound of Music*. He says, 'I hope they go and redo it in Austria so they can reopen the concentration camps and stick them in it.' But then he's a university boy, isn't he, so I suppose he just says it's 'ironic' and everyone thinks it's OK.

But just in case anyone's still in any doubt, let me spell it out: any man who is violent to a woman is a coward. End of.

Going back to the film, Nick did start to bollock Tamer at certain points. This is why I respect Nick; he don't give a fuck. Tamer had stepped out of line on a few occasions and he was just telling him straight. I don't know what Tamer had done, perhaps he reacted to a note badly or he said something to Nick that upset him. Mind you, Nick's notes can be quite direct. He'll say, 'What are you doing it like that for, you cunt? Why are you pulling that stupid fucking face? Go again.' It's a mad way to make a movie. It don't happen, directors just don't talk like that. You get these poncey directors that float around you, saying, 'Darling, leave me alone, I'm thinking.' You don't get that with Nick. You're more likely to get nutted. Well, not literally, but not far off.

Still, despite Nick having the hump, the shoot went well. I brought Joanne out there, Dani, Nan, my mum. We had a nice little apartment in a villa about an hour and a half from Marbella. It was a real moment for me being on a film set as the lead role and having the ability to treat my family to a holiday. One of the real perks of my job. They really enjoyed themselves. There were moments where Dani'd sit on Nick's lap and shout 'Action!' and 'Cut!' My sister came with me too and worked as an extra. It's something I'm proud of, that I can get my family involved in this sort of thing.

I like to get Dani involved as much as I can. I have a very interesting job where you meet all sorts of people and travel all over the world and it's OK for me to bring my kids to work with me. She's always been around film sets, and so of course, she now wants to be an actress herself. She'll have to work at it though. I don't want to her be an actress just because of who her dad is. She's got to do what I did, which is really want it, be passionate about it, and go down the right avenues. Mind you, I might give her a little more help than what I had.

She helps me learn lines – as long as the language isn't too bad – and really puts a lot into the role. She's acted out everyone – Tamer, Ray Winstone, Sean Bean, so you can't say she's not versatile.

As the lead role, I was granted a few bonuses on the set. One was that I had to sit in on the audition for the girl part and help pick out the actress for the role. It comes down to chemistry, who you chime with best when you're sitting there reading the lines off the page. Some people you have it with, and others you don't, simple as that. So I sat in my throne and all these beautiful girls came past. We had decided that the bird in *The Business* had to be a real stunner because she goes out with Sam, who is my enemy, and I end up having a little bit of a fling with her. The idea of the film is that she's so beautiful and irresistible that I just can't help myself, even though the consequences might be that I'm going to end up with a pair of concrete boots. The idea of that attraction being worth the danger had to be completely believable.

The bit of dialogue we used for the audition never made the film. She says to me, 'You know everyone round here wants to fuck you, don't you?' And I go, 'No, I didn't know that,' and she says, 'Yes, all the girls want to know what it's like to have your cock in their mouth.'

It's a really dirty, seedy scene of her trying to seduce me. So I just sat back in my chair all day while they wheeled all these birds in, all in their short skirts and high heels talking dirty to me. I've had tougher jobs.

It was nice to be on the other side of the audition, on the director's table, because obviously I've done plenty from the other side. I learned a lot about how to approach it. If you come in nervous, and it's obvious you're nervous, then it takes something away from your performance. If you've got a bit of nerves and you manage to channel that into the audition, then it's great because it gives you an edge. If you're really nervous you make the room uncomfortable and everyone can really feel it. That's bad news because they have to be happy that you're worth ten grand a week, that you're better than anyone else out there. They won't do that if you make them feel edgy.

So the first girl in was Georgina Chapman, a really beautiful and engaging girl – I'd never seen a face like hers. But she kept getting a little twitch in her eye, which took a bit away from the performance. Maybe it was that filthy line she had to say. She was all right though. She did it. Not too bad but I wasn't convinced she was 100 per cent right for this role. She certainly looked the part, though, I'll give her that. Lots of other girls came and read for the part, but I think Nick had settled on Georgina from the moment she came in. He saw something in her.

She was going out with Harvey Weinstein, one of the most powerful men in Hollywood. He turned up on the set and believe me, his reputation as a tough guy wasn't far off.

I had to do a sex scene with Georgina. That's difficult enough at the best of times without the most powerful bloke in your game, who happens to be her partner, standing looking at the monitor at the side of your eye. It was probably my paranoia – that and the fact that I'm in a film about stealing a hard man's bird – but I was glad to finish the scene and get out of his sight. Nothing Harvey did made me think he was jealous, but with a guy like that it's worth letting him know that the scene is strictly business.

This film was very well received. I got some great reviews for it and it earned a few quid as well. I think it did about £1.5 million at the box office and pretty well on DVD. It's a cult movie. I still have people today run up to me and say it's their favourite film of all time.

I think Nick got the look of the film completely right; we managed to bring out the sexiness of the eighties, the energy of the era. Just as *The Football Factory* brought hooligan movies streaming in its wake, *The Business* started off a whole influx of movies about the eighties. I don't think any of them are as good. Nick's attention to detail is unbelievable, the way he shot it. It has that eighties glossiness to it and all the clothes are bang on to the last detail. I love all that old Fila stuff, the tandoori-chicken suntans, the works.

After making such a great film, and having one of the best experiences of my career, then the yin and the fucking yang of the universe dictated I should make a shit one – once more with my old mate Vinnie Jones.

16

PONY AND TRAP

After all the football hooligan stuff and *The Business*, I was itching to do something a bit different. So when I got offered a romantic comedy – a film called *The Other Half* – I thought I'd go for it. It would give me a chance to stretch my legs a bit, try out something new. It's the first time me and Tamer had been up for the same role. I auditioned and got the part, which was good luck for Tamer and bad for me.

I was told there was no money in it. We got £100 grand to make this movie, which sounds a lot but, believe me, would just about cover the blue paint budget on *Avatar*.

We went to Portugal during the European Championships and we were going to try to base a film about what happens during the competition. The idea of the film, which had something about it, was that I get married to an American girl who knows nothing about football. I know the European Championships are going on just after our wedding so I plan our honeymoon to go to Portugal. The idea is that I'll I slip off to watch the games of football and she won't notice. Hilarious.

She loves the idea of Portugal and she thinks it's the most romantic place. I have to play this whole thing of keeping her sweet and then making up some ridiculous excuse for watching game on my own, getting a bit pissed, coming back to her and getting into bed at night.

What they wanted to do with the film, which would've been brilliant, is to make it as if England get to the final. She finds out what's been going on and I take her to the final, we win and she realises what the whole honeymoon has been all about. The end scene is of me and the girl dancing around with all the England fans.

Unfortunately, Cristiano Ronaldo and Co hadn't read the script and we got knocked out in the quarter-finals to Portugal. Now, I'd only agreed to do the film because the producers had tickets for the games. But that's about all they fucking had. They had no permits to film anywhere so they had to do it on the sly. They would give me the ticket, film me walking in to the stadium and then I'd go off and watch the game, which was perfect, just perfect. I was on my own, which was a bit weird, but my whole reason doing the film was to watch the Euros for free, so I wasn't complaining.

As much as I wanted to do a romantic comedy, I knew that making a film on only £100,000 was going to be a nightmare. I was sharing a flat with the lead actress and producer, which was a bit weird. I had a blow-up bed in the spare room. Glamorous it wasn't.

The director was called Richard Nockles and respect to him because he wrote it and raised a bit of money to make his first feature but me and him didn't really see eye to eye. In my opinion, he didn't know how to handle me. Since working with Nick, I need someone with an iron fist to tell me what he wants and when he wants it. I respond better to that kind of direction.

Also, I was quite famous at this point, and a lot of England fans recognised me because of *The Football Factory*. I was allocated a security guard, who was just Richard's mate, and he was useless. So I fucked him off early doors and said 'Look, you're making me look a melt by walking around with me.' I mean, he was a skinny fucker, he couldn't hold his hands up to save his life.

Being recognised made the job a lot tougher, because there are scenes of me walking through the England crowd all excited. It's a difficult shoot because the film-makers are blagging it and haven't got permission to film. As soon as the Old Bill clock us, we've got to stop filming.

The crew would be on a long lens hiding in some house overlooking the ground while I'd be walking through the crowd. Some of the fans would clock me and they'd be saying, 'It's fucking Danny Dyer,' jumping all over me and getting their cameras out to have photos taken with me. It was a real fucking mess trying to work with all that around you. It started to get me down that I couldn't focus on what I had to do, which was to try to make a film. It would've been great if I could have just had a jolly up and got on the piss. Which, to be fair, I did anyway.

We cracked on with filming it, and it's the first time I'd started to make a film and thought, 'This is going to be really shit.' I'd always had confidence in films I made and really felt a buzz about them, like I was fighting for the cause, but this one just left me cold. I honestly contemplated walking off the job. The only thing that kept me there was the England games.

I went to the first game and I think we played Denmark

and we smashed them 3–0. People were bouncing up and down, hugging each other, singing – beautiful stuff. But because they were shooting far away from a block of flats the director would say to me, 'We need you to walk past the turnstile, come back and do it again.' But I just fucked him off. I honestly didn't give a shit at that point, I just did it once and then I fucked off into the ground and sat down to watch the game, which was a bit selfish of me.

Still, I was enjoying the football side of it, until the game against Portugal. When we got knocked out then, it put us in a bit of a position. The script – maybe a bit optimistically – had relied on England winning the thing.

I had a bad time at that Portugal game. I went to watch the game on my own, and then I had to come out the ground and meet the crew. I already had the raving hump because the Portuguese were above where the England fans were sitting and they were spitting on us and throwing things at us throughout the whole game. And, to rub it in, they beat us on penalties. So I came out on my own having had all this grief and I was about ready to burst.

Eventually I got away from the ground, didn't bother to meet up with the crew because I was so fucked off, got in a cab, and then the cab crashed. Not a bad crash but still one more crash than you want after you've watched your team lose on poxy penalties while you're being showered in gob. I was shocked, angry, and pissed off, because we just been knocked out and I'd lost all faith in the film and I couldn't wait to get home to my blow-up bed.

So the director had to come up with something else to tie

up the film. It works out that my American wife, played by the lovely Gillian Kearney, runs away because she clocks that I only went there because of the matches. I go looking for her so we had this whole montage of me walking the streets of Lisbon with my England top on, bawling my eyes out, running down alleyways, pondering, remembering all the shit things I'd done, while she goes off with this English couple and learns about football. They go to the beach with her and tell her they were there for the European Championships and how great football is and she slowly comes down to an under-standing. So she comes back to me and we have this big reunion.

The film-makers thought that when Portugal won the final – which of course was inevitable – they could shoot us dancing around with all these Portuguese fans, them celebrating the football, us celebrating our togetherness. But Portugal lost. Greece beat them, and fucked up the end of the film. We had this massive street party planned. It would have been perfect – Portugal win the championship for the first time ever, in Portugal, cue the fiesta. And who goes and wins it? Greece, who have about five hundred fans there who fucked off home as soon as it was over. It's the only film that when people come up to me and asked me to sign a DVD, I write on it 'pony film'.

Vinnie Jones had to bookend the film, open and close it. He plays my conscience in these dream sequences. When I feel down about what I'm doing, because I really do love this girl, I have my conscience nagging at me who takes the form of a football manager, played by Vinnie. Every time I go into the dream sequence, he's sitting there in the changing room saying, 'Come on, boy, you can do it! You can get out there. She'll be all right, don't worry. We're talking about England!'

Vinnie only came on set for a day. Why I really fell out with him and slagged him off in the press was because I was meant to do a scene with him. They shot him first, and then they turned around to film me, which meant they had to change all the lighting. When it comes to my part, there's a runner standing in front of me with the script. I asked where Vinnie was. The director said, 'Vinnie wanted to go and watch the golf.' And I was like, 'What? You've let him fuck off?'

Obviously Richard, who seemed petrified of him said, 'Yeah, we didn't think you'd mind.' I said, 'You didn't think I'd mind? That's the most disrespectful thing you can do as an actor, you do your shot first and then you fuck off.' I was fuming.

The runner stood in for him and the irony is, he was better than Vinnie. It really put me on the back foot, actually. I did a bit of press for the film and all that anyone was asking me was what it was like working with Vinnie Jones. In the end I'd had enough of it and I said, 'He's a shit actor, to be honest with you, he doesn't excite me.' So I dug him out.

Of course, Vinnie heard about it and I got a message back to me through Tamer that Vinnie was pretty fucking upset about what I'd said. Tamer and Vinnie were pretty close at the time. And Tamer, being very protective towards me said, 'You won't touch a hair on his head.' This, had I known it, became the seeds of a dispute between Tamer and Vinnie that would finish up with Tamer and Vinnie having a tear up. Anyway, Tamer said he wanted to come and talk to me about Vinnie's beef. I explained to Tamer what had happened and he said, 'Well, you're in the right then.'

Tamer told me Vinnie was gutted because his daughter was a fan of mine and he felt let down. I said I obviously didn't want to upset his daughter but I'd just called it how I saw it. I've never come across Vinnie since. He's got a problem with me, I've got a problem with him. That's the way it is.

Vinnie seemed to think he'd done me some sort of favour by being in the film. What fucking favours did he do me? At the time, putting him on the cover of a DVD would sell a few copies, but this time around, it didn't work out that way.

Tamer bashed up Vinnie Jones recently. It's done him the world of good actually, put his profile right up. The press all loved him for it, because some of them see Vinnie as a bully.

I left *The Other Half* a bit disheartened. I didn't get paid much, but I did get to see the England games. You could say it was smart film-making for the fact that they did it on no budget, guerrilla style, and we actually got a film out of it, despite having no permit or anything, no right to be there. You could say that.

On the back of *The Other Half* I was feeling a little bit down about things. It's a saying in the business that you're only as good as your last film, so at that point I was completely fucking useless.

Then a script landed on my mat that lifted me from the depths to the heights. From doing the lowest budget movie I'd ever done, sleeping on a blow-up bed in a back room, I was about to make a film where money was no object and I'd feel like a proper movie star for the first time in my life.

17

ME AND MY MOUTH, PART 628

As soon as I read the script for the film *Severance* I thought it was brilliant. The director was Christopher Smith, who's a very good friend of mine now. He had made a movie called *Creep*, which is very dark. Chris is really into his horror movies, but he's not twisted, he's a lovely guy.

I came in to the audition and did my thing, but the producers – the people who finance the film – were unsure of me because I'd done *The Football Factory* and now – even in 2005, a year after that film came out – everyone thought I just played thugs. They were saying, 'Danny's not funny, and this is a comedy role.'

But Chris straightened them out and told them to watch *Human Traffic*, where he thought I pulled off the comedy very well. Apparently, the producers wanted people like Ralph Little from *The Royle Family* to be in it, more established comedy actors.

This was a chance for me to do something away from Nick, to stop people saying, 'He's a one trick pony. He wouldn't have a career if it wasn't for Nick Love.' This is the funny thing about my career. If you've read this far, you'll see I've done a huge variety of stuff – film, theatre, TV, even video games – most of it very successful. And yet when people think of me they just think I play hard men. In fact I've hardly ever played a hard man – yeah, a couple of films I've been a hooligan or a gangster, but even then they haven't been straightforward thugs. So *Severance* was a chance to remind people that I had a few more strings to my bow.

More than that, this was a chance for me to make a big budget movie, with £7 million riding on it. Also, I'm a bit of kid. Having the chance to be an action hero with a bit of comedy thrown into the mix wasn't something I was going to pass up. What could be better than running around, pretending to shoot people, and having a laugh at the same time?

I do think I've got a bit to give on the comedy side of things. I auditioned a couple of times for the part and I landed it, but I could tell I was on trial. They were saying, 'OK, we'll give Danny the part, but if he starts playing up or if he's not funny, then we'll just bring somebody else in.' No question, on this one I had to be right on it from the start. No drink, no drugs, no nothing that distracted me from the job. I'd grown up a bit and realised acting and living it up don't mix and I was determined to be completely on the ball throughout this shoot.

I had a big trailer and for the first time on a film set I was really well looked after. I felt like a film star. I hadn't really felt like that before. Like I said, people imagine actors are minted, pampered all the time, but that definitely wasn't the case with me. I was still at the blow-up bed stage. So this was the first really decent wedge I'd earned.

I felt I could really bring something to the film. I had myself a bit of a following after my last two films, *The Football Factory* and *The Business*, had done really well and earned a fair whack of cash. I was earning a reputation, and not just as a pillhead. So that's why they put me in it.

It was a strange process this film, because we filmed half of it in Hungary and half of it in the Isle of Man. It's all set in the woods. All of the cast were staying in a big pink castle in the middle of nowhere in Hungary. The thing that I loved about Chris, the director, is that he doesn't have an aggressive bone in his body, which is the complete opposite to Nick. On set he's like a kid in a sweet shop, wearing this shit-eating grin, with all these big toys to play around with. He couldn't believe he was directing it, and that enthusiasm fed the cast. He was so energetic and so good with the actors. All directors are different in what they choose to concentrate on. For instance, some are forever fiddling over the angle of a shot, while others are willing to leave that to the director of photography, if they have one. Some are about the actor, some can hardly speak to them, others just want you to stand in the right place and leave the rest of it up to you. Chris is an actor's director. That's where he focuses his energies. He managed to get a great performance out of me by winding me up a little bit, making me do lines in completely different ways, forcing me to really think about how I was delivering the action, and always keeping me on my toes.

I'm a massive fan of *Blackadder* and Tim McInnerny – who plays Percy in the series – being in it was a big thing for me. He's a comedy genius in my eyes and we had more in common than I thought. He enjoys a night out too, which was a bit of a surprise. I got on well with Claudie Blakley too – she's a very good actress.

Andy Nyman – who plays Gordon in the film, the bloke who loses his leg – is part of the Magic Circle. So in the boring moments between shots he would do some amazing tricks. He's a top-quality magician and he writes a lot for Derren Brown. Again, a highly intelligent bloke, quite sexy in his own little way.

Chris the director was a bit bored by the tricks, saying, 'Whatever, I don't believe in magic.' So Andy decides he wants to change his mind. We went out for a meal for Chris's birthday in this Hungarian restaurant and about halfway through the meal Andy pulled out a balloon, which he blew up. He gave Chris a pin and said, 'Pop that balloon.' Chris said he couldn't be bothered, but we all made him do it. When he did pop it, his eyes nearly shot out of his head. The balloon disappeared and in its place Andy had a bottle of champagne in his hand. It had come from nowhere. He opened the champagne and he started pouring it into glasses and we were all gobsmacked, sitting around with our jaws on the floor. I was on his case every day saying, 'Please tell me, please, I'll do anything, I'll suck you off, just tell me how you do that trick.' But he would never do that, obviously. He's a hilarious man and a great actor.

It was a chance to work with Toby Stephens as well. People were bit worried that me and him weren't going to see eye to eye, with him coming from an acting dynasty and me coming from a council estate. But we hit it off. Must have been the mutual respect we had for each other as actors, because I do think he's very good.

I was all set to expect the worst, and I thought to myself, 'If he starts getting tricky I'll tell him straight early doors.' But he didn't. What we had in common was I'd auditioned his missus for *The Business*. She didn't get the part and he wanted to know why. I told him I was rooting for her, and that if it had been up to me we'd have given her the job, which was the God's honest truth.

Severance was a fucking scream. Any moment I wasn't being funny with some brilliant dialogue they'd written for me, I was fighting and saving people. I enjoyed every second of that. It was a tough shoot in some ways, being away for so long, stuck out in the woods in the Isle of Man or Hungary. I didn't bring my missus out on that one, so I was away from her and Dani for eight weeks, which hurt a bit.

We flew straight from Hungary to the Isle of Man, which is an amazing place. In forty minutes you can drive from one end to the other and there are parts of it that are so medieval and been left completely untouched by the modern world. There are waterfalls you can drink straight out of. It's like something straight out of *Lord of the Rings*.

By contrast you've got the capital, Douglas, which is basically just a strip of kebab shops. I didn't warm to the people and I didn't feel they really warmed to us. This is their rock, and they're very proud and passionate about it. They don't exactly welcome you with open arms. They have their own parliament, their own money and their own flag, which is three feet with Wellington boots on. Who came up with that I'll never know. You can still be birched to this day and, doubtless if a few of the islanders got hold of me, I'd be feeling the lash across my back.

I found it fucking depressing but I suppose I should have kept that to myself. I did an interview, and I said that the Isle of Man is a shithole and that all the islanders were all fucking each other, and I found it disgusting. I just made a little comment in a three-page interview, but obviously the Isle of Man picked up on that. I was on the front page of the local newspaper, which said something like 'foulmouthed actor attacks our island'.

So again, and not for the last time, I had to retract my statement, because my agent said to me, 'Look, Dan, they do a lot of filming on the Isle of Man, it's not in your interests to upset them.' So I apologise to the good people of the Isle of Man, if they ever read the book. I don't mean anything bad by what I said. I just found the place pretty freaky and very strange. Probably says as much about me as it does about the island.

My mouth has got me into trouble on more occasions than I care to recall, so much so that I've had to hire a PR person to vet what I say in public. The thing is, she's not with me 24/7 and when I go out I have a habit of speaking my mind. People assume I slag people off for publicity but if I'd kept my fat fucking gob shut I might have a few more great roles behind me.

Take the musical *Oliver!* Now, I really would love to be on the West End stage and in this musical in particular. I auditioned for the part of Bill Sykes. It was a big thing for me because I had one song I had to sing. I've never really sung and I'm not confident doing it. Maybe I've got a voice in there somewhere but I've never practised at it, so going from singing in the shower to the Theatre Royal, Drury Lane is a big leap. I love the story of Oliver Twist. It's something I missed out on as a younger actor because I think I was born to play the Artful Dodger, and it didn't happen for me.

Unluckily for me, I started watching the TV show that was a live audition to select the girl to play Nancy in the show – it was called *I'd Do Anything* and was shown on Saturday nights during 2008 leading up to the show's opening in 2009, and was hosted by Graham Norton.

It's one of those things I watched more to shout at than anything. I love watching that kind of thing in a sort of 'chamber of horrors' way, because it smacks of desperation. Who do they have on the judging panel? For a start there's John Barrowman, some two-bob cabaret singer who just does covers of other people's music, and yet he's judging if people have got what it takes to be to be a West End star. I've never got my head around that to be honest with you.

I did one show with him, *Paul O'Grady*, I think. He does like the sound of his own voice. The only reason they were doing *I'd Do Anything* was to generate publicity for the musical, which they didn't need, because it's massive, it's *Oliver!* And why did they whittle it down to these ten girls who no one's ever heard of, who are straight out of drama school? Why didn't they audition some big stars? All of this is going through my nut while I'm watching the show.

Anyway, I got a call about it, do I want to audition for the part of Bill Sykes? I thought, 'Fuck yeah.' I was born to play that role. I loved what Oliver Reed had done with it in the film. Have you noticed, he's the only one who didn't sing?

I was hoping for that myself, hoping that they would think me a good enough actor that I wouldn't need to sing. No such luck. Bill Sykes has a song all to himself. Well, I'm nothing if not game so I thought I'd give it a go. It was a little number about him ripping people's heads off, if I recall correctly.

It took me a while to break down the barriers to be confident enough to do it. I practised on my own, downloaded it off the Internet and had it on my iPod. I kept going over and over it in my head. It was the first time in a long time that I'd really been out of my comfort zone.

I had to go for my first meeting, to show I could sing. There was me, the audition panel and a guy with a piano. I was bricking myself to be honest, but the audition went well and I was pleased with my performance.

Now, I hadn't been offered it, but I think I was close to getting the part. I did the audition singing off the page, then I had to go back and meet Cameron Mackintosh the director, do a spot of acting and sing without the paper in front of me.

I embraced it. You either do it or you don't, there's no mumbling into your chest instead of singing the notes, so I put my embarrassment aside and gave it the full bollocks. Cameron seemed to like me and by the end I could tell it had gone well.

The feedback they gave me was excellent and I knew it was down to me and one other geezer. Then I went to a party. That could be the story of my life, right there. 'It was all going so well. Then I went to a party.' They'll put that on my fucking gravestone.

It was for the launch of a mobile phone which I took my

missus to because she really wanted the phone. Sometimes the fame thing comes in handy when you get invited to things like that. Of course, the party is full of melts and these wannabe famous people, but I'm happy to sell out a little bit and take a cheeky freebie every once in a while. So I went there and got a little bit pissed, and started talking to this girl. What I didn't know is that it was a journalist with a Dictaphone in her top pocket. So, she said to me: 'What have you been up to, Danny?' and I told her I was up for *Oliver!* as Bill Sykes. She said, 'Wow, I think that's fantastic.' I should have shut up right fucking there. Unfortunately I went on to say 'I fucking hate all these Nancies in *I'd Do Anything*. What is that all that about? Why don't they audition people in a proper audition instead of doing this stupid show with Graham Norton where they're all crying every week?' The next day, there was a headline in the London paper that said 'New Bill Sykes attacks Nancies'.

My agent rang me up fuming and explained to me that I'd just blown it. I put the phone down and just took my head in my hands. I thought, 'You prick, you fucking idiot.'

I don't know where to begin to describe what a twat I'd been. For a start, if I'd have done it, I would've been working with whoever got the part for six months. It's not a very good way to kick off the show, is it?

Also, I've already said I loved *Blackadder*. Here I would've worked with Rowan Atkinson because he was the one playing Fagin. My agent gave them a call but was told straight off: 'It's not going to work out.' Why couldn't I have kept my mouth shut? I'd have been on the West End stage playing Bill

Sykes, and I know I would have fucking nailed it. It went to an actor called Burn Gorman.

Burn's not a bad actor, but not a household name. But then again, he doesn't open his mouth when he shouldn't and he's not known as some gobby cockney. I wished him all the best with it but I was quietly fucking gutted. More gutted for Dani, really, because she wanted to come and watch me in it. It would have been the first thing she could have come to watch, and I fucked it.

I was hoping that, because the show's been running now for a year and a half, they would've made the call and come back and said, 'All right then, all is forgiven.' But I never got the call. And since then, Omid Djalili has played Fagin and I would've loved to have worked with him because he's a good friend.

My missus actually took Dani and her friends to see it, which made me a bit jealous. It would have been about twelve grand a week for six months, and I would've been part of a massive thing.

It would have opened a lot of doors too, but you can't sit and stew on things like that, because that's the way of the world, that's the way life is. I learned the hard way. Journalists are there to get a good story, end of. Get used to it. Forget it and, to quote a song from the show, that's your fucking funeral.

It was about this time that I fucked up with *EastEnders* too. What happened was that I sat down to have a meeting with the head of drama at the BBC as they weren't putting any work my way. Believe it or not, I was quite interested in doing a bit of period drama – something like *Lark Rise to Candleford*, which I thought was great. I'd never been considered for it and I wanted to know why. They said 'Dan, your name does come up a lot, but we always think you won't want to do it. You make movies.' I said I loved TV and was up for anything they could throw at me. So they asked how I felt about *EastEnders*.

They said they were thinking about maybe putting me in for a couple weeks, not as a regular, just coming in to shake up a few characters. They said they'd make it a really cool part and I'd have a big say in it. I was really flattered and we left it that they'd come up with something and put an idea to me. The next day, the *Sun* ran a story that I was joining the show. That frightened the life out of me. It certainly wasn't me that leaked it to the press.

My defences, which were honed by then, kicked in. I thought 'I'm not even signed up to it and I'm getting this bollocks already.' And then the press went nuts and I was forever answering questions in interviews. 'Are you doing *EastEnders*? What about *EastEnders*?' At first I was quite diplomatic about it and I was saying, 'It might happen, you never know,' and then I started to get more and more pissed off at the constant stream of questions. To this one reporter, I said, 'I'll do it when I'm fat, bald and fifty.' It was more to get the interviewer to shut up about it than anything else, but it upset the BBC. My agent was getting phone calls from the head of drama at the BBC saying how disappointed he was with me and how hard they worked on that show. So, to make it right, I had to made a statement on *This Morning* saying how flattered I was and how there were some great actors in *EastEnders*, what a tough job they do there and how I really respect it. All that was true but I wouldn't have had to be sitting there on the sofa like a stuffed monkey if I'd just kept my mouth shut.

What terrifies me most about *EastEnders* is the way you're opened up to the press. Your entire life becomes public property. I know that sounds weird, as I'm writing a book about my own life, but the level of intrusion the guys on that show get is incredible. I wouldn't want to write it off completely; later on, who knows? I do respect the professionalism of the cast and crew, but I just don't think it's for me right now.

Anyway, these fucking gaffes aside, I was on a high when I finished *Severance*. I relished every minute of working on it and I loved working with Chris. I knew it was going to be the start of a great working relationship and we were going to go on and do different stuff together.

The film was a big success. It took a couple of mill at the box office, but it was number one in the DVD charts for a long time, and that's where your money is.

I just felt positive about myself at that point, because I was on a bit of a run, and I was now a leading man. I had to live up to that. I'd elbowed the drugs, by and large, was back with the family and was starting to get offered some parts on a decent wedge. But I was about to go back and work for five hundred quid a week. Why? Because I got a call from a director who was putting on Harold Pinter's *The Homecoming*. Pinter had told him he wanted me in it and the job was mine if I wanted it. It was a chance to see Harold again, so I couldn't refuse. It might have been better if I had – not because I didn't enjoy the role, I loved it – because my growing fame had an unforeseen influence on the kind of people who turned up to watch the play. I think it was the first time the West Ham away crew had turned up in force at the Almeida.

18

THE DEATH OF A LEGEND

I hadn't seen Harold in six years. I saw bits and bobs of him on the telly, and he'd become quite political around that time, campaigning against the invasion of Iraq. He'd also pocketed the Nobel Prize for literature – a million quid in your hand and a place alongside the greats of the writing world. So I was bowled over when he asked for me personally to play a character called Joey in his play. He's a boxer, inarticulate, brooding. It's a fucking great play, really weird, but you wouldn't expect anything else from Harold. You know where you are a little bit more than in *No Man's Land*, but not much more.

The Homecoming was directed by Michael Attenborough, Richard Attenborough's son. I went to meet him – he was a lovely man who sat me down and said he was aware of my work and that I came personally recommended by Harold Pinter. The job was mine, I didn't have to audition or anything like that.

I read the script and I have to admit I was disappointed with the size of the part – every actor always wants to be the main attraction – but I could tell it was quality.

I had to do it. How could I not? If a bloke like Pinter thinks you're good then that's more than worth £10,000 a week to me. Harold came in during rehearsals and it was nice to catch up with him again, although he did look a bit frail. We had a nice cuddle and a bond up.

His voice had changed, got croakier because of the throat cancer, but he was still himself – an impressive, intellectual giant of a man. The strangest thing, though, was what happened when the play opened. My career had gone up a notch since the last time I'd been in a Pinter play and now I had a big fan base who wanted to come see me in the flesh. That was a big part of why we sold out the play.

My audience doesn't understand Pinter, has never heard of him. Still, we were getting minibuses full of the JD Sports crew coming to watch me in this play, Krugerrand rings on, scars down their faces, a lot of *The Football Factory* fans. It was my mob coming to watch me and bringing their birds – White Van Man out in force.

At first I was really chuffed that my fans were a big part in selling this play out. But it started to get a bit tricky because my mob have never been in a theatre before and don't really know how you're supposed to behave, not that they'd give a fuck if they did.

There were people shouting out, 'Where's Danny?' when I walked off the stage. I had people like Kenneth Cranham virtually bursting a blood vessel on me backstage and saying, 'I'm not fucking going back out there with that mob.' I'd come on, and the girls would wolf whistle. It's not a fucking pantomime, it's a Pinter play.

I was apologetic. It wasn't my fault but there was nothing I could do about it. On the other hand, you can't have it both ways. They want to fill the theatre with paying customers, so they can't exactly complain about who those customers are. I totally understand where Ken was coming from though, and Nigel Lindsay, another great actor who was fucked off about as far as it's possible to be fucked off.

It was a bit embarrassing. I was getting all the attention, and I only had a small part in the play. I'd come out of the stage door, and there'd be a mob of people waiting for me who'd go nuts when they saw me. The other actors would walk out and they'd completely blank them.

Some would go, 'What the fuck was all that about then, that was a load of bollocks, wasn't it?' I'd say, 'Well, it's a particular sort of play, mate, ain't it?' It was a double-edged sword, because I was proud of them for coming to see me, but at the same time they were making my job very tricky.

I felt extremely guilty about the wolf whistling, but that apart it was an easy play from my side. I could have done it standing on my head. I'm not undermining it – it was what it was, a small part.

I found myself able to put a lot in to it, though, largely because the birth of my new baby – my lovely little Sunnie – had sparked a few rows indoors.

I have given some of the best performances in my life onstage when I've just had a row with Joanne. She'd throw me out of the house and threaten to chuck all my clothes out there on the pavement. Wasn't a regular occurrence but it happened a few times. We would have a screaming row, the kind that really gets your blood up, and not soon after I would walk out onstage in front of a thousand people. It made me channel all that emotional upset into the performance. During *Certain*

Young Men Joanne and me weren't getting on that well but it did seem to drive my performance to a new level.

I used to think she was selfish bending my ear just before I was about to go on, but if she's got the hump, she's got the hump – you can't pick and choose when you get pissed off with people. I think a lot of people would crumble in that situation, put the phone down after a row, look up at the clock and think, 'I have to be onstage in ten minutes.' But it brings out something in me. It's only when I come off that I end up sobbing my heart out. It's horrible. I'd go home and I'd be locked out of the house so I'd have to go to my nan's.

The baby brought stress because we were living right up each other's arses in Joanne's little house – two bedrooms, one teenager, a 50" telly in a 51" front room. We could argue about anything. We did have rows about my drug taking, which she disapproves of, even though I hardly do it compared to the madness I used to get up to before. We also row about the fact that very often when I do go out, I don't come back till the next day. She's completely right, of course. I haven't got a leg to stand on.

Take the well-publicised Lily Allen thing. I've always been friends with Lily Allen. She's been a good pal of mine since she was a kid through her dad Keith. So I've known her since she was twelve, she was like a kid sister to me. And then she cracked on and had her own show and she asked me on it. I happened to go to the one that was her very last show, so we had a party after it and ended up in a casino in Knightsbridge, staying out all night.

I went home and Joanne threw me out. She was right to.

I've got children and I didn't come in until the next day. It's irresponsible. It means I'm expecting her to deal with everything while I'm out having a laugh, and then I roll back home out of my fucking nut. It's not a good look is it?

I don't know who grassed me up to the newspapers, but there were paps waiting outside my house when I got back. I went back to my mother's, which was just round the corner.

I also had a night at the Olivier awards – the British theatre's Oscars. They asked me to present a gong and I felt very privileged. I was up about third in the awards. You come down the aisle and you have theme music, mostly classical or something like that. When I got up to present my award they played the theme from *Steptoe*. I couldn't believe it. You've got to remember this is a very snotty-nosed event. I walked up to the mike and I said, 'Are you mob taking the piss?' Everyone just cracked up laughing because it's such a stuffy event and I broke the ice. I said, 'It's a privilege to be here, I don't usually get invited to things like this. I can't think why.' And again, they laughed. I presented the award to this guy and fucked off the stage.

John Simm was there and I hadn't seen him in a couple of years. It was an excuse for me to cane it. I got bang on it, regardless of the fact John wasn't having any of it, then I went straight to the theatre and slept there for a couple of hours. It was a Friday or Tuesday, because I remember I had a matinee the next day. I did something which I'd swore I would never do again, and that is walk onstage fucked.

I was confident because of being able to wing it because of the small role but I was having heart palpitations again, thinking, 'Why have you done this to yourself?' I didn't fuck up but because of the coke my nose was dripping through the whole show. I'm in character so I can't wipe my nose. So I just had to let the snot drip out. It wasn't very pleasant.

It was a weird feeling, I felt very vulnerable onstage again. I was angry at myself. I don't think anyone noticed, but I knew what I'd done and that was the main thing.

I finished the play and moved on to some more film work but at around Christmas that year I walked into a petrol garage, read something on the newspaper stand and nearly fell over.

I think it was on the front of the *Star* or the *Mirror*. It just said 'Pinter dead.' As simple as that. With a picture of him next to the headline. That shows you how big he was. How many playwrights have the *Mirror* even heard of, let alone put on the front page?

I didn't think it'd affect me as much as it did. I'm not saying we were best pals or anything like that, but I loved the man. I always will love him. He meant more to me than I probably ever told him. He was a great writer, a great bloke, and an all round top-notch human being.

After he died I had a couple of days where I was just silent. I was devastated, gutted. I spoke to Keith Allen about it and he was just the same. As much as we got bollocked by him and had our moments with him, we couldn't have respected him more. He'll be sorely missed, I'll tell you that. That's one great British man we lost there, and he's in a better place now, no doubt about that.

19

OUTLAW

I have not, believe it or not, courted controversy during my career. By this stage of the book that may leave you thinking, 'Fucking hell, Dan, good job, if you had you'd have probably started World War Three', considering some of the shit storms I've managed to conjure up while aiming for a quiet life.

The next film, though, was to twist the bollocks of the whole middle-class liberal establishment – *Outlaw* with Nick Love.

The film had a bit of an edge to it right from the start, because Nick decided to go in another direction to the one he'd pursued so far. He'd always used the same actors and so naturally that gang of actors had come to expect a role in the next movie.

But for *Outlaw* Nick dropped Tamer, Roland, Geoff Bell and Frank Harper. There was a bit of ill-feeling going about towards Nick, I think. Tamer was quite disappointed and he couldn't understand why he wasn't in the film, particularly after the success of *The Business*. But Nick wanted to express himself in a different way. He wanted to use some big, established names and he managed to get Bob Hoskins and Sean Bean.

It's not good for the ego of people to hear, 'You're not big enough, we're going to go a different way now.' It hurt people, and I could understand that because I've had it myself in my career.

I was torn. These people are my mates, remember, and I really value them. On the other hand, it's a part in a film with one of my favourite directors, so I'm more than pleased to have that. Originally Nick said to me that he wanted something different from me. I was to play a smaller role, the nail bomber character, this nutty racist. I was well up for that because it would be a proper test of my acting.

I was starting to get into the idea of that role when Nick came back and said, 'Actually Dan, I'm going to have to put you in the bigger role, Dekker, the everyman character, and I'm going to give the nutty racist role to another actor called Sean Harris.' I was gutted by this because I always want to test myself and I've played the everyman character quite often.

Sean, who got the role, is a weird little geezer but, fuck me, what an actor! He's a method actor and he really immerses himself in the role. He was playing a racist and so he acted like a racist 24/7. There's a couple of black actors in the film and he wouldn't sit next to them at lunch. He'd come up to me and say, 'What are you talking to that black cunt for?' I was his mate in the film, so I was the only one he would talk to on the set.

He walked around in his costume constantly and he wanted to sleep on the set. I was thinking, 'You better be good, you better be very good if you're acting like this.' Luckily, he was. Like I said before, I don't get the method thing. I need to switch off. I can't live and breathe it, otherwise I start going a bit odd in the head. For another part, Sean Harris played the moors murderer and general nonce scum Ian Brady. Imagine being round him then.

He was a revelation to us all in a way. I've never worked with anyone that intense before. Luckily Lenny James, the black actor, who is a fucking amazing talent, took it all in his stride.

Sean Bean was in the film. He's an interesting bloke. To be honest, I didn't really rate him as an actor before. I never really got into *Sharpe* but my opinion of him changed radically when I worked with him. Bob Hoskins was on it too. He's one of my heroes and had the lead role in *The Long Good Friday*, one of my favourite films. I didn't really have any scenes with Bob, which was a bit of a let down.

There was a bit of a political message behind this film. Nick was trying to make a statement, to say something about the world we're living in. The film deals with what happens when you run out of options. For instance, what happens if you've got a group of kids sitting outside your house, taking the piss, keeping your baby up? Do you sit behind your curtain and suffer? No point in ringing the Old Bill because they'll do nothing. Or do you become a vigilante and start righting a few wrongs?

In the film Sean Bean has been fighting in the war and he's come back to a country that is more fucked than Afghanistan. I like the idea of him getting a ragtag army together to sort stuff out, which is what happens.

We started shooting and we all thought we had something

special. I suddenly realised how great Sean Bean was as an actor, and why he is this big time Hollywood star. He takes his work very seriously. He's an old-school Northerner as well. I like that about him, he has no airs and graces.

Bob Hoskins came in, and it was a bit disappointing, because we had less in common than I'd hoped. I tried to make conversation with him, because the World Cup was going on at the time, and I asked him if he was watching the England match. He said he'd never liked football. I was gutted about that.

I had another surprise coming from him. He came in on the first day to shoot a scene where he has to address us all. He did it and he was a bit off. He was stumbling over his lines. I was devastated. Nick being Nick took him outside the room. He never told me what he said to him. He obviously gave him a few notes and Bob came back in and sat down and fucking smashed it. I was very relieved because I don't think I could live with thinking Bob wasn't the actor I thought he was. He just took a bit of time to warm up. You have an expectation of someone like that, and it's sometimes unrealistic. Everyone has their off days and their on days, I guess. I'm sure I'm at the point in my career now where people who work with me have an expectation of me.

I'm not putting myself in the same bracket as Bob, but if people know who you are and they know your work, they expect a certain level from you. And if you don't hit the mark they're going to be a bit disappointed. Nick had the bollocks to take Bob out and have a word with him, which I think Bob respected him for. It was a great shoot, took place all round London, and it was fantastic being on the poster with Bob and Sean. That's my favourite poster of all time.

The premiere of the film was a bit tricky because Tamer came along and I could tell he still couldn't understand why he hadn't been in it. Him and Nick were both gentlemen about it but I could tell it was a bit of a weird situation and I was bang in the middle of it. I felt loyalty to both of them.

This is the problem, really, when you start putting your mates in films. They expect a part every time. And when they don't get one they have to be gracious, which can be difficult. Eventually it happened to me. Nick left me out of his last one – *The Firm*.

The whole situation around the casting of that was a bit weird because I was set to do something else. Nick was going to do *The Sweeney* first, with me and Ray Winstone. It was Americans who wanted to make the film – the money was coming from Fox.

They didn't know the show and they wanted a bigger star than me. I was more gutted about the fact that I wasn't going to do *The Sweeney* than not end up in *The Firm*. There was never any talk about me being in *The Firm*, to be honest.

To be fair, if Nick'd asked me to be in it I would have said no, because it was another film about hooligans and if I go to work with Nick again, I'd want to do something different.

He'd already put it to me about rereleasing *The Football Factory* and doing some more fight scenes to add to the extras on the DVD, but I put a complete block on it. Why should we go over old ground? I think Nick's a talented man and I thought we should be moving forward to do something a bit left field.

Outlaw came out and did OK, not as well as we hoped. I don't know why, really. I think maybe we held back a bit with the political side of things, so the film didn't make enough noise. It focused on us hunting down one man, rather than running around bashing up nonces and people who've got off lightly for crimes they committed. Nick cut all that sort of stuff out, which was a shame.

The press hated it, called it 'revenge porn' and said it showed an unrealistically violent Britain. I don't know what country they're living in. Perhaps they don't read their own papers. I wouldn't blame 'em.

Sean Bean and Bob Hoskins are big stars, no mistake. But in my next film I was about to work with someone who was a worldwide icon at the height of her fame.

20

HEROES

When I got the script for my next film, *Straightheads*, I liked it immediately but I was curious to know who was going to be the leading woman. When I found out I was completely gobsmacked. It was all my dreams come true, my ideal leading lady.

This is a film driven by a woman. She's the dominant one and controls the male lead. I loved that because I hadn't had the opportunity to play the subservient role before. I'd just been in *Outlaw* and *Severance* and both of them were pretty much Jack-the-Lad type characters. For once, I was going to play a laid back, sweet character.

The idea of the film isn't sweet, though, it's frightening. It's a love story that goes wrong. I'm doing a bit of work for her in her house as a handyman. She likes the look of me and takes me to a posh party and we fuck on the first night.

We're both thinking this could be the start of a blossoming relationship. On the way back from the party we hit a deer and we stop to drag it back off the road. A car pulls up with three geezers in it who bash me up and gang rape her. And so we're pulled together through this tragedy. She doesn't want to go to the police about the rape and I get bashed so badly that I lose my eye. It's a revenge story. It's about us getting a revenge on these men who have treated us so badly. In America it was called *Closure*.

I loved the script, but I couldn't think who was going to play the woman. I was really intrigued. When they told me it was Gillian Anderson, I couldn't believe it. I love this bird. I'm quite a sci-fi nut, and was a massive fan of *The X Files*, which she was brilliant in. Not to mention the fact that she is sexy as fuck. I remember buying *FHM* when she was voted the world's sexiest woman.

I knew Gillian was going to be there at the audition so it was going to add a real edge to proceedings. I thought, 'Do you know what? I've got to come in this room and I've got to really control it. Not characterwise, so much, but as a person.'

I guess that most men would be a bit overwhelmed by meeting her. I'm sure she's had a few drop to the floor and go, 'Oh Gillian,' but I thought I had to go in there with a bit of bollocks. So I made sure I looked the part. I had a bit of stubble going on and I wore something a bit sexy, the old Fila gear, splash of aftershave, you know the score.

I walked in the room and I controlled it, let my confidence show, looked everyone in the eye when I shook their hands, made sure I came over as bright and breezy, a bit cocky even. The scene I was reading for was an odd one, because she is comforting me. What happens to my character is that once I lose my eye, I can't get it up. I have these severe insecurities going on because I don't feel like a man as I didn't protect her. She's just been raped, so she's not up to the sex thing.

In the scene, I try to get myself hard by grabbing her tits really violently. It's a pretty dark moment because she's just been raped and the only thing that gets my character going is me being quite violent with her. The whole film is pretty dark, to be honest.

I needed to do something to stand out, and I had a plan. I'm sitting in the chair and Gillian's stroking my hair, telling me it's going to be OK, and I start stroking her hand. We slowly build up and then I just went for it. I grabbed her tit. Luckily, she started laughing and went 'Whoa, whoa, whoa.'

I think she liked the bravery of it. I said, 'Look, you could have picked any scene but you picked that one. It says I grab her tit, so I grabbed her tit.' The director said he understood but that I was the only one that had gone for it. 'The others had asked first,' he said. He looked a bit stunned and I think he was worried about Gillian. He needn't have been because I could tell she'd found it funny and also that she could sense a chemistry between us.

I walked out of the room and I could tell I'd got it. I thought this was the start of something massive for me and that it would really open me up to America. I was looking forward to going toe-to-toe with a serious actress. I've worked with a lot of good actors, and I've worked with a lot of shit actors and all, but to go and have it with a well-established multi-millionaire Hollywood A-lister, that was a big deal for me. She wasn't aware of my work but she then went away and watched a few of my movies and she really loved *The Business*. So we had a mutual respect. Also, it was a dark, moody film, so we really needed to bond up on that film to get each other through some of the darker scenes. We got on. She's a great bird and a good laugh.

I needed someone to cheer me up because I went to some strange places on this movie. It was the first time I had to deal with sitting in the make-up chair for three hours and having a prosthetic over my eye. Because I go blind in one eye, they put this big white contact lens in. Because it was so hard to get in and out I would leave it in all day. I started to get really moody because when you lose an eye you can't work out distances, and you begin to feel disoriented. You start to feel sorry for yourself. At least I did. So I was quite unapproachable on that job and I was a bit of a ratty fucker. But I needed to be, I suppose. In a way, as much as I dug out Sean for method acting, I went a tiny bit method on that one. I thought, 'It's OK, I'm playing this character. It's fine, I can get away with this sort of behaviour.' At the end of the day, when they took the lens out of my eye, it was as good as an orgasm. I've never been so fucking relieved.

When the film came out, it died a death. For me, it all felt a bit too familiar. It was a re-run of *The Great Ecstasy of Robert Carmichael*'s problem – leaving the audience with a bad taste in their mouths.

The last scene of *Straightheads* features a guy getting raped up the arse with a gun. That's the image you're left with as you leave the cinema. I've realised that the last thing you leave an audience with is the most important, because that's what they remember. In this case it was a man with a rifle up his Khyber. Not one for a general audience.

I was towards the end of the shoot when a chance to work with Ray Winstone came up. Ray has always been one of my idols. He was sort of one of the reasons I started acting. I'd been in the game for a long time and I'd met my fair share of stars and a few idols too, but I'd never met Ray. I'd met Kathy Burke and other people associated with him. I'd even met his daughters, but I'd never even been in the same room as the man himself.

An audition came up for something called *All In The Game*, where I would be playing Ray Winstone's son. This was all my dreams come true. I couldn't believe I had to audition for it, that it hadn't been offered to me exclusively. But my agent said the fact that I did *The Football Factory* counted against me. This was much gentler. It's an interesting one that. You do a film like *The Football Factory*, really successful and with a big following, and it can come back and bite you in the arse. As much as that film has been massive for my career, it's sometimes hindered it too.

The producers were wary about the hooligan thing. I was begging my agent to get me in the room with Ray. I read the script and I loved it. Not only was I going to be playing with Ray, I was going to be his son. I couldn't have hoped for better.

I was telling Gillian about this, pouring my heart out. She was a massive fan of Ray's as well. She couldn't understand why I wasn't being offered it and was telling me I'd be perfect for the role.

I went to the audition, sat down with the director, I read and he said, 'That's great.' Then he took me aside and told me something that made my jaw drop.

He said: 'I'm going to be honest with you. I had a call from Gillian Anderson at the weekend. It's not why I'm making this decision, but she sang your praises. I thought I'd tell you that so you could thank her. I don't know how she got my number, but she'd obviously done a bit of homework on me. She rang me up and she said, "You've got to give the job to Danny Dyer. He's brilliant and professional and he's a massive fan of Ray's."' I was so taken aback by that, it meant so much to me.

The professional thing really made me feel proud. I'd cut right back on the drugs and booze by this point. It was just a very occasional thing for me by then. I understood that the work was the important thing, not having a line of gear up your hooter. I'd become a leading man and that brought some responsibility. If you're coming in just doing cameos maybe you can get away with that kind of behaviour, but not when the whole movie's resting on you. The days of the wildman are fucking over, let me tell you that.

Gillian wanted to do me a favour, a massive favour. I am indebted to her.

There was a downside to this, though. The director said, 'I'm going to give you the part but I want you to do something for me. I want you to dye your hair ginger. I want to give you a totally different look, glasses, ginger hair.'

I said, 'Listen, if it gets me playing Ray's son, I will do it, I will do whatever you fucking want.'

He explained that Ray was ginger when he was younger and so it would look natural. It was horrible. It was a while since I'd had to do something quite as drastic. In one way I was excited about the fact I was going to have a different look. But at the same time I was walking around with a ginger hairdo. I was forever having to explain myself to people. I looked like a fucking prat.

I got it done and I went to the read through and there's Ray in the room. The very first words he spoke to me were, 'Look at, you ginger cunt.'

That was his opening line to break the ice. I said, 'What are you talking about? I've had to do this because of you. You was a ginger cunt when you were younger.'

He went, 'I've never been ginger, you've got to be fucking stupid haven't you, dyeing your hair?'

And that was it, me and him hit it off immediately, like we'd known each other for years, and he ripped the arse out of me throughout the film for dyeing my hair.

Just to be around him was terrific. It's hard to explain what it meant to me. And to have become friends with him like I have, it was just perfect. I didn't go for a drink with him at the time because he was on the wagon during the job, and he wasn't boozing at all, which was a bit of a disappointment. We'd get to that though.

I thought he was amazing in it, but some of the reviews said he was over the top. I disagreed. I think he based a bit of it on Harry Redknapp and, if you knew that, you could see exactly where his performance was coming from. It was all about the way that football is run by money now and how agents are running everything.

I play an agent in it. Ray's a manager and I'm his son – I was never any good at football as a kid and he was always disappointed in me, so to make up for it, I become an agent. I start telling him to sell our best players so he can take a few backhanders and buy himself a swimming pool and a jacuzzi, all that.

Ray's character uses the word 'cunt' in it a lot, which reduces its audience. Plus it was a Channel 4 thing, after the watershed. I thought it would have opened up things for us to be together more often, but that hasn't happened. I would jump at the chance to work with him again.

Working with one of my heroes, I was always going to be nervous. But Ray's not perfect and he got his lines wrong sometimes. When he did he'd get really angry with himself, start effing and blinding. Seeing that even he made mistakes allowed me to relax about my own performance a bit and let me do my thing the way I wanted to.

Ray and me swapped numbers. I went round his house a couple of times. He lives out in Epping, which is not too far from me, but a million miles in terms of what sort of houses we live in. People imagine I have some huge pad, but that couldn't be further from the truth. I live in a suburban semi on a modern housing estate. I've made a bit of wedge but I've spent a bit too. I certainly haven't got enough to get some gaff out of *Footballers' Wives*.

To be honest, the move to a semi is a massive step up for me and one that I wasn't exactly falling over myself to make. If it had been left to me we probably wouldn't have moved out of Canning Town. I was all right in Joanne's little council house near to my mum, my dad, my nan and all my mates. We'd done it up nicely, a bit over the top maybe. Like I said, the telly was a fuck off plasma screen that almost covered one wall and we had a Porsche and a Merc sitting outside but at the end of the day, we were living on a council estate. Having no space with two kids running around wasn't a sensible way to live.

Canning Town was a great place to live. Everyone knows me around there, so no one is going to fuck with me. People appreciate the fact that I grew up in the area and haven't really changed as a person. Still the same old Danny Dyer. So it wasn't my choice to move – Joanne's the one who set the ball in motion for us to get a house somewhere else.

I knew it had to happen but I wasn't looking forward to it. We had to move out because I was on the settee and she was in bed with the baby – little Sunnie had come along by then. It was only a two-bedroom flat. Dani had her own bedroom, obviously, being a teenage girl, but we had nowhere to put the baby.

That would be our routine. Joanne'd put the baby to bed in our room, then she'd go up after a while, and I'd go to sleep on the settee. I'd wake up in the morning feeling like someone had kicked the shit out of me. The settee wasn't big enough for me so I had had to sleep with my legs bent. I could barely move. Not exactly what people expect from a film star, but there you go.

So after thirty-one years of my life I was finally moving out of the flats and the East End for good. It was a weird feeling but it's not like I've moved to a foreign country – we've only gone up Debden, so it's a few more stops on the Tube to get home.

It was mad how we got the mortgage because no one was handing them out at the time. I was in *The Homecoming* at the Almeida. They're supported by Coutts, who are the Queen's bank. They put a Coutts night on to watch the play, and I got approached afterward, and they said they'd love to take me on. At that point I didn't have any money, because it was a four-month run, and I was on £410 a week.

They said all I needed to open an account was five grand. I had to do *Mr and Mrs* on ITV because I was so skint from doing a Pinter play and it was an easy way to scare up some cash. They offered me and Joanne twenty grand to do it, ten grand each. It was a bit muggy, but I needed to do it to keep the account open and get the mortgage on my house. Coutts were the only people who would give me a mortgage. It set me off on this whole new thing of taking control of my life moneywise. You see I'd never owned anything. My name wasn't on anything. If I'd have died at that time, I literally would have had nothing to leave behind. And so I got a credit card for the first time in my life. I'd never had one, not even to slice up the coke.

Anyway, Ray's gaff's on another level. He has his own big place, massive, with its own swimming pool. He has a little bar outside in a big shed at the bottom of the garden, which is called Raymundo's. It's like a gentleman's club. It's got a huge TV, a radio and no clocks, so you never know what the time is until you walk out. It's beautiful in there. He serves you from behind the bar with 'Raymundo' above his head in neon lights. It's covered wall-to-wall in West Ham memorabilia. He's got all the shirts signed, pictures of players with him. That for me is one of the lovely things about becoming famous – you get to meet a lot of your heroes. Some of them live up to what you expect; some of them let you down a little bit. One of the bad things is that everyone has an opinion on you and some of those opinions ain't very nice. Also, when things go wrong in celebrities' lives, you can find yourself caught up in that circus whether you like it or not – as I was to find out when I was there the night when a future England captain got himself in a spot of bother.

21

CELEBRITY

I suppose this is as good a time as any to discuss what fame has brought me, good and bad. Among my favourites is getting to meet and becoming friends with a lot of footballers.

Finding out that some of your footballing heroes are actually fans of yours is a weird one though. I love West Ham – Come on you Irons! – so when Bobby Zamora, who played up front for us for a couple of seasons, walked up to me and called me a legend, I was pretty blown away. It was a real moment for me. I got quite pally with Bobby but then we drifted out of contact. I think it was because of what I'd come to represent to some people. It wasn't in his interests to be seen with me. I was in a film about football hooligans. Nowadays, these footballers have to be clean cut, although as we all know, a lot of them end up fucking it up for themselves anyway.

Sometimes you can find yourself caught up in stuff that makes the news, even when it's got nothing at all to do with you. I had a moment with John Terry a few years ago when he got arrested for allegedly bottling a geezer – John was found not guilty.

I was there on the night. It was at a place called the Wellington in Knightsbridge. I was walking out and this geezer came up to me and asked me for my autograph. I went, 'What's your name, mate?' He looked at me and said, 'What? Don't you know my name?' And I said, 'What's your name?' And he said, 'John.' So I wrote, 'To John from Danny Dyer' and started walking out.

I saw him say 'fucking wanker', and he screwed up the bit of paper and threw it on the floor. It was John Terry. He was in there with Jody Morris. He was only up-and-coming then, we're talking 2000, 2001, and I honestly didn't recognise him. The bouncer Trevor was a pal of mine. He turned round to John and said, 'He ain't a wanker, you've had too much to drink, fuck off.' John didn't like this.

I heard plenty about what went on that night, but I didn't see anything more. I had the police round my door asking if I would testify in the case but I couldn't help them. Nothing showed up on the CCTV and John Terry was acquitted in court, so it wasn't him who bottled Trevor – definitely not. Someone did though.

I saw John Terry a couple of years ago when I was with Tamer. He came up to me and he called me a legend as well. He didn't really speak about that night. He had Ashley Cole around, all that mob, little Shaun Wright-Phillips.

Another side of fame is that everyone has an opinion on you. I don't go on the Internet no more because you can read such shit about yourself, things you know to be untrue. Some people love me, some hate me. There's even a Facebook page saying Joanne's the wrong girl for me. How do they know? It's up to fucking me, isn't it? I read here and there that people want to take a pop at me, punch me in the face. None of

So young and untouched (yeah right!)

Me and the big Turk (he's always grabbing me boat).

Me in *The Business* – love that eighties clobber.

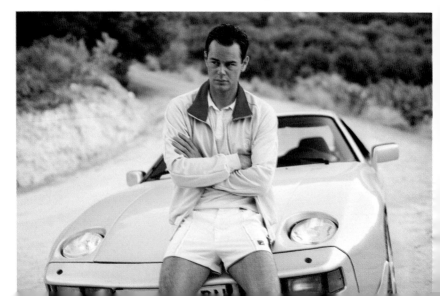

A rare picture with Harold. We lost a great man there.

Me and Nick on the set of *Outlaw*. I owe him more than he'll ever know.

On the set of *Doghouse*.
Believe it or not, that's my
Dani as the zombie.

Me and Sean in
Kurt & Sid.
I loved every
fucking moment.

Man love in its truest form
– go on the Ray!

My daughters Dani and Sunnie. Don't be fooled, underneath that beauty are two terrors. Only joking, they give me a drive and passion I cannot explain.

Mum and daughter.
They're so fit!

Me with my beautiful
babies. I'm nothing
without them.

Me at the Soccer Six trying to play football, with Dani and little Jack.

them ever do though. It's easy to be brave at a computer keyboard, it takes a bit more nuts face to face.

Being in the public eye means you come in for quite a lot of piss taking and criticism. I actually don't mind quite a lot of it, up to a point. Take Frankie Boyle, for instance.

Now up until it all went wrong with *Zoo*, he has been quite funny about me and I don't mind that because, despite his picking on people who aren't in a position to defend themselves, I do quite like him. Not to look at, obviously, because that is one ugly mug. I close my eyes when he's on TV and just listen to him. It makes it difficult to eat my dinner but I don't want to risk being sick if I catch a glimpse of him. Frankie's a laugh though, which I suppose he kind of has to be because he's never going to pick up a bird any other way – he looks like the third Proclaimers brother, the one who was too ugly to get in the band.

Ugly bastards seem to line up to have a pop at me. Take the film critic Mark Kermode. With a face like his it's easy to see why he chose a career that involves spending a long time in the dark. If you've never seen him think of Timothy Spall – Barry from *Auf Wiedersehen, Pet* – dressed up like an ageing ballroom dance instructor. Kermode has a haircut that I honestly thought he was wearing for *Comic Relief* the first time I saw it. It's a sort of teddy boy look, a greasy looking thing that would make you think twice about allowing him anywhere near the headrests on your car. It has the one advantage of being so revolting that it takes your attention away from his boat. Perhaps that's why he chose it.

Apparently he does some sort of impression of me and thinks

that I'm a fucking mockney, not a real East Ender. Well, I might be a tosser – and you can form your own view on that – but I am an East Ender, born and bred, no question. I could be more cockney, I suppose, but short of my mum dropping me out of her on the clapper on the Bow Bells, I don't see how.

What gets me about Kermode is not that he thinks I'm a bad actor. That doesn't bother me at all because Harold Pinter thought I was a good one and he won the Nobel Prize for fucking Literature. It's not even that he doesn't think I'm a real cockney. If he wants he can go round and ask my nan about that but I'd warn him, she's only four foot ten but she'd batter him. I've still got the same mates I had when I was eight years old and I still drink on the old manor. I know where I come from and what I am.

What annoys me about him, in my opinion, is the contempt he shows. Take his impression of me. Clearly he thinks I talk funny so he takes the piss out of it. Well, that's how cockneys talk, as he'd know if he ever spent any proper amount of time with them.

It reminds me of some of that country house stuff I did early in my career – it's like the toffs taking the piss out of the way the servants speak, the posh people thinking they're so superior to the working class, laughing at the 'little people'.

I shouldn't find Kermode's contempt for me surprising. Privileged people like him have always looked down on people like me. They laugh at our accents, they sneer at us and treat us like shit when we work on their houses. They find the sort of entertainment we like crass or obvious and turn their noses up at it. Kermode hardly watches TV, despite showing his face on it far too much for my liking. He doesn't like *Star Wars*, doesn't like *Titanic*, doesn't like *Pirates of the Caribbean*. He does like foreign art house movies, just like you'd guess he fucking would. He thinks I'm a contrived cliché. What the fuck is he?

Kermode lives in a world where words don't mean anything, not really, where you can say what you like about who you like without any comeback. I don't live in that world. If you're going to call someone a cunt you better be prepared to back it up. So, if you're reading this, Kermode, carry on. If we ever meet we'll see if you've got the bollocks to do your impression while we're toe-to-toe.

Glad I got that off my chest. Now, where was I? Oh yeah. So fame brings good things and bad. Above all, it's just a bit weird.

Fame has never been annoying but I almost feel I'm not real to people. They look at me like I'm a cartoon character. It would be so easy to get wrapped up in it. You are – wrongly – looked at as better than other people. You walk into a room and everyone knows who you are, everyone points.

That's a strange feeling, because you know you're no different, you just work a job that you've your face up on a screen. I'd go to a normal boozer and I'd be constantly asked, 'What are you doing drinking in here?' like I should always be in some West End bar. I know I'm no better than anyone else and I don't want to be better than anyone else. But the more real you try to be, the more you feel you're acting at trying to be real. It's not healthy for your brain.

People that crave fame, and in my business a lot of them do, are setting themselves up for a fall. When they haven't got it any more I can't imagine where their head goes. An example for me would be John Alford who was in *London's Burning*. I'm not saying he was a fame nut, just that he had it and then it went away. He's not a bad actor, and he was in a massive show on about £300,000 a year. Then got set up by the *News of the World* in a drugs sting. In a moment his whole career was gone. He was a nice kid and they snatched that away from him. I saw him in Canning Town putting scaffolding up. The only reason I knew it was him was that a couple of kids were throwing things at him. I thought, 'Not only has he lost his whole career and he's having to put scaffolding up, people are being horrible to him.'

I said hello and we had a chat. He said, 'You know what, Danny, I can't catch a fucking cold at the moment.' Everyone's at it now, but in the nineties it was a big thing for him to get caught. It was a family show and all that. A shame.

People even found it a bit strange I moved into the house I did – a normal, modest semi on a normal street. The thing is, people assume actors all make millions. You do one appearance on *The Bill* and they think you're minted. It don't work like that. Most actors are skint and I'm lucky to be making a decent living from it, never mind hitting the jackpot in Hollywood.

I am an ordinary person, I just do an unusual job. I'm not knocking the fame thing because it has brought me some great opportunities. Take my TV stuff – *Danny Dyer's Deadliest Men* and *The Real Football Factories*. They might not be everyone's idea of high-quality TV but they've put the fucking dinner on the table for my family and, more than that, enabled me to see extraordinary places and meet extraordinary people.

They've also brought me a sack load of trouble, which is the reason I won't be doing that sort of thing again.

22

HOOLIGAN ELEMENT

The Football Factory was a huge success as a movie. I got a lot of attention from it, and in acting terms it put me back on the map. It opened me up to a new audience, including some people from an aggressive, young and lost culture – that of the football hooligan. This culture had been around during the eighties but it had faded from view. It had always been there, but *The Football Factory* cast a spotlight on it again.

Off the back of its success I was approached by a company called Zig Zag who asked me if I'd be interested in presenting. My first instinct was to tell them to do one. I take acting very seriously and I could never understand actors who did presenting. My worst nightmare would to have been known as Danny Dyer, actor/presenter.

But they offered me a nice bit of money – about fifty times more than what I was paid to do the movie. That made me prick up my ears, I can tell you. All my career I've been skint, up until very recently. I don't mind, it's not about the money, and God knows you can keep the fame, it's about the work for me. However, I'm a family man and I do want to provide for my kids. Dani was in a school I wasn't too keen on in Custom House and doing the presenting gig would be a chance to get enough dough to get her out of that.

So I asked them what they wanted me to do. I wasn't keen when they told me, to be honest. They said, 'We want you to tour the country talking to all the different football firms.' It was going to be called *The Real Football Factories*. I thought, 'Jesus Christ, logistically, how is this going to work?'

I wondered about how you run around talking to hooligans that are still active, from a legal point of view. Also, I grew up around people like that. There are some dangerous geezers involved in that game, let me tell you. Still, I needed the money. I didn't want to do it but a lot of people have to work doing things they don't want to do to put food on the table so I thought, 'Let's have it.'

I made sure I didn't sign a contract so that any point it got too heavy I could walked away. It's a big ask this programme. Zig Zag don't like me to meet any of the hooligans before we put them on camera. I have to go in there cold, the camera over my shoulder. They want the freshness that gives. The trouble is, if you're going into a pub full of nutters, inevitably you get big attention if you're dragging a cameraman behind you.

I would meet these hooligans in various strange places, whether that would be under an archway somewhere or walking into a pub in Burnley. It was all very guerrilla filming in a way.

The first episode I done was Rangers vs Celtic, the old firm derby in Glasgow. Now I'm a football fan, so I know that's one of the most intense rivalries in sport, certainly the most intense in British sport. I thought, 'OK, straight in at the deep end.'

They briefed me about how the day was going to work. We were told Rangers didn't want to know. Celtic were more up for it and were going to accept me into their group and take me to the game.

The problem with dealing with middle-class TV people is that when it comes to this sort of thing they haven't got a clue. Their first suggestion could have potentially got me killed as well as ensuring I could never look at myself in the mirror again. I was told I was going to be given a secret camera to do some undercover filming. I said, 'Bollocks, I'm not doing any of that. I'm not a grass.' In the end I agreed to just take in a little camcorder and film out in the open. If people know they're being filmed that's OK, they can object to it if it bothers them, but I'm not acting like a snake for any amount of dough.

So I bowl up outside the ground and start doing a piece to camera. I can't stress how much hate there is at this game. Between these two clubs it's another level. It's a political and religious thing for a start, Protestant against Catholic. Doing my first piece to camera was the first glimpse of how famous I'd become in certain circles. Every fucker knew who I was. I'm not the sort of actor who buzzes off that kind of thing but I understand that you need to have fame if you're going to be successful. It's something I put up with rather than enjoy most of the time.

The idea of me walking around with a camera in my face wasn't one I was comfortable with, particularly in that environment. Even if people didn't recognise me immediately, they'd see the camera and think, 'Who's that? Oh, it's him off *The Football Factory*.'

Zig Zag had written me a script. In the later series I'd just make it up, but they'd written me some good stuff, quite articulate. I learned it and was trying to say my lines. But we're outside the away end and there are masses of these hard-nut Celtic fans recognising me, coming up to me and putting their arms around me and wanting to have photos taken with me. If someone wants a photo I'll have it, and if someone wants an autograph I'll do it. I'm not a snotty-nosed bastard but this was becoming ridiculous. It was an overwhelming experience, something completely new for me. I don't think Zig Zag realised how well my face was known either.

So I finally manage to do the piece to camera and then I get in with this Celtic mob, some who I can understand and some I can't because of their accents. They take me in and they embrace me and look after me, so I start to relax a bit. The game was actually at Ibrox, Rangers' ground, so I was in the away end. I remember standing there thinking how intense the whole thing was. The players didn't get the ball when it went out for a throw because the people on the hoardings were trying to grab them and spit at them. It was savage.

Still, I went with the flow. Celtic won 1–0, and I got a chance to jump about a bit. I got the camera out and saw the general nuttiness of it and I could feel the hate coming off the Rangers mob, like a hot wave sweeping over the pitch. It all went off OK though. I came out, interviewed a few of the Celtic boys and they were all happy.

Then I had to go to a Rangers pub and interview a few of their mob to see how they feel about it because the idea of the show was that it's not about one club, it's about an area.

By the end of the game, I was on a buzz. I'd had the opportunity to watch the Old Firm derby, which I'd always wanted to do, and I had a bit of a spring in my step. I was thinking 'This is a piece of piss.' I thought I'd do a few more quick interviews and go home, nothing to worry about. I was about to be reminded of what I should have been worried about, and in no uncertain terms.

We met this fixer for the Rangers mob and we went into one of their pubs. And, fucking hell, from earlier in the day and getting all this attention, all this love and people wanting my photo, I just felt hate drive towards me as soon as I walked in the room – Rangers-style hate, and believe me, those boys are experts at it. It obviously had got back to the Rangers mob that I saw the game with Celtic. They had lost, against their bitterest rivals, and the idea of a clueless cockney walking into their pub was not one they liked.

I had thought that if I was going to go to these mad places with aggressive people they'd have given me security, but did they fuck. It was a cameraman – a very middle-class cameraman too, just ripe for bullying by this sort of geezer – some bird with a clipboard, and someone with a little boom mike for sound. That's it, that was the vibe. I later realised it was a better move, because walking around with two big blokes in suits would make me look like a prick. Plus it gives the hooligans an excuse to have a pop. Not that they need an excuse.

Let me tell you what it's like in these Glasgow boozers. They don't have any windows so you can't throw nothing through them and nobody can be thrown out of them. It's very dark, very rammed, very fucking hot. I started to interview this fixer guy and I just remember another guy coming up to him and whispering something in his ear. This guy, this fixer, he went white as a sheet and then disappeared. We couldn't find him nowhere. The director was walking around the pub and getting cutaways, nice pictures of the pub, faces drinking, and I could sense the vibe going sour. He was oblivious to it, absolutely fucking oblivious to it.

All of a sudden, I felt someone grab me, turn me towards the door and kick me up the arse really fucking hard. So I was standing there like a prick all of a sudden. I thought, 'Fuck this, this isn't what it's about,' and I got the fuck out the pub. I remember getting outside and pulling this director to me and saying, 'Come here, this ain't going to work. I don't think I can do this. This is a fucking dangerous situation.' He said, 'No, Danny, it will be fine, we just picked the wrong pub. That's all.'

I had to point out to him that people have died picking the wrong pub. I did this big spiel to the director telling him I didn't think I could do it. It was only a day into the shoot, and if this was the start, then what was the rest of it going to be like? I didn't think I could do six weeks of it, six episodes and twenty clubs around the country. After a while, I calmed down a little bit and reined it in. I'd said 'yes' to the show so I thought I should be a man, stand up and get on with it. And, after all, it could only get easier than the old firm derby.

The tough thing for the rest of the series was I'd just finished doing the Ray Winstone thing and I still had a bit of a ginger hairdo going on, which made me look like a complete weirdo. I did think of having a skinhead, but I'm not a thug, and I didn't want to look like one. It was always my mission that I had to remain neutral and not try to pass myself off as a hooligan. It would be a false image. To be honest, sometimes I was pretty scared. I'm not acting when I'm presenting, so when I look scared, I am scared. And believe me, it is scary sometimes. A TV camera affords you no protection against these people whatso-fucking-ever.

As an audience member hopefully you're watching it sitting on your settee thinking, 'I wouldn't want to be in that position.' The trouble is, I'm thinking the same, and I'm right there in that position.

The rest of Scotland went fine. The Dundee and Dundee United mobs were great with me and the Hibs mob was sweet as a nut. It was more about the past with them, hooligans that are not active now. It was about redemption, all that. I met Bradley Walsh there, who was a former Hibs hooligan and who now has his own gym. He gets kids off the street, takes them in and trains them, gets them to stop running around with knives and all that. He was an interesting bloke, had something about him definitely – quite inspiring to young kids.

Bradley had been a lost soul and he had to do a bit of bird to realise that hooliganism wasn't the life for him. The idea of the show was to ask why it went on with these men, especially when some have never committed a crime before in their life. They're happily married with three kids, they work all week, look after the kids, all that, and then on a Saturday afternoon they get together and turn into complete lunatics, smash places up, then turn around and go home to the wife for a bit of dinner. Why do people do it? I've got to say, we never really did put our finger on it. For some people it's about territory. For other people, it's about race. For others it's about belonging to something, to feel part of an army, but there's absolutely no single explanation for it. Abroad it's a different thing, you've got the legacy of wars playing out on the terraces, but the Old Firm aside, that's not the case over here.

Glasgow set me up nicely for the rest of them. I'm not saying it got easier but it couldn't have got any fucking harder, let's put it that way – an Englishman who was known to have spent all afternoon with Celtic watching Rangers get beat walking into a Rangers pub and saying 'How do you do?' Stick that on *Challenge Anneka*.

When we went south to the Midlands I learnt a lot about the actual rivalries, the intensity that exists between Derby and Nottingham Forest. There was this really sweet story about this Derby football hooligan and this Nottingham football hooligan who were best pals growing up on the same estate. One of them got put in prison and they hadn't seen each other in a while. After years apart they met on a battlefield when Derby and Nottingham Forest were coming together for a tear up. They remember this moment, locking eyes, fists clenched, ready for some action. But instead of a rumble, they wanted to embrace each other, throw their arms around each other and have a few beers. They did meet up on the sly later but since then they have actually fought each other, because they get a laugh out of it. They would never take the piss and if they saw the other one lying on the floor getting kicked they'd go and help them. But yes, they gave each other a clump and then they sat back and pissed themselves about it. Strange world.

I interviewed them at the same time in a neutral pub because they didn't want to be seen by the opposite firms, which surprised me because I was thinking, 'It's going to be on the telly so all this cloak and dagger bollocks ain't going to be worth much.'

A lot of the firms we did were quite notable one way or another. I'm not going to mention every single one of them here because this is a book and not a fucking encyclopaedia. The stuff's out there on DVD so it would be a cheat to just go through every programme telling you what went on.

I'm only going to talk about firms where I've got something to add that you didn't see on the telly. So no disrespect to anyone if they don't get name checked. This stuff comes off the top of my nut and I'll just mention the firms that come to mind when I'm writing – these are the ones that I remember today, could be a different bunch tomorrow.

One firm that sticks in my mind was the Zulu Warriors out of Birmingham, as much for its racial mix as anything. We were told we going to meet them in a pub. They were playing that day, the game was to kick off in a couple of hours and they'd already got a meet, which meant they were going to have it with another firm. We went into the pub and there were loads of them, all races as well, really big blokes – some on banning orders, just got out of prison, the works. They were very black orientated, a lot of Turks and Asians as well, which I thought was unusual, with a lot of football hooligans being big fat white fuckers with the bulldog tattoo thing going on. This was coming from a different place.

I got a big cheer when I went in. These are people who look on me as someone who has represented them. I'm only an actor, not a hooligan, but because the film was so successful and so honest and I'm the lead character, they show me respect. Sometimes I feel I have to play up to that image a little bit, of course. I'd walk into these places and immediately get a pint thrust into my hand, and I'd have it with them, even though it would have been better for me not to. You've got to remember, I have to remain straight. I've got to do pieces to camera and all that, so I can't be pissed.

I could sense that the couple of Zulus I was talking to wanted to get out the door and have the tear up, they couldn't wait. Then two Old Bill walked in the pub, and the Zulus were 150 strong. A couple threw pint glasses at the police and they just put their heads down and walked out. I thought 'Fucking hell, this is a powerful, powerful firm.'

From there we did Stoke. They're called the Naughty 40. This was a very young, still active group. They actually used the footage of this group in the title sequence running towards the camera because the lads didn't give a fuck about their faces appearing on TV. They don't want scarves or hoodies covering their faces up, none of that.

I remember they couldn't wait to get me in the khazi straight away because they wanted to whack a line of gear up my nose. I had about eight of them round me all with a wrap of coke in their hands, shoving it up my nose going, 'Here, Dan, have it!' And I am going to be straight with you, I had it. I thought it was the easiest way to get on with them. I remember walking out of this khazi, feeling like the top of my head was going to come off, wired off my fucking nut. Luckily, my previous experience had prepared me for that one. It's not like I'm Judith Chalmers, so I just about managed to keep it together.

Buzzing like a lunatic, I went to interview their top boy, who was about fifty. And, fuck me, did he run this fucking crew? He's written books about it and all that kind of thing, though he's not active any more. There were about fifty kids in there, all charged up to the eyeballs on gak, all eighteen-to twenty-five-year-olds. So I sit down, buzzing, to this interview with this top boy. It was noisy, and they were chanting and all that and he just said, 'Shhhh!' And it was silence. This geezer brought them under control immediately. I was trying to get into their heads, to see what made them tick but, to be honest, the only conclusion I came to was that they were very proud of Stoke. Not an insight that's going to win me a prize for social comment but there seemed no real cause of it beyond that.

Then we went to Burnley, The Suicide Squad. I met their top boy in this pub and all I could smell as I walked in was this really strong smell of hash. They were all playing pool at the back. Again, I got a good reception but I always felt guilty that I was going in there with a camera. I knew some of them would want to show off to it, but others would book me a grass. It's only because I'm always in with the top boy that they behave themselves. This geezer sat there and he said, 'I am an artist, I'm like Van Gogh, violence is my art form.' I couldn't see the similarity between smacking someone's head in and painting masterpieces myself but there again philosophy has never been my strong suit.

He went, 'Where's my boy, where's my boy?' and this young kid came through the crowd, sixteen, puffing away on a fag, a bit nervous. The dad said, 'What are you going to be when you grow up, son?' And the kid said, 'A hooligan, Dad,' and he said, 'That's my boy.'

It was the only time I heard that. A lot of hooligans say 'This is the last thing I'd want for my son, if I found out he was running around doing this, I'd batter him myself.' So hearing a dad push his lad into hooliganism did surprise me.

The top boy's parting shot to me as I left the boozer was to say 'Do you want my book?' I said. 'Go on then, mate.' He charged me fifteen quid for it. Being honest, I've had more enjoyable afternoons.

Having done these firms, I was right in the job, hitting my stride and getting used to presenting. I really wanted to make sure the programme had something about it, because I knew this sort of thing has the potential to be pretty bad TV. That said, I was wondering if I'd given too much away on the show by stepping out from behind the façade of a character and showing myself. I was turning into a celebrity, I could see that, and I never wanted to be a celebrity, I wanted to be an actor. By this stage the whole thing was pretty much unscripted so I had no one else's words to hide behind. I knew I was putting myself in the firing line and that if people didn't like it I couldn't say, 'Oh, it's just the character,' because it was me on the screen. People slagging me off personally would hurt a lot more than critics having a dig at my films. I also wondered if I was milking the hard man thing too much.

There was a lot I was having to think about. I was going down a route I had never wanted to go down. I've always been so passionate about acting, about honing my craft, and I had to ask myself if I was throwing all that away for a pound note.

This show didn't come from me, it wasn't even something I was particularly interested in. It just came from a TV company, who said, 'We've put this together, and we will give you this much dough.' But when the show came out people began to believe I was some sort of violence junkie, some bloke who gets off on hanging around with hard men. I don't. I get off on earning a few quid for my family. Maybe that was the wrong motivation, but Joanne and the kids had gone long enough being poor.

Going from town to town I didn't really get any grief off anyone other than in Glasgow. I got a lot of love, a little bit of piss taking about my ginger hair now and again, but nothing heavy.

The hooligans did tend to bully the director more than anything, which was pretty horrible. They'd slap him around the head, throw things, basically call him a cunt, because he wasn't working class and he wasn't one of them. We used three directors in the six-week period. I don't think one would have lasted the whole thing.

That was the first series, and I was fucked by the end of it. It had taken six weeks and I had met a lot of naughty people in that time. I'd done it, I got my money and was prepared to move on to the next thing. But they were so happy with this series that they couldn't wait to go to work again. And this time I would be on unfamiliar territory, working with people who had never heard of me, miles and miles from home.

23

INTERNATIONAL NOT-SO BRIGHT YOUNG THINGS

A year before *The Homecoming* at the Almeida, Zig Zag came up with the idea of *Real Football Factories International*. I always knew that I was fairly safe with British hooligans because a lot of them had watched *The Football Factory* and had liked it – liked me enough that some of them came to see me in a Pinter play – so they respected me and cut me a lot of slack.

Now, I was going to go into the realms of hooligans that hadn't got a fucking clue who I was. Some of them had seen the movie but the majority of them didn't know me from fucking Adam. Now I sat and thought long and hard about this because my missus had just become pregnant again, with Sunnie. But they offered me three times as much as the first series. I thought, 'Oh God, how am I going to turn that down?'

I remember finishing the first one and thinking, 'I never want to put myself through this again, don't milk it, don't milk it.' But I did it, I fucking did it. The money was just too much.

Plus, on the bright side, there was something appealing about travelling the world, even in the way I was going to do it. We were going to Turkey, Italy, Russia, Poland, Brazil, Argentina, Serbia, Croatia and Holland.

And there were parts of me that quite enjoyed the presenting side of it. Because I am an actor I could learn the lines and that made me sound more articulate, like I'd really done my research on this stuff. So we went forth on this mad tour. I did four continents in six weeks.

I was straight in the deep end again with Galatasaray of Istanbul. The Turks are a lovely people, friendly and hospitable, but anyone who knows anything about football will know that that all takes a back seat when it comes to supporting their teams. They are lunatic fans, putting it mildly.

Galatasaray wanted the whole show to be about them – the firms are often like that – but the fact we were also doing their arch-rivals Fenerbahçe meant they wanted nothing to do with us and couldn't guarantee our safety. I took that on board and thought, 'Let's stay away from that mob.' So we went in with the Fenerbahçe mob. Their crew had the charming name of 'Kill For You'.

We had to involve Galatasaray somehow, though, so we did one segment with me just walking outside their ground doing a piece to camera. I couldn't believe it – I was getting bricks thrown at me and everything. There wasn't even a fucking match on.

In one piece they edited out I walked past this pissed bloke. He clocked what we were doing, and he made a phone call. I'm walking towards the camera, saying my lines, and he had a beer in his hand, which he threw at my head. I was like, 'Fucking hell, what was that?' He started shouting at us in Turkish, and I said, 'Let's do one.' The director was like, 'We just have to finish this piece.' By the time we did finish there were more bodies there and things were looking a bit tasty.

People were hurling all sorts of shit at us. Luckily we did beat a retreat before any major damage was done. I'm not going to lie to you, I was shitting myself. There were a mob of them and me with a couple of TV types with only a furry microphone to defend ourselves with. I was glad to get out of there because, as the presenter, I was naturally their main target. Mind you, they weren't too fucking accurate so any of us could have got bricked.

I always thought of Galatasaray as the more glamorous club in Istanbul, but it's not. The ground's falling to bits really. We went over to Fenerbahçe, which has a much more modern ground. They took to me because they wanted to celebrate their club. They were all laying into Galatasaray the whole time, saying how shit they were. They all drink Ouzo out there, don't they? So I got a bit pissed up with this mob before I went in to watch Fenerbahçe against Galatasaray – one of the great derbies in club football.

What fascinated me was that every time Galatasaray got the ball the Fenerbahçe mob would start whistling. This went on for ninety minutes. It was designed to be very offputting for the players and it worked. Fenerbahçe won. The Galatasaray mob was in their little pen and they smashed the fuck out of it.

They had a net all over their segment so that people couldn't throw things at them, which was lucky, because chairs were going over. It was a weird thing, because I got in with the firm, and I got a bit pally with them. I was thinking, 'If it goes off, what the fuck do I do? Do I have it with this mob or do I have it on my toes, risk the Fenerbahçe boys turning on me?' I just really hoped that wasn't going to happen. But it was an incredible experience being in that ground, the noise, the colour, flares, chants in a language you can't understand, the strange rhythms to the songs they sing. Fenerbahçe won 2–1, thank fuck, because it wouldn't have been fun to be around a firm after they'd lost a derby like that.

We met this other guy called Rambo from the Fenerbahçe mob. He once hid in the hoardings all night with a kebab knife. Just as the game was going to kick off, he came out and started waving it at the Galatasaray mob. He was like a legend over there, a tiny little guy with a 'tache, but in my opinion a complete sociopath. He's like a mascot for the club now, and he hangs around the ground at all hours of the day or night. They love him there and give him money and food, cigarettes and things. He's a glorified tramp, really. He's always said that he has a price on the soccer pundit Graeme Souness's head, that if he sees him he's going to kill him. That was because Graeme Souness was the manager of Galatasaray and he once planted the Galatasaray flag in the centre circle at Fenerbahçe – proving to me that Souness is a braver man than I.

Turkey was mad but it couldn't set me up for what I had coming when I went to Poland. Now, I am never going to have Cambridge University phoning me up asking me to take over from Professor Stephen Hawking, but even I was unprepared for the lack of education out there. It was Wisla Kraków vs Cracovia and the fans were very right wing, Nazi salutes and all that sort of thing. That really surprised me. It's Poland! One of the first countries that Hitler invaded. Why would they celebrate the ideology that sent tanks crashing through their country not all that long ago?

All year round before the derby game the Wisla lot would beat up any Cracovia fans they saw and they'd take scarves and shirts and any sort of memorabilia. At half-time against Cracovia they would put all this stuff over the fence by the pitch and set light to it. The police don't do fuck all. The fans are there singing all these songs and stuff and the whole fence is on fire.

The Poles look at English hooligans as fat, drug-taking, disorganised wasters – all of which are better than being a fucking Nazi in my book. A lot of the hooligans around the world felt like that about us. When you start getting into the realms of Italy you can't get into their firm unless you are a martial artist or a bodybuilder or something like that. If you take drugs or drink then they won't let you in, as simple as that.

We were looked on as a joke. I didn't know that but I found out when I had a little bit of a moment with the Wisla Kraków mob. Cracovia were a bit cagier about meeting me – I got to talk to a couple of their old hooligans, but that was all. They were very chilled, actually. I met up with them in a nice little pizzeria.

But the night before I had been with the Wisla mob and they have a segment of the ground where they have a sort of club shop. They have a party there after the game. They asked me if I wanted some coke. Like I said, I didn't know they have us all booked for drugheads but I thought I'd go through the motions and be pally. They said I had to come outside, so I went outside with this mob – on my own, obviously, no filming. There were a couple of geezers waiting in a car and immediately my instincts kicked in, and I thought, 'This ain't right. Why have I gone off the beaten track here?' It was over, we had finished filming, I was having a couple of beers with them but I had no need to be there.

I walked around the corner with them to this car and, as soon as we were around it, one of them pulled out a knife and said, 'Give me pound! Give me pound!' I said, 'What are you talking about, mate?' He just stood there looking like Igor off Frankenstein saying 'Give me pound!' He turned to his friends and said something in Polish and they all laughed and I thought, 'Ooo, right, fucking hell! What is the outcome of this? Is this a wind up, is this part of their banter or are they for real?' He didn't put the knife up to my throat, just stood there waving it about. I was looking for an escape route more than anything. The last thing I wanted to do was to get fucking plunged. Mad shit was going through my mind – my missus is pregnant, she hasn't even given birth to the kid and she gets a phone call saying that I've been stabbed to death in Poland. I had a result because the Old Bill turned up at that minute, raided them. An incredible and lucky coincidence for me. They didn't find nothing, they didn't have any coke on them, so I don't know what their game was. I just skulked off at that point, counting my blessings.

In retrospect, I can see the geezer with the knife was just bullying me. I tried to laugh it off and say, 'I got no money, mate,' standing with my chest out as much as I could because I realised that if you show them a weakness they will jump all over it. You've got to stand up a little bit, show them you're not afraid, but he was pissed up so I had no idea where it was going. In the end, I think it was just a bit of banter. Later on I asked myself, 'Who do you think you are swanning off with these people?' It certainly made me be a bit more careful in future. I'll tell you this for free, I was happy to get out of Poland.

After that, we went over to Russia. Hooligans are the least of their problems really. It's a crazy fucking country, where you have the richest and poorest people in the world living right next door to each other. It was so cold too.

When we got off the plane, the fixer was waiting for us to introduce us to people. He took us around and showed us the sites because we like to do some establishing shots of me walking through Moscow taking in a bit of the scenery, in order to flesh out the documentary.

There was this dog there around one of the tourist bits, begging for food. There were a lot of dogs around, just like there were when I was a kid. You don't see it as much now. I love dogs, I love all animals. I went up to the dog to pat it and the fixer started shouting at me, 'Don't touch the dog! Don't touch the dog!' He said, 'Listen, these dogs are scavengers, they eat tramps.' I can't imagine being a tramp in Moscow, you ain't going to last long when it's minus twenty outside.

These dogs get on the subway in packs. They live out in the suburbs a little bit, they wake up and jump on a train. This is accepted. They know what stop to get off and they'll look for tourists. They'll either give you the puppy dog eyes so you feed them or they'll use a new technique, which is to walk up behind someone who is eating and bark very loudly so that they drop their food. I found that fascinating. I'd rather have done a documentary about the dogs than the hooligans.

That run in with the dog made me feel quite vulnerable. You have these moments when you think, 'What am I doing here? If this is what the dogs are like, what are the hooligans going to be like?' Not exactly what I'd expected, was the answer.

I met the Spartak Moscow mob. They had the only female hooligan I came up against, this really beautiful Russian girl. She was part of a firm and her boyfriend was head of one of the mobs. I did an interview with her and she showed me a picture of her jumping on a bird trying to take chunks out of her. Something about a bird being violent made me think even more, 'What is the point to all this? Why does someone bother to go around acting like that?'

The Russians look on our hooligans as fucking idiots, so when I'm doing this documentary I'm not getting any respect at all. They're all laughing at me, at the English way of doing things. There was one bloke called Vassily the Killer. Lovely name, not so lovely guy. When I interviewed him he had a balaclava on – to disguise his identity, although he might have been wearing it because the weather was Baltic, literally. It was very intimidating. He was talking about how his brothers had been killed and this was why he became a hooligan himself. I didn't know the full extent of what he had got up to, because it was very limited what he could tell me. Let's put it this way, he wasn't called Vassily the Counsellor, and I was glad to get out of his company.

In Russia they would have organised meets and they would pay a doctor to come down. He'd patch them up after it had all gone off. I watched some of these clashes on film, and you see some archive on the show where they just come in and they'd play it out like a football match. One team would take their tops off, go skins. And then they would bash the living shit out of each other. Then they would shake hands, and fuck off. This is violence to the extreme, men who just want to punch the fuck out of each other for no reason whatsoever.

The Football Factory was quite a success in Moscow. I'd been all over the world and no one recognised me. I could do pieces to camera without too much going on. But in Moscow, they knew who I was, and I got mobbed a little bit, which was quite nice for the ego, really. A little pat on the arse. I didn't realise how religiously that film is watched by hooligans all over the world.

We only had two or three days in each country and then we had to move on. From Russia, I had to go to Brazil. Now, how the fuck do you pack a bag for that? You're just getting used to some sort of dialect and you're whisked across the world to somewhere completely different, sunshine in place of the freezing cold, more strange accents, different languages.

Brazil took it to a different level. This is the home of beautiful football. I notice on their beaches, they have little floodlit pitches so you can play football twenty-four hours a day if you want. You haven't got to pay for it, it's encouraged. In the UK, nowadays you get bollocked for kicking your ball down the street. There are no facilities for you to go and play football and, if there are, you have to pay money. That's the reason the Brazilians produce the footballers they do, no two ways about it. Like I said, the beautiful game. But there was nothing beautiful about the hooligan side of it.

They've moved on to guns. That was what Brazil was about. Guns. The most fascinating thing for me was to be allowed into the favelas – the slums of Rio. When you go to Rio, you've got this coastline, which is like paradise. You sit on the beach, watch the beautiful women walk by and sit at these little stalls where you get a coconut that's been put in the fridge. They chop a hole in it and put a straw in it and you drink the milk from it. But that's the only safe part, that little strip.

You walk two or three streets in and you're fucked. Every car in Brazil has a blacked-out window. It doesn't matter if it's the shittest car in the world. That's because the kids come out of these favelas with guns, look in the cars and they will shoot you in the head and take your purse, your watch, whatever they can get. And then they'll fuck off back to the favela, because they know the police won't come up there.

I went into the favela with the Fluminense firm. None of them spoke a word of English, and none of them had any money at all. The favela was exactly as I expected it to be, these little rat runs, dogs running past with their ribs sticking out, kids in the street all filthy. As we approached the house all I could hear was these drums banging. As much as this Fluminense mob like to have a tear up, they're all into the music side of it too. It was like a rave when I walked in.

To be honest, I got a very nice reception from them and they were all good to me, but I never once felt safe, especially with the camera, because that's worth three or four grand. We had twenty-five minutes to get what we could and then we had to fuck off. It was tough seeing that level of poverty but these people followed their team to the end of the world, buzzed off it, fought for them. In a way it gave them something to take their mind off how hard their lives were.

Then we went to Grêmio, where Ronaldinho used to play. When they score they do a thing called The Avalanche. They have a stand that seats six thousand people and when they score they all jump forward to the front. People at the front break arms, some break legs and get squashed, but they carry on. If you're at the front it's quite a privilege. I made sure I got out of that shit. That's the sort of privilege I can do without.

There are weird little differences about the game out there. The referee, for instance, because of the disputes that can flare up over players trying to nick a few yards at a free kick, carries this spray can around with him. Where he wants the ball to be put he sprays a circle and the ball is put exactly in the middle of that. I thought I knew a lot about football, but I'd never seen that before. The spray dissolves very quickly and leaves no mark behind. It's to stop any disputes. Very strange.

They won 4–0 that day, Grêmio. Four avalanches. I went into the other stand and watched it from a distance. It freaked me the fuck out. That's passion. It didn't kick off at that game but you could have got killed just being part of the celebrations.

Then I went on to The Green Stain, Palmeiras. That's in São Paulo. I didn't realise how big this place is. This is 30 or 40 million people in one city. It's quite a sad story with The

Green Stain because they'd lost a lot of people through shootings. You walk into their clubroom and you see a lot of pictures with RIP on them. I interviewed one of the fathers who had lost a son about six years before and he was still crying over it. The pain was still there. I can't remember what mob it was that had done them, but they were out for revenge. They also had a tattoo parlour in there because one of their hooligans is a tattoo artist and does them all for free. They were all smothered in tattoos.

I'd done my bit and went home when I had finished up. The director and crew, though, wanted a bit more and stayed on. They went to another clash with The Green Stain and got on the away coach with them. You get a police escort so far on the way out of the ground after the match. They got to a point outside the city limits where the other team ambushed them and shot their coach up. The director was on it, bless him, he's got some bollocks about him. It's like the old Wild West.

Zig Zag tried to shoot it to look like I was there; they put the voiceover on it and all that. That's not because I want some sort of brownie points for getting shot at but because they don't want the film to look all bitty, with me in and out of it. But I wasn't there, thank fuck. That would have been the final straw for me, getting shot at. That's taking it to extremes, it's not about having a tear up to three miles from the ground, it's about ending up dead. Too heavy for me.

So from Brazil I went to Argentina. It's a country I would never have visited if I hadn't done this documentary. There we basically got robbed by this guy. He was called Big Baby.

He was from the Independiente firm in Buenos Aires. He wanted two thousand American dollars to look after us over there, introduce us to everybody.

When we met him he had these two enormous bin liners with him. I didn't know what they were, but he gave me one and said, 'Follow me' – after getting his money, of course. I had this little bracelet on, and he said, 'You better take that off, because I can't guarantee it will still be on your arm when you leave.' I'd thought he was the top boy, that he was meant to be guaranteeing our safety. Clearly not.

So I follow him along with this black bag, it's fucking heavy and the day is roasting hot. We get into the ground and he knows everyone, everyone is saying hello. There are a couple of geezers in suits who look quite important who seem to know him. What he's got in these bags are loads and loads of balloons. I sit down with him, ready to do the interview, and he gets a kid, who has no shoes and socks on, and gets him to come and sit on his lap while he does the interview. These balloons say, 'Say No to Violence'. He's used us to cover himself with a friendly image so he can crack on with his underground hooligan activities. He wants us to film him, saying, 'I don't believe in violence here, it's not what I'm about.'

I later found out that he was on a banning order, not for violence, but for selling illegal tickets. Didn't stop him swanning into the ground. This stadium was made of wood, it must have been twenty pence to enter, through an old turnstile thing. Everyone in the crowd looked like Kempes – mounds of jet black permed hair on their nuts, unshaven, like your nightmare cell mate if you got sent down – who used to play for Argentina and no one had any shoes and socks on, it was such a deprived area. They were playing Racing Club, which was their derby. I'd never heard of any of the players but they all seemed brilliant to me – a very high standard of football.

I started off in the Independiente end, but this guy was starting to get fucked off with us being around. I'd done an interview with him and asked if he could tell us about any memorable battles they'd had. But he just said, 'We've never had any battles here. We don't believe in violence.' I realised we'd been knocked, that he wasn't going to talk about hooliganism at all, so I just thought we should do one out of there. The producer was fucked off and was having a bit of a fit about it, but I thought, 'What are you going to do? What the fuck are you going to do? This is what it's about, we are running around the world looking for hooligans and we've come unstuck here. Deal with it.' So Big Baby ushers us off and we go round to a safe, soft-core stand. Independiente go 2–0 up and you can see that Racing Club aren't as good as a team. So the Racing Club mob just smashed their end of the ground up. They start ripping up lumps of concrete and throwing them about. The game gets suspended for a bit and the referee clearly does not know what to do. Mind you, who would? Now the police have to do something. You should see the police. They've got old roll-ups hanging out of their mouths, droopy moustaches and a 'couldn't give a fuck' attitude and they just walk on to the edge of the pitch and start firing tear gas into the crowd.

We are meant to be in the safe part of the ground but the

tear gas just comes drifting over us. When you get tear-gassed, it's a horrible feeling. It does exactly what it says on the tin. You can't see a thing for the water pissing out of your eyes. It was awful, there were little kids next to me crying. But this is how they deal with it out there, you kick off, and the Old Bill shoot tear gas at you, they don't give a fuck who is around you. If there are kids in the ground, they suffer the same as the hooligans who are causing the damage. Eventually, the game was suspended, and so Racing Club had got what they wanted; the game was void.

At the time we were there in Argentina, because of this Racing Club and Independiente thing, they were having a clampdown on hooligans. And we got it all on film. We heard on the radio that there was a BBC crew, who had footage of all the rioting. They meant us, because BBC is the only British channel they know. We had to get out of the country with the film lively, because they wanted to impound it.

The idea of hooligans in Argentina is that they run the club. At one lower division club, we were allowed on the pitch in the afternoon to interview the hooligans. They had a butler, who served beers while we sat there and discussed how they like to crack heads.

I made a point about that on the show, how hooliganism is not just tolerated, it's almost celebrated. In their version of *Match of the Day*, they commentate on when the hooligans arrive. You'll see the hooligans come in on their coach. And say there was a stand of 16,000 people, there'll be a perfect square space in the middle where the hooligans stand. It looks like it's perfectly roped off, but there's nothing there at all.

Everyone knows that that is where the firm stand, and you do not stand in that area. And on their version of *Match of the Day*, they commentate on how big some of the hooligans' arms are. The subtitles had one commentator, your Alan Hansen type, saying to their Mark Lawrenson, 'Look at the size of his arms, they're as big as your legs.' It's a celebrated thing, something they accept.

From Argentina it was back to the former Yugoslavia – Croatia and Serbia, which was a horrible experience, to be honest.

Dinamo Zagreb in Croatia was really an eye opener. There was a game with just three thousand hooligans in the stadium. Without them there would have been no other fans in the ground to watch the game. And this is the power they had: one time, just once mind you, the team played bad, really bad. So these hooligans got on the pitch and dug eleven graves there. That's the particular brand of fucking nutter I was dealing with.

They were big enemies with the Serb teams, although they obviously don't play them since Yugoslavia broke up. I thought I'd seen hatred before, but not like that. Just a few years ago they were at war, killing each other, raping each other's mums and sisters. That's why they can't play in the same league, it would never work.

There are no flights to Serbia from Croatia so we had to drive. When you cross the border into Serbia, the first thing you come across are graves of Croatians that they've killed. They were basically saying, 'We've killed your mob', flaunting it, really. Serbia was a fucked-up place, because next to a

McDonald's you have a big building with a rocket hole just left in it, holes in the ground where bombs have landed. Belgrade tries to be all cosmopolitan but they've just left it for some reason. The place is battered.

I met a mob from Partizan Belgrade called The Gravediggers who really disturbed me. I just thought, 'This ain't what I'm here for.' Their big enemies were Hajduk Split, the Croatian team. You can tell this is serious stuff by the names of the teams – if you translate *partizan* or *hajduk* into English, apparently the nearest you'll get is 'freedom fighter' or 'paramilitary'.

The Gravediggers once caught one of the Hajduk Split mob. They were telling me this story, all laughing and then speaking to each other in their own language and cracking up again. That makes you very uncomfortable; you don't know what the fuck they're talking about and it could be that they're working out the plans they had for us lot. They said, 'We gave him the leather bullet.' I said, 'What do you mean, the leather bullet?' This bloke said, 'We fucked him in the arse.'

How do you react to that? I mean, I'm there, I don't want to get on the wrong side of these lunatics, but I don't want to be laughing along at what they're saying either, making them think I agree with it.

They took him to a cemetery, and they asked him to kiss the gravestone of one of their ex-leaders and he wouldn't do it. So they fucked him, about fifteen of them. And they were laughing about this. Now I thought it was all about being a man's man, this idea of standing up for each other, having a good old-fashioned tear up, not raping people. But that's what they did. They fucked him up the arse and sent him back to his mob. They said the guy later committed suicide, which doesn't surprise me.

I remember this right fucking fat prick with a beard giggling because he was the first to fuck him. And I'm sitting there, in their pub, looking at them with hatred. I looked around to the director, saying, 'Get me the fuck out of here.' He didn't know how to react either; the director had no idea that was coming. The point of The Gravediggers mob was that, since the football's died off for them – their league is nowhere near as competitive as it was in the Yugoslav days – they go to basketball games, or anywhere else where they have an excuse to kick off. They are just evil fucking people and I was glad to leave them behind and get on to Italy.

I've always wanted to go to Italy. I'm quite into old shit and all that, and it was great to see the Colosseum. That was the theme of that show, really, it was like the old-school gladiators coming together. The one thing I really liked about the Italian hooligans is how fucking good-looking they are, handsome, stylish.

They take it very, very seriously being an ultra – which is what they call their hooligans – and they are a massive problem in Italy. Juventus was a big moment and very scary. I went to meet them all, but none of them spoke a word of English. I went to their little hideout and they immediately said to me through the translator, 'We fucking hate you, we hate your camera crew, we hate the English. From left to right, up to down we fucking hate you, the only reason we're giving you the time of day is because we want to put our story across.'

I thought, 'Nice.' I knew it was good telly, but at the time

I'm thinking, 'This is embarrassing. I don't want to be put in these situations, this is shit. I've just been spoken to like a child by these people, and I'm having to sit here to grin and bear it.' It was bugging the fucking life out of me.

The big coup of the Italian episode was that I got to spend time with the Lazio and Roma mobs. They share a stadium, the Stadio Olimpico. While I was there, the Rome derby was on and we thought it would be sweet to see how both sets of fans went about their business. I was to spend the first half with the Roma mob, sneak out, go to the other end of the ground, change scarves and get in with the Lazio mob. Now that's a dangerous fucking thing to do, very dangerous. I'm not aware that anyone has ever done that before and there's probably good reasons for that.

I went in with the Roma lot first. Their main guy took me there. He couldn't come in because he was on a banning order, but he introduced me to a couple of youngsters, up-and-coming, not too full of themselves. This is a massive game, Lazio against Roma. There's a lot of fireworks, flares, smoke and generally things being set alight. They love all that. So the game kicks off and straight away there's a couple of tear ups within the Roma mob; they're just throwing punches anywhere. This apparently was a common thing, just the boys letting off steam.

Roma went 2–0 down and fuck me, did the atmosphere change, towards me more than anything. People started asking why I was there with a camera, and I had to move positions three times. The big thing was getting out at half-time and going round to the Lazio end. I had to make my excuses with this mob, saying I was going outside to do a piece to camera, which was always a good cover for disappearing.

I was feeling very didgy as I left, thinking someone was going to attack me at any time. As I'm walking around, all I can hear is bottles smashing. *Bash! Smash! Crash!* I thought, 'What the fuck is that?' It was actually the police. At half-time they take any bottles, anything that can be used as ammo and they smash it. But they were just behaving like a bunch of little kids throwing them up in the air, and they were landing four feet away from us. The police were really enjoying smashing these bottles.

I met the Lazio geezer at their end. Obviously I'd dumped my Roma scarf lively, no disrespect to Roma fans. Now, I was with the Lazio. So, everything changes. We couldn't say we'd been with the Roma, so I had to say that my plane was late. The Lazio mob were ecstatic that they were 2–0 up. It was like seeing the game in a completely different light, jumping up and down with the Lazio and feeling the hate and anger from Roma. Lazio won 3–0 in the end, and I thought, 'Thank fuck I'm not over there with the Roma.' I did feel a bit of a snake going between the two clubs, even though I didn't particularly care about either of them, but I was relieved to be with the side who won rather than in the other end where me and the crew would have been a major target.

Italy was the last one. They don't put them on TV in the order that they were shot. They start with the most interesting programme to get people hooked and go on from there.

Normally, I wouldn't watch a whole series of a show like that but I have to watch mine, because I do the voiceover on it. They send me the programme with the director's voice on it so I get a feel for it and then I come in and do it the next day. That's the only time I watch them. I didn't watch them when they aired. A fair few others were watching, though. Bravo were over the moon with the show because they were getting an audience of 500,000–600,000 people. That's a massive thing for them. It didn't sound a lot to me, but you have so many options if you've got Sky then to keep people interested for an hour just doesn't happen. It sold worldwide as well. I was in Norway recently, and they were showing the first series.

With the hooligans thing you are always under stress. I'd get up and I'd never know where I would be going or who we were meeting. And you'd have to trust these researchers and Zig Zag as an outfit to put me in situations that could be interesting, safe and that have some sort of structure within the story.

After those two series, I was done with it. I said to them, 'It ain't going to happen now. I appreciate the amount of money I earned out of this but no more.' I'd had to work my bollocks off for it and during this time I'd been receiving some death threats from different organisations, different hooligans abroad and in this country. There were some comments on my website asking how could I run around grassing people up. We didn't grass nobody up. We were totally upfront with people. Everyone who was filmed knew they were being filmed, and no one said anything that they didn't want to.

I explained the shit that was coming my way to Zig Zag and sat them down and said I was going to pack it in. I have kids and I'm not putting them in the firing line for all the money in the world. There was a 99 per cent chance that it was all complete bullshit, but it wasn't a chance I was willing to take. I'm not putting my family at risk, I couldn't bear the idea. So I knocked it on the head. I changed my numbers and everything solely so Zig Zag couldn't ring me up. I just didn't want the temptation. I didn't know, though, that Zig Zag weren't prepared to let me go that easily.

24

DEADLIEST MEN

Zig Zag were devastated when I turned them down. They were on a run with me; the show had earned them a decent amount of viewers and they thought it could run on and on, series after series. I ducked out, forgot about it and was cracking on with other jobs. It was around 2008 and I made about six films that year.

So one day there's a knock on the door to the flat in Canning Town and there is this kid standing there. I thought he was a fan or something. I asked him what he wanted and he said, 'Can you just open the box?' I said, 'What's in the box, mate?' He said I just had to open it. Now remember, at this time I've had a few people tell me they are going to do me. So I'm wondering what is in this box. He said, 'I'm not allowed to tell you, you just need to open the box.' He seemed like a sweet kid so I did open the box and there was a phone in it. He said, 'You've got to ring this number.' So I rung it and it was Peter Day, who was the producer at Zig Zag. They'd gone to these lengths to get me to talk to them. I was quite impressed by that. Peter said he wanted me to come in for a meeting, that he had this great idea. They'd had this kid knocking on my door for four days and I hadn't been in. I sort of laughed, but I was quite flattered.

So I went in and I sat down with them. I knew I held all the cards and could charge a serious amount of money for this one, whatever it was. I thought that if I could run around with hooligans all over the world, I could deal with anything, fuck it. So they put this idea to me: *Deadliest Men*.

The idea is I go out and meet the deadliest men in the country and find out what makes them tick. I wondered what they meant by 'deadliest men'. I was keen that if we were going to do this we shouldn't just go to villains. What is a deadly man anyway? Could be someone in the forces, could be a policeman. It was nice readies, a lovely bit of dough. It was going to be eight episodes, which I thought was milking it a bit. It was just me spending three days with these deadly men, listening to their stories, that sort of thing.

Again though, I knew it would have implications for my career. This is the second TV show I'd done that centred on hard men and so I'd be coming over like some sort of violence fetishist. Still, there are those moments in your career when you think of your family and the good things it could bring them. In the end the money was too good to turn down.

I'm going to go through a few of the deadly men, not all of them, for the same reason I didn't go through every football firm. If I leave someone out, it means nothing. These are just the ones that come to me while I'm writing, the ones that for some reason or another stuck in my mind or the ones I have something to say about beyond what was in the programmes. So no disrespect to anyone who doesn't get mentioned.

The first one we did was Stephen French. He was a shock

to me really though not in the way he looked. He's a big, fit-looking black guy, bald head, air of menace, an unmistakeable hard man, really. They found this guy because of the book he wrote, which was called *The Devil*, his nickname because of what he was capable of. He would run around taxing drug dealers, torturing them and getting money off them. Robbing them, essentially. He was clever and would only ever do people once, because if you back a man into a corner, and keep on pushing, what's he going to do? He was quite philosophical, this geezer. His whole thing started with the race riots in Liverpool, the black community coming together to stand up and be counted. He was part of that mob. Then he discovered kickboxing and went on to become the world champion. It seemed that anything he put his mind to he excelled in, and later in life that thing just happened to be taxing drug dealers. He was good at it.

Again, I'm back on home soil, half the job is done because he was a fan of mine, and he opened up to me a lot, which helped.

The first day is the most difficult. It's uncomfortable to be sitting in a car with a complete stranger with someone with a camera in the back looking at you. You feel you need to speak but you can sometimes find yourself lost for words, saying things for the sake of it and coming over as a twat. It's great when they just rabbit on, as some do, but some people, no matter how hard they are, just clam up when they get a camera in their face. And you can't blame them because they don't want to say anything to incriminate themselves.

Stephen, though, was chatty. He had gone through a big

conversion and now was all about trying to tackle knife crime, getting the kids off the street and telling them that crime is a mug's game. He's all about redemption and telling stories to the up-and-comers about things that have happened to him in the past, how a life of violence is nothing clever. On the surface he was a changed man. But then he would just flip out when he was talking passionately about something, and you could see the danger in his eyes.

Because he had written a book about his criminal life, a lot of these youngsters in Toxteth and Croxteth, fucking dangerous areas, view him as a grass. We interviewed a lot of the youngsters and they had the scarves disguising their faces and the pit bulls and all that. They were saying they were going to glass him. Maybe they will one day, but as far as I know the man's still walking the streets in one piece. He was an intelligent bloke and very careful about protecting his house. The amount of security he had there was unbelievable, CCTV, alarms, locks, vicious dogs – dogs you don't stroke.

It was an interesting one to start with because he did have a lot about him and I think we got on pretty well. I suppose the most talked about bit from the episode is where he tells me what he would have said to a drug dealer to get him to reveal where his money was. It didn't really do it for me, because obviously I knew he wasn't going to hurt me. All he said really was that he would chop my cock off and make me eat it. I mean, that's quite a horrendous thought, although I've been trying to nosh myself off for years, and I just can't do it.

Obviously, I heightened up my response for the cameras. If

he had me tied up and had been beating me for real then my response would have been a little different. But, like I said, I got on with the bloke and I had a camera crew there so I knew I wasn't in any danger.

In fact, the worst thing that happened to me on that show had nothing to do with him. I had a little moment when I was doing a piece to camera in Toxteth. A couple of Scouse kids came round the corner and said, 'It's that cockney cunt off *Hollyoaks*.' *Hollyoaks*! That was the nastiest thing anyone's ever said to me! Worse than being tear-gassed.

When I was with Stephen French I felt quite safe, it's when I wasn't with him it got a bit more dicey. Nothing really prepares you for walking around with a camera in Toxteth – it's not a good move – but we needed it for the film, for a backdrop. We got no real trouble but there was plenty of people shouting at us, plenty of intimidation.

It was a good one to start with because it was a bit more thoughtful than what was to come. A lot of people said that in *The Football Factory* documentaries we were glamorising violence, which we definitely weren't. If you're a normal guy, why you would watch the show and then say, 'I'd love to be part of that, I'd love to be raped up the arse by fifteen blokes'? I have no idea.

What we really needed was people who had lived it and had special stories to tell. You couldn't hold the audience's attention for a whole hour just talking to a straightforward thug with a few stories about some tear-ups down the pub. You needed people with real charisma.

Of course, there was a moral side to this whole thing. I

always had these little moments of guilt, because when they're talking about chopping someone's ear off or the big fight, I always had to bear in mind that there are victims involved.

What do the families of these victims think, while I'm walking around with this guy, with sexy music in the background and montage shots of me and him walking along the street? I can imagine, if it was one of my uncles or something that he'd tortured, I'd be royally fucked off.

The episode with the UDA guy took it to another level. I'm not told anything about these men before I meet them. So I'm waiting for him on the seafront and the crew tell me he's actually an exile, that he can't go back to Belfast because the paramilitaries have ordered him out. I know a lot of people think I put on some of the nervousness in the show, but that genuinely did throw me. Gangsterism's one thing, terrorism's quite another. These paramilitaries are a fucking army.

The bloke was Sam McCrory, an openly gay former paramilitary. He did seven years in the Maze Prison. I struggled to understand what he was talking about, because of his thick accent. He was a fan of mine, which did help. It's always easier with gay guys anyway in day-to-day life, because I quite like flirting with them. They seem to like flirting with me and I have a good relationship with them.

Skelly – Sam McCrory's nickname was Skelly – tried to wind me up quite a lot. There was a lot of banter between us and, to be honest, I felt a bit like a twelve-year-old girl around him, a little bit vulnerable and shy. For me, this episode wasn't just about the guy. It was actually about The Troubles. I knew nothing about them. I was aware there was something going on in Ireland, of course I was, I'd seen it on the news, but I never quite knew the ins and outs of it.

I never knew how this community of people became so divided, how a wall split Belfast on the Shankhill Road. It was a horrendous fact that these two communities that lived so close to each other had so much hatred towards each other that they needed a wall to separate them, that these gates would open for a couple of hours a day and once they shut, the people would be divided again. That wall is still there, though the gates are off it now. But the legacy of those times remains, the hurt, the pain that these people have gone through. You could almost feel it when we went there.

I found it amazing that they were brought up as children, to be told that's what you are – a Protestant or a Catholic – and you hate the other mob for whatever reason.

Skelly said to me that he remembers hating the Catholics and not quite knowing why, he just knew the hate was there. His big dilemma wasn't worrying about being killed by the IRA, it was that he was gay. Protestant, gay, paramilitary. Quite a mix. He had to hide that. I don't think he still feels like that today. He's a different man now.

He was the best friend and right-hand man of Johnny 'Mad Dog' Adair. This is Mad Dog Adair, the former Loyalist para-military leader. He's nearly been assassinated about twelve or fifteen times. He's had a bullet in his head and he's always got away alive.

Skelly told me about the moment when he came out to Mad Dog, who was absolutely fine about it. He said he thought he knew all along. After revealing that, though, he was always paranoid that someone was just going to take him out for the sake of it. So he would have to have the secret little liaisons with guys here and there. I found all that stuff much more fascinating than the violence. The guy now has his boyfriend and he goes to all the Mardi Gras rallies dressed up in all the pink gear – a complete turnaround.

Skelly came back to Belfast to help us film a little segment and he took us to a cemetery to talk about some friends he's lost. He introduced us to Mad Dog Adair, up where they both live in Ayr. Mad Dog is not a big bloke, though again he's a hard looking bastard, shaven head, muscles like Popeye and the full set of Loyalist tats. You could see he had a charisma about him, and why people wanted to follow him. I'm making no comment on his politics here, or what he's done. I'm just saying you could see how he got to be a leader, that he has a personal magnetism to him. I only spent an afternoon with him, and he was telling me about some of the assassination attempts he'd survived, which the others all found fucking hilarious. I couldn't understand what they were saying beyond a few sentences because they were talking a mile a minute in their Northern Ireland accents.

I had a couple of death threats after that programme went out which supposedly came from the IRA. I'd told Zig Zag that this would always be the problem with doing this sort of thing. They said that maybe we should do one on someone from the IRA as a balance. I was like, 'For fuck's sake no, let's not push our luck with it.' It was horrible to have the threats made against me but when I got to think about it, I realised that if it was the real IRA, I just wouldn't be around any more.

There wouldn't be any threatening about it, they'd just come and pop me off. I'm an actor, for fuck's sake, and I don't mind pretending a little bit, but when that kind of shit gets real, it doesn't exactly warm your heart.

For me, the focus of the programme was not the violence. All right, Skelly was with the UDA but surely having a deadliest man who is openly gay is the most interesting part of the film.

After Skelly we did Vic Dark, who was someone from my area. Again, Vic's another of these fellas who's never going to be mistaken for a social worker. He's another big bloke, only 5'9" maybe but about that wide as well, the shaved head, the Ralph Lauren sports gear. He looks what he is, a proper geezer. You could line ten blokes up naked and say, 'Which one is the armed robber?' and you'd pick him every time. He was brought up in Leytonstone, which is just a stone's throw from where I grew up. Now this guy was an old-school face. He's done a lot of bird. One of the things that got him sent down for a long time was that he decided to hold up this nightclub on his own, just because he was bored.

He was one of those fellas who needs an adrenalin rush. As a youngster he started to run with the ICF – the Inter City Firm – for a little while, but much as he enjoyed punching the fuck out of people, he couldn't see the point in it because he wanted to earn money out of violence. He was a getter, so he became an old-school bank robber. He'd run around with a sawn-off shotgun, and they'd hold up maybe three or four post offices a day.

He just liked the thrill of it, scoping the gaff first, sitting outside the post office, waiting to see when the security guard came in and out. It was all a game for him, really. And then one night he decided to just run into a nightclub and rob it. It went horrifically wrong and he shot a manager twice in the arm and in the leg. Then he took a police officer hostage and the cops chased him through London. It all spiralled out of control.

He was about fifty when I met him and he'd done twenty-one years of bird. So he's really used to the prison system and he's met everyone inside from Ronnie and Reggie Kray to Charles Bronson, and they all respected him. This guy, I loved him. I loved everything about him. I loved his warmth, I loved that he was another one who was going, 'Look how my life has ended up. I've got kids, I haven't seen them grow up, I'm fifty-odd, and I'm just getting my life on track. It's a mug's game, you're either going to end up dead or sitting in prison cells wanking for twenty-one years.'

I found him quite touching and he would get quite choked up. He would sometimes go on a rant about paedophiles and nonces because he had seen them on the inside. Obviously, he wasn't with them because they're segregated, but he would say, 'If they're going to give them eighteen months, why not put them on a normal wing, then the eighteen months will feel like eighteen years. Let them have the shit and the piss in their food. They rape and kill children.' That was the only time I really saw the fire in his eyes.

Other than that he was all about getting the kids off the streets and showing them that a life of violence and crime was not the way to go. So, I had a lot of time for Vic. I know he's hurt people, and I apologise to anyone who has read this book and thinks that I've got no considerations for the victims of his crimes. I do. I liked him as the human being he is now, not as the thug he was then. Also he's from my manor and we spoke the same language, so I never felt uncomfortable around him.

I enjoyed the three days with him. When Vic says he's sorry and he's trying to make up for it now, I defy anyone who says he's lying, because he isn't. I haven't spoken to him since the programme but I do wish him all the best because he was a lovely geezer.

I was pleased we didn't do all criminals or hooligans. Doing an episode on a policeman was a tense thing for me because I honestly didn't think I was going to get on with him. I thought a copper would be a stuck-up snobby bastard, just trying to condemn all villains and all criminals. The copper we chose, though, was the complete opposite. Peter Bleksley was an undercover copper. He's not someone that, coming from my manor, you're going to instantly fall in love with, because his whole career has been spent grassing people up. He's a man who gains someone's trust, eats at their house with their missus and then gets them banged up.

But this guy got so involved in the undercover thing that he lost who he really was and started to believe the character he was playing. He became a major coke addict. The coppers leave you to get on with it if you're undercover; you might not speak to someone from the police for three or four months at a go. You've got to integrate into these people's lives, and gain their trust.

This geezer had some charisma and nuts of the purest shiny stainless steel. He was also very honest. He lost his marriage and his kids because he didn't know whether he was coming or going. And it was fascinating to me because essentially he was acting, and I could relate to that. The difference between us was that if I get my dialogue wrong, I get another crack at it. At worst, I maybe get dug out by someone like Nick Love. Not for him. If he got his lines wrong, he got shot in the head.

He banged up some pretty dangerous people. His story was that he had to go into hiding because some senior copper had all these documents with information about his real identity, what he was doing, who he was trying to nick and who he was pretending to be and left them in his car. His car got stolen, and so Peter, bless him, was a marked man. He had just done a massive drug bust, sent some guys from a big heroin gang down, and this information got back to them. Obviously they came gunning for his blood.

He had to hide away and had no support from no one. That's when he hit the bottle really bad, because he was no longer a police officer. They were funding and giving him money but he was completely cut off. They put him in an old people's retirement home. He had to do that for six or seven months on his jack until it died down, supposedly. Although, in truth, he knows it will never die down.

You have to be a very rare breed to be able to deal with that.

I then went on to Spud – Nigel Spud Ely – who is ex-SAS. Now, right from the start he had plans for me. He now does close protection work, and the reasoning for this is that he went so far in the army that he couldn't really go any further. Promotion up the ranks would have meant tying him down to a desk job, and bureaucracy isn't an option for a person like Spud. Getting involved in protection work meant that he could do what he was good at, what he had been trained to do. Besides, he got accepted to the SAS, and did his time there, so where do you go after that? It's the elite of the elite.

Now this was quite an emotional one for me really, because this guy had some issues to deal with having come out of the army. I understand it's all about mental strength being a soldier but when you get out, things can come back to haunt you. When you've got time to think about the things you've done out in the field, the death and destruction you faced, it can bring even the hardest man to tears. If he was talking about military things and weapons, tanks, he was on it. He knows everything about everything. But when you start talking about personal things, he's slightly less comfortable.

I remember he made a point that more British soldiers died after the Falklands War, when they came home and killed themselves, than died during the conflict. That made me think about the pressure these guys are under. In the Falklands Spud had this moment when he dropped down into a trench, lost his weapon and then came across this Argentinean kid. It was kill or be killed and he had to improvise. The way he killed him was by head-butting him with his helmet on. He remembers the smell of the flesh when he killed the guy. Very harrowing.

The director wanted him to tell the story again because he

wanted to shoot it from a different angle but Spud wouldn't do it and I don't blame him, because it was such an emotional thing for him. He's another man who has lost his marriage and his children. You commit to those elite units and it can be tough on your personal life.

Anyway, like I said, he had plans for me. The crew and me got to the hotel the night before we were due to meet Spud and I had a few beers because it was a new director and I hadn't met him before. We ended up staying up really late. I bought a couple of packets of Scampi Fries – I do like a Scampi Fry – and I munched those just before I went to sleep. I woke up with this massive dose of heartburn, a terrible hangover, and I was not in the mood for filming, but I had to get on and get the job done. Anyway, we drive out to this deserted place and I'm not really taking anything in, I'm just concentrating on the raging hangover I've got and trying not to be sick.

Anyone who's seen the show will know that I walk up to Spud and everything's nice. He's at this fort and he says, 'Hello, Danny.' I say, 'Hello, Spud' and all of a sudden some people are shooting at me and he's screaming 'Get down get down!' He throws me to the floor, a car pulls up, he gets me and tosses me on the back seat with these shots ringing out around me and the car guns it out of there at top speed. Oh my word, I was all over the place.

Sometimes people think I ham it up on these first meetings, but I can tell you, it was all I could do not to throw up. If I look scared, then it's nothing to do with thinking I was going to get shot, it's to do with me thinking I was going to make a mess of the upholstery in the back of the car.

He was just trying to give me a glimpse into what he does now and how he would have protected me. His best way of protecting me right then would have been to give me an Alka Seltzer. Spud was very hands on, he wasn't very good at sitting down and doing the one-on-ones, he had to keep it active. Fair enough, he's a man of action, not words.

We did the one where he kitted me out in all the gas mask and stuff. As soon as I put it on I started panicking because I felt so claustrophobic. The idea was we would run around, jump over a few things, plot up and then run into this old building and he was going to throw CS gas in there. I don't know if you've ever put a gas mask on, but when I did, I felt like I couldn't breathe. In goes the CS canister but I just have to take the mask off because I feel like I'm suffocating. Spud was there screaming at me, 'Don't take that fucking mask off!' Luckily, the CS gas didn't go off, there was some kind of fault with it. I thought, 'These are superhuman people, who the fuck do I think I am to mince around in this gear?' You try that game after a skin full the night before. No fun, believe me.

So, because the CS gas didn't go off, he wanted me to experience what CS gas was like. I've had tear gas before, but this was different. It's like tiny shards of glass in the back of your throat. He was spraying it on the wall and sniffing it and saying, 'Come here, Dan, have a sniff.' I had to do it, to save face, and it was absolutely horrible. It doesn't last very long, but while it does you want to rip your own throat out. Spud, though, he does it for fun.

Again, I really did bond with this guy. I felt that by the end of the three days I'd got on well with him and he'd opened up to me. And that's a weird thing, because you become close to these people over the three days. And then that's it, you never see them again. At the end he gave me the pin from the CS gas canister that hadn't gone off as a souvenir.

It's weird, perhaps you'd like to remain friends with some of these blokes but you just don't. That's just how blokes are, I suppose. In some cases, though, it's a good move. Even though I've got on with the overwhelming majority of people that we covered on *Deadliest Men*, they ain't called the deadliest men for nothing. There is a price for entering into that world, because if you're seen as mates with someone, you can also pick up their enemies as well. With some other blokes we featured, that puts you into the orbit of pretty heavy geezers. I'd rather stay in my lightweight world.

With the boxer Bradley Walsh up in Edinburgh, who I'd already met on the *Football Factories* thing, the director wanted me to spar with him. I was like, 'Are you fucking mad? He's a professional boxer. Do you want to see me get bashed up?'

He said it would be great, that I'd be all nervous when I was meeting him and we'd be getting on but I'd know that by the end of it we were going to get into the ring together. I told them that I wasn't going to let them make me look like a complete twat.

I accept that, for the money, I'm sometimes going to look like a bit of a twat, someone who is ridiculously interested in violence, but there is a point at which I draw the line and that is pretending to think I'm hard enough to give Bradley a go in the ring. I mentioned this to Bradley, that they wanted us to spar, and he didn't like the idea one bit. He said, 'How dare you embarrass him and me?'

Bradley was a bit tricky this time around because he'd seen the *Football Factories* thing we did about Scotland. He wasn't that happy in the way that he'd been portrayed and he wanted to really put it right this time. So he was refusing to talk about most things, and he wanted to make the show about his gym and the work he did in the community. He talked a little bit about when he tried to take over the doors of the nightclubs at age seventeen, about ending up in prison, but the director was unhappy and was asking me to push him more. I told him to fuck off, I wasn't pushing Bradley nowhere. I said, 'He's bang on, I get on really well with him. All I'm willing to do is sit there and have a chat with him. If you want more out of him ask him yourself. Don't make me the bad guy.'

We only had a couple of days together but I got a few things out of him. And then I had to go and do the next one. They came back and filmed him again three months later to try and get some more stuff. The irony is that his episode got the most viewers of anyone, because he spoke about his childhood and his mum, who was very charismatic. He's an interesting character, and he holds the screen without having to talk that much about violence. And he's funny as fuck. Whether the viewing figures are down to the Scottish mob backing him up or not, I don't know, but there was a point at which Zig Zag thought they would have to cut it and do a 'best of' for the eighth episode. They stuck with him and they turned up gold.

Going into the second series, we did *Deadliest Men: Living Dangerously*. Again, I asked for more money, because this time they wanted me to stay at these hard men's houses, to sleep there. To be honest, I thought the idea was bollocks. I said, 'What do you want me to do? Hide under a quilt, pretending to be scared that he's going to come in and kill me? It's bullshit.' They sold it to me by saying that it was more about me trying to get into the blokes' shoes as much as I possibly could.

The first one we did was Paddy Doherty, the gypsy guy. Of all the people we covered, he's the one I would least like to tangle with. No disrespect to anybody else at all, because everyone apart from the fraudster we covered in this series could chew most blokes up and spit them out, certainly me included. The difference with Paddy is that he might chew you up but he definitely wouldn't spit you out.

He talked about the organised gypsy fights, the 'clean go', where there's at least some idea of rules, and the 'dirty go', where there definitely fucking ain't. Basically, in the dirty go, Paddy used to, in his own words. 'Eat you up like a Rottweiler' – that is, bite chunks out of his opponent's face and swallow them in order to disfigure him. He didn't want to spit a bit of nose onto the floor because there'd be a chance it could be sewn back on.

Now this makes him sound like a completely nasty fucker, which I'm sure he is if you get on his wrong side, but he was sweet with me. He's a genial bloke, the governor on their site, a sort of father figure for everyone. He makes sure all his nieces and nephews go to school, he won't have rubbish on his site, no drugs. He's got a great chalet as well, like the White House, really plush. But he oozes violence and, I'm not going to lie, he scared the living shit out of me.

He's quite a character, a force, no mistake. They were a law unto themselves, the gypsies, and if I was going to live on their site I was going to play by their rules. It was a fascinating insight into their world. We're known as country people or gorge. They don't want to know us really; none of their kids would ever marry a gorge. They have their own way of doing everything. If they have a dispute with each other they have a tear up to settle them. What really got me was the love they have for their kids and that their kids have for them. Their kids are quite aggressive, running around hitting each other over the head with sticks and stuff, but you know they'd die for each other. In a way you're a bit jealous of not being involved in such a tight-knit community like that, but you'd never be accepted into it. They look after each other, they don't go to the police and they don't go to hospitals. It's such an old-school way of life. Paddy said the day of the traveller moving from place to place has gone, that went out with the dinosaurs – those were his exact words. Now they have a little plot, where they live, bring up their kids, keep animals.

The most random thing was that Paddy was related to Shane Ward, who won *The X Factor*. That was a surreal thing, sitting in this pub on a Manchester estate with Shane on one side and Paddy on the other. In the episode I look like I'm shitting it in that pub and I bloody am. I was one cockney in a pub full of Mancs with only Paddy there to protect me. All right, he can have it and no mistake, but there were about 150 of them in that pub and the atmosphere was nasty.

Mind you, Paddy is an intimidating fucker and when we met him the next day he was right as rain. It hasn't always been the case. He was once shot in the head. He said that when the guy who has the gun in his hands is more scared than you, you know you're going to be all right. I have no idea how you can read a situation like that. It was just a smack-head somebody had sent to do the dirty on him. He came out of a coma after two weeks and straight away wanted to do a dirty go with the guy who had called it on him. But the bloke disappeared, never heard from again. Wise move, I'd say.

This was my first time living with one of these blokes and, though they couldn't have made me more welcome, I found it tough – you have to give a lot more of yourself in these one-on-ones than you do when you're just meeting different hooligans all the time.

Living with a family you don't know is a bit weird, no matter how welcome they make you. It's like you're on your best behaviour for three days straight. And although Paddy was a really friendly bloke, it's always at the back your mind who he is and if, for whatever reason, he takes against you, you are royally fucked. Anyone who thinks that someone like Paddy would think twice about giving you a clump just because you're on the telly, or that you happened to be filming him, has clearly never met the bloke. And the same goes for most of the blokes about him.

All this said, Paddy and his family were very good to me and it was an incredible experience. The horse fair at Appleby I went to was something I could never have seen any other way. That was an amazing event, watching the geezers race their horses up and down the road, just so many gypsies in one place.

So it was on to the rest of the series, where we met some fascinating blokes. But by this time, I'm just doing it for the money really. The shows all started to become too similar, the same beginning, middle and end. It starts with me shitting my pants wondering about if I'm going to get on with this guy, if he's going to be all right with me. Then I meet them. We're a bit awkward with each other, then we start learning about each other and by the end, we're best pals, patting each other on the back. Like I said, I met some amazing people, I'm proud of every show and I think they're interesting individually but I was just getting bored with the format of it. It was becoming predictable.

I knew I was flogging a dead horse now. I was on episode twenty-six of this hard-man thing, and it was starting to wear me down. I couldn't wait to get the last series over with. It was just the whole process of it, being away from the family, trying to keep things sweet with the subject while having a director yakking in my ear. I'd had enough.

Zig Zag sensed it was coming to an end and were doing their best to get their money's worth out of me. We did identical twins, the Butlin brothers, who were kick-boxers. I had to meet these two in the middle of the Moors up north. I've got no idea who I'm meeting, so I'm waiting, waiting, waiting there and then all of a sudden I see two twins walking towards me with shotguns.

Dave Butlin was the better fighter of the two but he had a car accident that put him out of the game so he started to train and manage his twin brother Ian. He and Ian were very different. Dave was intense, very focused; Ian was a bit more laid-back, doesn't quite have the same drive as his brother. Dave was solemn and didn't want to smile, whereas Ian was happy-go-lucky, and bit of a womaniser. The dynamic between them was very interesting and could almost have made a movie in itself. I'm sure they love each other but there was a tension at the heart of their relationship. Dave expected Ian to go off and fulfil his dreams for him; Ian was game for that up to a point but, fair play to the man, he liked a beer now and again too.

They told me this story about how Ian went on a bender when he should have been training for a fight, and Dave went looking for him and found him in someone's house. He was so angry with him that he gave him a clump and broke his jaw. I thought that if me and my brother had a fight like that and he broke my jaw, I'd never talk to him again.

This was just natural behaviour between the pair of them. I tried to train with Ian for while – like I said, Zig Zag wanted their pound of flesh on this one – but fuck me, was it hard work. I went to Dave's house to have a bit of rabbit stew and straight from there I went to do the circuit training, where I threw up. You can see perhaps why kick-boxers don't chow down on a bunny before getting into the ring.

I tried to be sick on the sly, to nip out the back, but I had a radio mike on and they heard it and shot around there to film me coughing rabbit out of my nose. Next thing I had to do was go jump off an eleven-metre diving board with Ian, because he'd always been afraid of heights. It didn't occur to me until I got up there that I'm bloody afraid of heights too. You might think eleven metres doesn't sound too bad but when you're looking down at that tiny swimming pool from up there, you do have a moment. I did it because I didn't want to lose face but I can't say I'll be rushing to repeat the experience.

With my next deadliest man, I gave the people who hate me a right treat when I got smacked in the mouth by a bloke who's had the practice. Mo Teague was a mercenary, he's been in the services and he's been a bouncer. He came out of the army, didn't know what the fuck to do with himself, but was still a fighting machine. He decided to become a bouncer because he thought it was a legal way to crack skulls, which of course it isn't – you're there to prevent trouble.

He found himself starting fights because he wanted to have tear ups. This man is built like a barrel, a round awkward object. He teaches a weird martial art called Jeet Kune Do, but if you want to be taught it you have to feel pain. Zig Zag, surprise, surprise, wanted him to demonstrate a few things on me so I said, 'OK, I'll do it.'

He started throwing me around a bit, showing me how to put someone on the floor using their head and twisting your fingers. And then he said that he would show me the one-inch punch. Now I've heard of the one-inch punch from Bruce Lee movies, and seen demonstrations of him doing it in black-and-white, grainy footage. He does it to a guy's chest and the guy goes flying across the room and you think, 'Hmm, that might be bullshit.'

So for those of you who've seen this on YouTube – and it had a fair few hits, rather too many for my liking; I suspect some of you might be enjoying it – you'll know what I'm talking about. Now, the camera crew knew what was coming, so he must have discussed it with them first, because they set up the camera in two places – one behind my head, and one from the side. They wanted to do it in slow motion, so you could see my head ripple back. He told me to shut my mouth and clench my teeth together and before I knew it, he clocked me. I remember the noise, this big pop. Now of course he could have hit me a lot harder and knocked me spark out but, bloody hell, it hurt enough the way he did it. I fronted it and tried to make it look like I hadn't felt it, but I hated him at that moment, really hated him.

He demonstrated the rest on this kid who was helping him, and the kid was covered in blood by the end of it. There was a part of me that was thinking, 'You love pain. You love inflicting it.' But on the other hand, I could see his theory, that if you want to protect yourself against pain, you need to know what it is. I've got another theory, though. If you want to protect yourself against pain, don't stand in front of Mo Teague and say, 'Go on then, do what you like.' When him, or anyone like him, shows up and says 'let me show you this technique', do one out of there before you've copped it on the jaw and all the little lights are dancing about your eyes.

Mo was all right, though, I got on well with him despite the fact he'd punched me in the face. And I had asked for it, literally. If you say, 'Smack me in the gob with the famous one-inch punch,' you can't really complain when it happens. But Mo was a really decent fella, and he later sent me a chimnea – a clay barbeque you can put out in the garden – which I thought was a lovely little touch.

I finished *Deadliest Men* and was glad to be done with it. I had time for everyone I met on it and there were some guys I really respected for trying to put stuff back to make up for what they'd taken out. Elijah Kerr, who used to be in the Peel Dem Crew in South London, for instance, doing his best to set the kids around him on the straight and narrow. I met mad characters like Dave McMillan, the drug smuggler and the only bloke ever to escape from the Bangkok Hilton prison, Dominic Negus who had one flash of temper fighting Audley Harrison and headbutted him, ruining his own career, Barrington Patterson from the Zulu Warriors, everyone we covered on the show. They were proper geezers and I liked them all.

However, I felt I'd become trapped in the hard-man image or, worse, the image of someone who sucks up to hard men.

My next foray into documentaries was something I was much more interested in than violence: UFOs. Instead of big angry men I was moving to little green men and I couldn't have been happier. I was about to fulfil a lifetime ambition and see a UFO. I definitely saw one, no question. I clocked a UFO and it was one of the best experiences of my life.

25

NO DOUBT ABOUT IT

I was quite surprised when I got summoned by the BBC. Now I've done a few bits and bobs for them but not that much. So when they said they wanted to meet me to discuss a project with them I was intrigued. I thought it would have something to do with acting. As it turned out, it was another presenting thing.

I went to a meeting with these two birds. I sat down with them and one said to me, 'How do you feel about UFOs?' I thought it was a mad question, but the funny thing is, I've always been fascinated by UFOs. She said, 'We watched you on *Never Mind the Buzzcocks* and we thought you would be right for this.' They said some flattering stuff about liking my style, thinking I was witty and relaxed. Even though you know they're blowing smoke up your arse, it does make you feel good.

I told them that I thought I'd seen something as a kid, it was probably nothing but I did think I saw something. I'd been over the park playing football late on my own when I saw this light in the sky. We lived really near to City Airport but you never saw the planes because of the smog. So I saw this light hovering in the sky. I know it was probably a plane but, as a kid, it scared me and I ran home quickly, thinking

I might have seen a UFO. It set up an interest in that sort of thing that has lasted my whole life. I always watch *Star Trek Voyager* and things like that too, things that aren't all that cool, but fuck it. I like them, so I'll watch them.

They wanted me to go on some sort of journey to see whether there is life out there. I'm not big-headed enough to think that I'm going to answer a question that's been perplexing the finest minds – and a few not-so-fine minds like my own – throughout human history but I thought this could be a good move for me. The only presenting and documentaries I'd done around that time were about violence, about hooligans and hard men, me being on the edge of my seat saying, 'Fuck me, this geezer's a lunatic, isn't he?' This was the chance to show another side of myself.

Not everyone who comes out the East End is a violent criminal. Some of us are quite nice, or try to be. This was a chance to show me as I really am – a bit of a big kid, really, so I signed up.

We started by going to see Sir Patrick Moore, which was a major thrill for me. I've always looked up to him and been intrigued by him. His intelligence, his curiosity, and his affection for everything space-related – people like him are a real inspiration. The thing about smoking dope from an early age is that you watch a lot of late night TV. I'd watched an awful lot of *The Sky At Night* and it was a thrill to meet the man himself.

We had to drive out of his place. He lived in this fucking mansion. As you go up his drive he's got this enormous telescope in his garden, with the dome and all that. Fantastic stuff, right up my street. I fucking loved it.

Again, it's all over-the-shoulder camera work but much less stressful. It's a different vibe for me, I don't have to worry that someone will come and bundle me into a car. Sir Patrick Moore is very unlikely to nut me. I was more confident as a presenter by this time so I was really looking forward to it. I knocked on the door of his house and this lovely young girl answered the door, aged about twenty. She showed me through and there he was sitting in his office with all trinkets everywhere, with signed photos from the Queen and major figures from all over the world. He's eighty-six, and seems to have it sorted to me. He was sitting there in his chair, watching the cricket and drinking wine while this young girl ran about after him. Not a bad life at all.

They gave me a list of questions for him. But my only question was, 'Is there life out there? You're someone who has been studying the stars for very many years. What do you think?'

He said he didn't know if we were being visited by aliens, but there was definitely life out there. He broke it down for me and said that for every grain of sand on the earth there are one million stars. I thought if you put it like that there has to be, it's arrogant for us to think we're the only ones here. It's also a pretty depressing idea to think that we're the most intelligent things in the whole universe, given the state of the place.

Sir Patrick is an old fella and we couldn't take up too much of his time so it was a short visit. But he gave me a book, which I have indoors now. His mother was an artist and she'd draw aliens and space ships in the 1920s or '30s. He signed it, and I thought that was a really sweet gesture of him.

He was the first Sir I'd ever met, and it was just brilliant to be around someone who is that intelligent and who'd been a hero of mine from a young age.

The next stage for me was the crop circle thing. This was the biggest revelation, because I did come across a lot of bollocks, things that you think, 'Come on, man, this is just too far-fetched, I want it to be true but I just can't believe it. It's like a cartoon.'

We went to this crop circle. I walked into the middle of it and it's a fascinating thing, because the wheat is not laid flat, the stalks are all tangled round each other. I actually did meet these guys who have done crop circles themselves. They do it three- or four-handed in the early hours of the morning, using a bit of wood with a rope attached and they stamp the crops down. All that does is flatten the wheat, it doesn't twist it.

The crop circles they do are simple things too. These guys are pretty chilled out, hippie types. They're not saying that aliens don't do crop circles either, they're just saying it is possible for humans to do them.

But I can't believe three pissed hippies with a plank could have done all of them. I went in one that was 1,500 metres long, that's a ridiculous size for blokes just to do on their own. I was shown this wheat, which wasn't broken. When you make a circle with the wood you snap the stem of the plant, basically kill it. The ones I saw weren't killed, they were still growing. And there's not one mistake in the pattern. Every time I open a newspaper and I see another one of these intricate designs I think, 'Why the fuck is it not a message from up there?'

I met this guy who's absolutely dedicated to the idea of crop circles, no missus, no kids. He's spent about thirty grand on the equipment to film it. He showed me footage of one actually happening. He was a fucking lunatic, this geezer. I liked being around him, though. He sets these cameras up and sits there filming all night, filming fuck all really. He showed me this film he has: there's a shot of this field, there's lightning going on or something and you slowly see these indentations forming in front of your eyes. It can't be a trick of the camera. He didn't give us that footage because he thinks he's going to do something with it himself. He's also adamant something very big is going to happen soon with the alien mob. I don't know whether it's something that ties into 2012 with the Mayan calendar, all that bollocks.

When I was doing it, I'd switch off and think, 'This is bollocks, actually,' and then something would happen that would drag me back into it. Unfortunately the night I spent with him nothing happened. I sent one of the runners to get us some beers and I just lay around getting pissed. He had these night-vision binoculars and I was lying on the floor, staring out with those just feeling spacey. It was a long night, and it was quite disappointing.

I then went to America and, obviously, the Americans have to take it to the next level, don't they?

We were only there for four days and I was pretty jetlagged. The crew were a good bunch of kids, but I didn't really have that much in common with them, so I was sort of on my own. None of them believed in UFOs so I didn't have anyone to talk to about it and nobody was as excited as me. They were just there to make a documentary. First of all we went to this guy called Stan Romanek. He's the number one alien abductee in America. Poor bastard.

This geezer had a fascinating story. He said he had been abducted over a period of nine years starting in 2000. He claims hundreds of alien contacts.

Stan Romanek believes that aliens will choose you as a child. They are not there to harm you, but they will come back to visit you in later life. He remembers being a kid and sitting on a swing. This woman came up and sat next to him on the swing and he remembers she had these massive beautiful blue eyes. She said to him, 'You're a very special little boy.' He then saw her again when he was coming out of the shopping mall with his mum and dad. The woman came up to his mum and dad and said, 'You know you've got a special little boy there.' And they said, 'We know that', and she said, 'If you want me to take him off your hands, I will.' It was a jokey sort of thing.

When people in later life claimed to have been abducted, they all reported the same experience of having a strange woman with big blue eyes, or a strange man, come up to them when they were children. They all got together and remembered that this woman never opened her mouth once when she spoke. That gave me a little tingle up my spine that story, it's quite a mad idea that they would come and visit you and then come and take you later on.

I sat in this guy's house for over four hours, looking at all this stuff he's got. For instance, they found an implant in his hip, this strange thing that he went to the doctors about. They took it out, and they'd never seen anything like it, they had no explanation for it. He took it away with him and he said to his missus, 'Just hide that.' And she did, she hid it in the back of a stereo player. But they kept hearing this whistling through the back of the speakers. He took it out and it had changed colour. He said this thing, in front of his eyes, just broke in half. He was frightened about going to anyone because he thought he was going insane himself. He gets strange phone calls, these messages from somebody with a mad computer-type voice that warns him of things. He's got a missus and twin daughters, and it's either true or they're all in on it and they're fucking brilliant actors.

It goes two ways, it's either complete bollocks, or it's real. Only he knows that, there's no grey area. The thing that fucked me off about him was that he wanted $50,000 to show the most convincing alien. He said it was time to tell his story, he said he gets followed by helicopters, he said he's been bashed up by the army for no reason. But then he wants a load of money, which makes me think he isn't interested in telling the story at all, it's all about the money.

After that I went to a hippie commune in California, where I did see my UFO. This is the place that Robbie Williams famously went to. Anyone can go and stay there. Their idea is that you have to be quite spiritual and to open your mind to understand what's going on when you see these things. The BBC wanted me to sit round and meditate with these people, and I was quite worried about that. I thought the documentary was just going to be me standing around on a load of hills.

I didn't really get into the meditation side of it. There was one girl next to me sobbing her heart out while she was doing it and another guy laughing hysterically. A bit strong, I thought.

Obviously, when you close your eyes for a while you go in to yourself. You just start thinking shit, which is why, when you've been doing it for twenty minutes, you've got some mad voice in your earhole. You're always going to come out of it feeling a bit weird, but I certainly didn't think it took me to a spiritual level.

Still, it was a very chilled-out vibe. I brought a crate of beer with me, but none of them drank. I nipped out into the forest and had a crafty drink, and it was a very relaxing place, right under this enormous mountain called Mount Adams.

The guy who organised the commune told me that they saw UFOs every night. I was like, 'So you're telling me that tonight I am going to see a UFO?' And he was like, 'Yeah, no doubt.'

So I was surrounded by all these chilled-out people, they had all got their kids with them, some of the kids were called things like Orion, there were these little dogs running around. It was a nice vibe, actually.

We go outside to look out for these UFOs and the main guy's got this laptop that shows you where all the satellites in the world are, so we can absolutely rule out that it's one of those. You watch when the planes come over, because they're on a flight path and they always take the same route across the sky.

The BBC crew are sitting around, they think it's going to be a load of bollocks. And then, amazingly, incredibly, as the night goes on, you see this massive light in the middle of the mountain about halfway up. Now it could be that a geezer has gone up this mountain with the brightest fucking torch in the world and he's shining it but I don't believe they'd go to those lengths.

The top boy said, 'You're very lucky tonight, the mountain's opened, that doesn't happen every night.' I was quite mesmerised by it all actually. And then, I saw a UFO! All a UFO is is an unidentified flying object, something you can't explain. And I certainly couldn't explain this. It was like a massive star in the sky. You're looking at it and it starts to move. It changes direction and then goes up and goes past another thing that looks like a star and that starts to move too. They said sometimes the UFOs like to play with each other. That was not an aeroplane or a helicopter or a shooting star, definitely not. It absolutely did my nut in.

I finished the documentary just as confused as when I'd begun. What was it over that mountain? It was some experience, a real moment for me. I really do feel that stuff is going on out there. The BBC crew were quite freaked out because they'd seen it as well.

I'm now in the UFO world, like it or not. I must get about twenty letters a week from UFO nuts. I get drawings, I get people who want me to join a group, I get pictures that people have taken. I quite enjoy it, actually. Maybe it'll become more obvious to us in the future some time. There's definitely aliens out there, the issue is whether they can be fucked to come and see us, whether they look on us as like little ants.

All in all the UFO thing was a positive experience for me. I do get grief now and again from people shouting, 'Seen any aliens, Dan?' Obviously that doesn't bother me and I even find it quite funny as long as it doesn't happen too often every day.

But UFOs are a personal thing for me. I was really moved by seeing the lights over Mount Adams. Whatever they were they made a beautiful and eerie sight. That alone was worth doing the documentary for, and I feel blessed to have seen it.

26

NEVER MIND THE BOLLOCKS, HERE'S DANNY DYER

Nothing sharpens you up as an actor like the theatre. It's an unforgiving place where your mistakes are there for all to see and the only way to deal with that is not to make any.

I was asked to do a play called *Kurt and Sid* about Kurt Cobain and Sid Vicious. I've always wanted to portray someone, a real person. I look at actors like Michael Sheen and they've had this rare career where much of what they do is portray real people. It's a skill, not exactly an impression, but just catching the essence of someone. I buzzed off the idea of that.

So when I got the chance to play Sid Vicious I jumped at it. Sid was an enigma. He was called Sid Vicious, not because he was vicious, but because he was the main attraction in a band where he couldn't play an instrument and he couldn't sing. He was hedonistic, loved to lose the plot on drugs, he had this real couldn't-give-a-fuck attitude. He had a great look, but there was something more than a look that made him magnetic. He was a unique spirit and it's up to anyone portraying him to capture that.

I did a lot of research for this one and found out a lot about Sid. Half the time they'd take the plug out of his bass so he didn't even know that he wasn't playing. He'd stand there on the stage and cut himself, abuse the audience, but you couldn't take your eyes off him. He does what a rock star is meant to do onstage – he generates excitement.

I think I was destined to play him because when I was quite young, I must have been eighteen, before *Human Traffic*, these American producers came over. They were going to make a movie called *Pretty Vacant* and they wanted me to play Sid Vicious. Chloe Sevigny was going to play Nancy Spungen, Sid's girlfriend. It was basically about the Sex Pistols' last tour, which was a fuck up, a long and unpleasant journey of drugs, backbiting and recrimination. It finished with that famous line from Johnny Rotten in San Francisco: 'Ever get the feeling you've been cheated? Goodnight.'

San Francisco, which was rife with heroin – or brown as it's known – was the worst place for Sid, as he was bang on drugs. I was so into this role I was even thinking of having a little dabble on the brown. Now that's something I've never done, but I did consider giving it a go just so I could act it properly.

I was so young and impressionable and wanting to get the part right but I thought I couldn't do it unless I had a little taste of that drug. Now that's a bad move, I would not advise anyone to do that, but that's where my mind was at the time. I was so excited by this film, driving everyone mad talking about it and then the rug was just pulled out from underneath my feet.

I was all ready to go. I'd done my research, though I hadn't met Chloe yet, and then this Hollywood strike happened, the Screen Actors' Guild strike. Everything just shut down and they pulled the plug on the film. They just cancelled the whole thing. I was absolutely devastated; it could have been a great opportunity for me.

Then about three or four years later, I get given this script called *Kurt and Sid*. It was a two-hander between Sid Vicious and Kurt Cobain. A producer wanted to try and get it off the ground, so we did a reading of it, me and another actor. This is quite a common thing. You read a script in front of people who might invest in the play. Sometimes when you do these readings, and I did a lot of them as a kid, they'll use you for the reading and then they'll fuck you off and get another actor for the role.

So I did it and it was a hilarious piece, I remember everyone was laughing. It was at the Old Vic. I thought it had gone really well, but then I never heard another thing.

Then, out of the blue, last year I got a phone call that they wanted to put it on. I don't know whether it was because my career gone to a point where putting me in a play would sell it but I was amazed they'd come back, I'd forgotten all about it. My dream had come true, because at the age of thirty-one or thirty-two it was my last chance to play Sid. Sid died at twenty-one, he was a young gun. I was like, 'Sign me the fuck up.' Now I hadn't done a play for a while, and I was nervous about it because I'd had my worst experience onstage, when I dried up. The fear of that feeling was still there, of feeling so lost and thinking I'm in the wrong game. You've got to remember this is two actors onstage, an hour and a half, dialogue rattling back and forth. There is nowhere to hide. At least when I dried in the Pinter I had the chance to go offstage and get my head together. From the moment you walk out in *Kurt and Sid*, apart from the interval, you're out there. This was a real test for me as a human being and an actor.

I knew the massive thing would be who's going to play Kurt Cobain. That happened to be an actor called Shaun Evans, a Scouse kid. He was in a mini-series called *The Take*, which I turned down. That turned out to be a wrong move, because it was a good programme.

I met Sean and I thought that it was very important that we got on. This is the sort of play that can turn into two actors having an 'act off' onstage. It could be a competitive thing but that would ruin it. We had to get on, have a bond up, a man up, if you like, say to each other, 'Listen, man, this is me and you together, let's get out there and help each other, if one of us comes unstuck the other one has to be there for him.' Luckily Shaun is as good as gold and we got on really well and started to bounce off each other.

We only had a three-week rehearsal period. That was a worry. But I got more and more confident with it as the rehearsal went on. I learned the dialogue really well, and I watched *The Filth and the Fury* just to get the feel for Sid's character again.

The idea of the play was that it's set just before Kurt Cobain blows his brains out in the attic. Kurt Cobain would sit in this attic and he would get his daughter's dolls and cut them up and make scenes with them, stick three heads on one doll, cut one up so it had a womb in it. He was a weird guy, fucked in the head.

The idea is that he's had his last hit of smack before he's killed himself and this is his last smacky dream. So I'm Kurt's idea of what Sid Vicious would be like. I'm very articulate, I speak Latin, and I'm there to convince him not to kill himself. It's a debate between me and him. It's a funny piece, but it's also very dark, two raving smackheads sitting there having a heart to heart before one of them tops himself.

You have to remember that Sid Vicious killed himself, and maybe killed the person he loved – Nancy. I don't think he did, but there was a possibility. He couldn't have hurt a fly but when you're smacked off your head, you don't know what you're doing. In *The Filth and the Fury* there are these amazing scenes where he's so smacked up, he's burning Nancy who's sitting next to him and he doesn't even notice it. The dialogue for this was tough to learn and I could only do certain segments with my normal soundboard Dani, because some of the stuff that is coming out of my mouth is filth.

I was very nervous every night. It was at the Trafalgar Theatre, which is a very small space – it only holds about a hundred people. It was almost like going back to the medieval days, like being in a barn, you might as well chuck some straw on the floor. It's a lot harder doing a play in that environment than it is in at 2,000- or 3,000-seater. At least you have that detachment. Here you can hear someone raise a glass, ice clinking, another person coughing.

I was shitting myself every night. It never changed, even after I nailed it on the press night. I'd never understood actors who get up before a play and do their warm-ups. They go on the stage, and they need that half an hour in the dark with their shoes and socks off, humming and doing these mad voice exercises. I just feel like a prick doing that. My way of preparing is to sit there with a copy of the *Sun* in front of me, a fag and a cup of coffee. In this play I felt that I needed to get into it a lot more, to try a bit of that warm-up stuff myself. I slowly became Sid Vicious as I put the costume on, started adapting his mannerisms, his way of always falling about the place, holding one shoulder higher than the other, that sneer he always wore, arrogant but charismatic.

We did thirty shows in twenty-five days, and it was great for my fans to get to see me doing something like that. They'd only ever see me doing Pinter before and they didn't understand Pinter, they just didn't get it. This was something they could really see me being what I'm known for, a bit of a bad boy, a bit reckless. We sold out and it was a huge success.

I fucked up twice in the whole run; that is, I jumped a couple of lines. I had a couple of moments where I didn't know the line and it just came to me on the point I thought I was going to dry up. That's quite a weird feeling, like you just hear the line yourself, almost like you're not saying it. I was proud of myself to have done this play. It picked up great reviews and got put up for an award.

However, at the end of it I was fucked, my family life was suffering because you do eight shows a week and only get Sunday off, it's a weird existence when you do a play, because you don't do the show until evening. So what do you do? You can't go for a drink, your kids are at school, you want to sleep as much as you can because you want to remain alert for the evening. I was missing dinner with the kids, missing bath time and bedtime. It was a struggle and I know Joanne struggled with it. Also, I'm playing Sid Vicious, which does get to you after a bit. Good job I didn't go method round it and start slashing my arms in front of the telly.

On my Sunday off the family want me to do things to make up for a week of not being around. I can't do that; all I'm thinking about is Monday. I don't read the lines again on Sunday, once the show has started I never look at the script. You have to get rid of the script at some point because the more you get used to having that in your hand, the more you come to rely on it. I don't want that script anywhere near me during the run, that's for the rehearsal process. You have to trust yourself.

It was great working with Shaun, he's a terrific actor. The tragic thing is they wanted to do it again but they wanted to get rid of Shaun and use some bloke who had been in *Hollyoaks* and in *Dancing on Ice* just to get some teenagers in. I said, 'No, I'm not doing it unless Shaun's in it, because half the job's done that way.' I wouldn't disrespect Shaun like that.

I think they assumed I was going to do it because they offered me more money but theatre's never been about money for me, it's about honing your craft and getting out there and testing yourself.

I still feel you should get paid a lot more for theatre then you do for film. Film, you get twenty goes at it; theatre, you get one shot. That's what makes theatre exciting but scary too. I would love to do more of it but the money makes acting onstage an indulgence rather than a living.

So, as I tie up this book, what about the years to come? Where do I go from here? Well, as I write I'm going to America to do a film called *Guns of the Dead*. Now this is well out of my comfort zone, because I have to do an American accent. When you're acting in your own accent then all you have to think about is the performance, but a different accent adds another dimension to it. I'll spend a couple of weeks with a voice coach first and a voice coach will be with me on set. If he or she feels something's not quite right, then they'll come up and have a little word. I'm a perfectionist, so I'd rather have it locked down so I don't have to worry about it.

It's great to get a run of work now. I've been skint for most of my adult life. I started when I was fourteen and I had a good run as a child actor, but most of my career I've had no money, and it's been a struggle. The last four or five years I've got on to a real roll and finally I got a bit of clout in the business. Putting my face on the cover of the DVD sells a certain amount so I've not auditioned for a British role in two years. I get offered a lot of stuff and can green-light a film just by saying I'll be in it. That's a privileged position, I'm very aware of that, and I'm determined not to make a dog's arse of it.

The future will be about making the right decisions. Being an actor is such an insecure job and you go for so long not knowing where your next pay cheque's coming from, all of a sudden when people are throwing scripts at you left, right and centre, you say, 'Yeah, yeah, yeah. I'll do it' because you want to earn. And you learn eventually that that's not a very good move. I've been in one or two films that I'd rather forget. Plenty I want to remember too, but it's about choosing the films that I and other people will want to recall and recognising the ones that aren't so hot before I see my face on the DVD cover in a shop.

Sometimes I can feel angry about the way I've been used and my fans have been treated. I suppose it's naive really but it never used to occur to me if I did some little bit in a film that they'd stick my face on the film poster and the cover of the DVD as if I was the main actor in it. I did a movie recently called *Just For The Record*. I did it as a favour to a friend and also because I was playing a posh producer, so I got an opportunity to change my accent. In the film I had a slicked back hairdo, a pencil moustache, I looked like Clark Gable, but they put me on the cover with a shot out of *The Football Factory*. I've got stubble and they're trying to sell it on that hard gritty image. It fucked me off. I can see why the distributors do it – because they want to get their money back and they need to sell a certain amount of DVDs. People like me in the tough stuff so the punters see me looking a bit moody on the cover and buy it thinking it's going to be a film about gangsters and it's not. It's the complete opposite and sometimes I'm hardly in the movie. So they're left feeling cheated. But that's the way the game works. At the end of the day, it's all about money and figures.

I'm not interested in directing or producing or anything like that, I love acting too much. I come in the morning, do it, smash it hopefully, and then fuck off. I don't want to get involved in the rest of it. The idea of being an executive producer, which I've had offered to me a few times, is too much on the brain.

In this game, you really have to watch out for bullshitters.

I did one film, which I won't name, but it never came out. This director approached me and told me he'd got the next *Da Vinci Code* on his hands. I liked his energy, the script was a bit confusing but I trusted he could sort that out. The second we started filming it became apparent that the director was a complete prick. He was walking around with a cap with 'Captain' written on it and it was also clear to me that he was a raging alcoholic. I also found out that a lot of villains had put money into the film. He offered me a quarter of a million quid to do it, which turned out to be bollocks. After six weeks of filming, he had forty minutes of footage, he couldn't use it as a TV film, couldn't use it as anything. It was a complete waste of time and money. I later found out he's gone into hiding, which in my opinion is the best place for him, because I don't want to see him again.

I've got a few films that are in the pipeline as I write. There's one called *Devil's Playground* coming out that I'm really excited about. It's with Craig Fairbrass – who I've acted with before and is a terrific fella – and Steven Berkoff. Craig used to be in *EastEnders* but he's also done a lot of great film work, and Steven Berkoff is a legend of the theatre and film. He's probably best known to my audience as General Orlov in the James Bond film *Octopussy*. He's done a lot of other stuff – really groundbreaking theatre – and I confess I was in awe of him slightly. People study him in drama school.

It was interesting to watch Steven's style on set. He takes it extremely seriously, likes to ask the director a million questions to make sure they're on the same page, and he nails it every time. You won't get a bad take out of the man. Seriously, I never once saw him fuck up. Remarkable, really.

I have high hopes for this film. It's about a battle for a group of people to get out of London, which has been taken over by the zombies, but not the shuffling zombies, these are like free runners, and can leap over gaps between buildings and up walls.

I didn't have to smoke in that film but I have in others. In *Human Traffic* I always had a fag or a spliff on. It's quite hard to smoke on-screen, because you have to remember that you might be doing ten or fifteen takes. For the sake of continuity, you have to take a puff on a fag at exactly the same point every take. Some actors are very concerned about continuity; Sean Bean is one of them. He wants to know exactly where his hand was in any given take. He's very technical, like that. I tend not to bother about it until I get pulled up by the continuity person. That is an intricate job. You have one person, whose sole purpose is to look out for things like how did you tie your tie in that scene, how long you cigarette was, the exact point at which you took a sip on a drink.

Being good with props is a skill in itself. David Jason, for instance, is well known for being comfortable around props. If you watch *Only Fools and Horses*, you'll often see him speaking while making a bacon sandwich or something.

I've also got *Age of Heroes* coming out, which could be a big thing for me. I'm playing a commando, along with Sean Bean. It's based on the life of Ian Fleming, who wrote James Bond. In the Second World War, he put a crack team of soldiers together from all different units. They weren't called commandos at this point but that's effectively what they were. They were sent out on these very difficult missions, and if the mission failed no one ever would have heard about it.

It was fascinating, because the film concerns the whole training process of a top soldier, the beasting, the milling, where they stand there and punch the fuck out of each other, the hikes of the really high mountains and then on to the mission.

We were ten-handed in the middle of Norway against two hundred fucking Nazis. It's a true story, unbelievably. You wonder how blokes handle odds like that, what it does to their heads. They didn't have a lot of money to make the film so we had to do it in twenty-six days. That is some going, believe you me. A war film with explosions, guns, at the mercy of the weather in Norway in twenty-six days. We went straight into a training camp, which I was happy about, because I was a bit chubby at the time, a little bit puffy around the chops. We did four days of training and then straight to Norway. We had a half a day with forty commandos, blokes who are in service in Afghanistan at the moment.

They showed us how to use the commando knife; they don't really like to use guns if they can help it, they're all about stealth. They were telling us about laughing in the face of adversity. One had his arm blown off and was complaining that he couldn't roll his cigarette. The other was saying, 'Stop moaning, I haven't got any legs.' It's all about mental strength with them and I have enormous respect for them.

So we start this job and it's all going well. We land in Stavanger, where there is no snow, and then you take a six-hour drive up into the mountains and you start to see it. Metres and metres of it.

We get to where we were shooting the film and it was fucking freezing but it looked beautiful. But we arrived at the exact same time as the volcanic ash from Iceland. Norway was at a standstill. We couldn't film and get the rushes back to the UK. The rushes are the raw film of that day's shooting. You need them to see what you've got, to tell you if you need to do something again.

We were staying up in the mountains in a large camp, all of us together. It was part of this Jobs for Heroes initiative, where soldiers who have been wounded are given work. It's a great idea and I'm proud a film I was in was associated with it. The soldiers – from a variety of regiments – are playing the Nazis, which was a worry for me, because we're this bunch of mincey actors poncing about and they are the real deal. Makes you feel very self-conscious about getting stuff right.

We did start to get a bit of cabin fever, because we were cut off. There was nothing to do on your day off but drink in the bar. You can whack a few DVDs on, but that's about it. We started to go crazy, but then this illness started to go through everybody, a forty-eight-hour bug where you're spewing your ring up. Horrendous. Everything was against us. We had twenty-six days to film, when people were getting ill and we couldn't fly out replacements because of the volcanic ash. Four people out of sixty didn't get the bug and I was one of them. It was as if there was an act of God, telling us not to make this movie. The director fell ill on set and he was trying to fight through it. And then the director of photography got it, so we couldn't film. The annoying thing was that the little we were getting on film was special.

The marines were getting pissed up in the bar, starting to head-butt each other. These men are fighting machines and they were very bored. I think they were starting to realise that making movies is not as glamorous as it seems.

I refused to really drink on the job; this was a big opportunity for me and I needed to stay focused. The last thing you want is a hangover a thousand metres above water, freezing your bollocks off. Also, I was playing a commando, and the boys who trained us said to us as we left, 'Don't let us down.' I took that very seriously. I wanted to put them in the best light I possibly could, so I couldn't afford to turn up looking like I'd been on one.

This was one of the most knackering shoots I've ever done. We're running around with these 1940s rucksacks on, Bergens, they're called. Most of the time on a film set you're treated like a king. But here we had to lug our own stuff up the mountains – they were trying to get us to be a bit method.

Sometimes there's rotten snow under the snow you're standing on and you fall in up to your neck, other times we had to swim through the snow, we got caught in blizzards, all sorts. It was worth it though because it looks great. I think this may be my best film yet. I hope so, anyway.

I missed my little Sunnie's third birthday, which was a fucker, and I did start to really miss the family on this one, quite badly. I came home and, fuck me, did I see the change in my daughter. You spend a month away from your child you see the difference.

Joanne told her that I had gone away to get her some presents, and I had got stuck up the mountain, so she bought a few little presents in for her when I came home. It was a very emotional thing for me; I missed them all terribly.

The change when you come home from this kind of thing is quite great. You're with a crew of people, living out of each other's pockets, with them 24/7 and suddenly it just stops, they're gone, and you come home and you're Daddy again. It's a big adjustment.

Still, I should get used to it because, while my luck and talent holds, this is my life. I can't do nothing else. I come from a working-class family who are grafters, they all have a trade behind them. Well, this is my trade, acting. I've had a result, because I'm a man. As an actor, if you are a woman then you can struggle to get work by the time you're thirty-three. Some really talented women go beyond that but it's a fact that a lot fall away at that point. It's a crying shame and there really should be more good roles for women, ones that don't require them to look about twenty-one. Male actors have it easier and can go on until they're eighty years of age, which is something I'd love to do.

If I have one real ambition it's that I'd love to be in something with my daughter Dani one day. She's always helped me learn my lines and I love sharing that with her, and I think that's why she's got the buzz at the moment. She's just got into a little drama school at the weekend, which she's done off her own back, nothing to do with me giving her a leg up. She auditioned with two hundred kids and they picked thirty-four. She was one of them. There'd be no better feeling than sitting at the awards ceremony at the BAFTAs and seeing my daughter pick up an award for something. That would be better than getting something myself.

For me, I've got no set plan, you can't really shape your career as much as you'd like. You can only do what is in front of you, try to shine in that and hope it opens a few more doors. I love acting and I want to stay in it, to get better, take on more challenging roles. Hopefully at some point in the future I'll learn to think more before I open my mouth a bit as well. If I can avoid any controversy at all for the rest of my life I'll be a happy man.

I've made a great start to my career, in some ways all my dreams have come true – and a few of the nightmares as well. But that's all it is – a start. I hope and believe the best is in front of me. I'm thirty-three now and if I'm still working as an actor when I'm sixty-six, still testing myself and trying new things, I'll consider my life a success. I've got a lot of love around me, from my family and from my fans. That's a brilliant springboard into the future. I want to use that to push myself on to better and more demanding work. Maybe I'll manage it, maybe I won't. But I tell you one thing for sure: like the people in the family I come from, I'm a grafter and if I don't get there then it won't be for want of trying.

ACKNOWLEDGEMENTS

I'd like to thank my mum and dad, my brother Tony and my sister Kayleigh, my nan and all the rest of my family. I'm proud to be part of your clan.

And I'd also like to thank Jack Fogg, Paul Stevens, Natalie Higgins, my agent Kate Buckley, my lovely publicist Pip Gill and Dennee and Gemma, who worked so hard for me. And Carol and Tolo, for having faith in me.

I'd also like to thank the actors and actresses I've worked with who've shaped me into the actor I am today.

And finally, to Mark Barrowcliffe, who had to sit there and listen to my bollocks for far too long. I couldn't have done it without you, mate.

LIST OF ILLUSTRATIONS

Dead Man Running Premier (© WireImage) *Human Traffic* (© TopFoto) / Danny Dyer and Tammer Hassan (© Toby Melville/Reuters/Corbis) / Danny Dyer in *The Business* (Courtesy of Vertigo Films) / Danny Dyer following the press night of *The Homecoming* (© Getty Images Entertainment) / Danny Dyer on the set of *The Outlaw* (Courtesy of Vertigo Films) / Danny Dyer in *Kurt & Sid* (© TopFoto) / Danny Dyer and Ray Winstone (© Getty Images Entertainment) / Danny Dyer at the Soccer Six (© Getty Images Sport)

All other images are courtesy of Danny Dyer.